Women Singers
in Global Contexts

Hello Liz

The fruition of the Special Initiative Fund!

see p. 34. Thank you.

Very best wishes,

Ruth

(rhellier-tinoco@music.ucsb.edu)

Women Singers in Global Contexts

Music, Biography, Identity

Edited by
RUTH HELLIER
Afterword by
ELLEN KOSKOFF

University of Illinois Press
URBANA, CHICAGO, AND SPRINGFIELD

Library of Congress Cataloging-in-Publication Data
Women singers in global contexts: music, biography, identity /
edited by Ruth Hellier; afterword by Ellen Koskoff.
p.   cm.
Includes bibliographical references and index.
ISBN 978-0-252-03724-5 (cloth: alk. paper)
ISBN 978-0-252-09436-1 (e-book)
1. Women singers. 2. Women singers—Social conditions.
I. Hellier, Ruth.
ML82.W687   2013
780.92′52—dc23 [B]   2012022030

Contents

The Companion Website

www.music.ucsb.edu/projects/womensingers

Audio examples of all the singers featured in this volume can be heard via the dedicated website that accompanies this volume. In addition to audio material, the website includes video material, still photography, links to further resources and recordings, and updates on tours and events featuring many of the singers.

I gratefully acknowledge the University of California, Santa Barbara, for hosting this website.

*Women Singers
in Global Contexts*

Introduction

Vocal Herstories: Resonances of Singing, Individuals, and Authors

RUTH HELLIER

Prelude: Warming Up

Ten Unique Women

Akiko Fujii   Amelia Pedroso
Ayben Özçalkan   Ixya Herrera   Kyriakou Pelagia
Lexine Solomon   Marysia Mąka   Sathima Bea Benjamin
Sima Shokrani   Zainab Herawi

Ten unique women constitute the heart of this volume: each one has engaged her singing voice as a central element in her life, experiencing manifold opportunities, tensions, and choices through her vocality. Her stories encompass relationships, encounters, and journeys entailing jubilation, struggle, suffering, excitement, fervor, drive, and generosity. Her singing—the action of producing musical sound through the expelling of air causing vibrations of the body—involves profoundly personal and individual experiential, sensory, and signifying processes that resonate with contexts ranging from local to global. Through narrative ethnography, biography, verbatim text, and analysis to convey fragments of these women's lives, we reflect upon ways in which these ten women make their literal and metaphorical voices heard. Engaging the interface of music-making, politics, and ideology, and dealing with aspects of vocal aesthetics, gender, and multiple identities, the narratives convey accounts of agency, activism, risk, childhood, familial relations, legacies, and the profound pleasures and passions of singing. These themes and threads are interlaced through this collection, offering valuable insights into issues raised by women singers in their private and performing lives, in a range of sociocultural contexts, as each woman vocalizes her individual subjectivity, simultaneously shaping and articulating her place in the world through singing. Through each chapter we invite a sense of engagement with one woman and with salient aspects of her vocal stories.

Taken as a whole the volume coheres around three elements: first, each chapter focuses on a unique woman; second, singing plays a major role in each woman's life; and third, a biographical and lived-experiences approach of specificity provides the overarching framework. The material is varied in terms of musical genres (encompassing jazz, rap, traditional, folk, devotional, and classical); geographical areas (Afghanistan, Australia, Canada, Cuba, Cyprus, Germany, Iran, Japan, Mexico, Poland, South Africa, Torres Strait Islands, Turkey, the United States of America); and the role of singing in the life of the singer (including a locally known community singer, an internationally renowned priestess, a professional wedding singer, a national star, and a regional entertainer). We embed these individual women in the personal, familial, local, translocal, and global environments in which they live, sing, and work, focusing on notions of multiple selves in specific situations. We develop our ideas around the proposition that "our current understandings of what and how music means could be expanded by more flexible and socially based notions of 'selves' as locally articulated in specific contexts," as propounded by music scholar Elizabeth Tolbert (2003, 80). Recognizing that "people's voices change over time," as Simon Frith, scholar of popular music, observed (1995, 6), we trace transformations and personal journeys in the life of each singer. In mapping these occurrences we encompass major events, life markers, moments of decisions, and elements of vocality, all placed in a broadly chronological life-story framework, encountering women at different stages and ages of their lives and careers.

Every account was written by a single author, drawing on a one-to-one relationship with the singer, using interviews, short- and long-term interaction, and shared music-making. Reflecting our engagement with individuals and relationships, here we present the authors: Shino, Amanda, Tom, Ruth, Nicoletta, Kate, Louise, Carol, Gay, and Veronica, each documenting and celebrating the particularity and specificity of these singing lives.

This introductory chapter is divided into two parts: Part One, Creating a Context, deals with the conceptual and methodological issues that underpin this volume, covering vocality, subjectivity, individuals, theorization, contextualization, feminist theory and politics, understandings of woman and gender, identity politics, and authoring. Part Two, Personal Encounters, is separated into two sections: first, an overview of each singer's life and the relationship between each author and singer; and second, a summary of predominant threads, themes, connections, and clusters.

Part One: Creating a Context

A Singing Voice: Subjectivity, Identity, and Vocality

Singing is a corporeal, sonic utterance, produced as air is expelled from the lungs and the vocal folds come together, creating vibrations that are sonated by the cavities of the head and throat. This process and act enables an audible and felt sensation for both singer and listener, with immense communicatory, emotive, and kinesthetic powers. Each singer's voice is ephemeral and yet wholly located in an individual person, tendering representational and sensory possibilities. A solo, singing voice presents vulnerability and connectivity, offering a raw, unmasked, and naked presence of significance. Each woman in this collection offers up her voice to be heard and listened to, placing her singing and her self in front of audiences or with a community of other musicking activities.[1] Listening to a singing voice as a creative act and process provokes and activates memory and perception, enabling an encounter (conscious or unconscious) with self and others.

A major thread in this volume concerns how each individual woman chooses to vocalize—within, through, and beyond traditions, conventions, boundaries, and genres, expressing a personal life in song. The narratives that emerge reveal and explore relationships between a singing voice, subjectivity, and agency, telling of close associations between voice and identity. We pose these questions: "[H]ow does a voice signify a person? What is the relationship of someone's vocal sound and their being?" And if "the voice is usually taken to be the person," how is singing an expression of identity? (Frith 1995, 6). Covering issues that concern cultural meanings of the human voice as an instrument or medium of expression, and exploring how vocal aesthetics shape and define notions of "woman," we discuss the individual properties, codings, techniques, and aesthetics of these women's singing voices, relating to matters of production and process (sometimes in terms of timbre [tone quality], register [pitch quality], and volume [loudness]). We deal with phenomenological aspects of singing, particularly in terms of individual flavor or texture, influenced by ideas of Roland Barthes, French literary theorist and semiotician, in his essay "The Grain of the Voice" (1977). Such individuality of expression is at the core of this volume, as each woman strives to create a form of vocality through her singing voice that is at once enabling and empowering, yet often constrained and bounded by multifarious controls. It is also noteworthy that one woman's voice—that of Ayben of Turkey—is associated more with speaking rather than singing; as a rapper she uses a form of vocality encompassing a speaking voice in musical form, blurring the boundaries between singing and speaking.

We often hear and consciously or unconsciously classify a voice in the first split seconds in terms of "woman" or "man," subsequently moving to other associations and axes of identity. As ethnomusicologist Martin Stokes has observed, "one searches 'in' the voice for something," with voices offering "reassuring, politically resonant gender stereotypes" (1995–96, 57). Such classification concerns the "expectations of an alignment between voice and gender," as discussed by musicologist Judith Peraino (2007, 63). Vocal gendering is a product of a complex interplay between anatomical differences and socialization into culturally prescribed gender roles, expressed as "the contrasting possibilities for expression for men and women within a given society" by Leslie Dunn and Nancy Jones in their collection examining the representation of female vocality in art and classical music contexts (1994b, 2). According to Frith, "we learn to hear voice as male or female and the singing voice carries these codings with it" (1995, 3). Physiology affects the sheer literal pitch range that is possible and when connected with cultural and ideological specificity encompasses what has been called the "hegemony of male vocal range" (Sherinian 2005, 8, 9, 12).[2] Frith captures some of the complexities of vocal identity, coding, and reception, observing that "when it comes to the singing voice all such readings have as much to do with conventional as 'natural' expression, with the ways in which particular gendered singing voices are coded not just female but also young, black, middle class, etcetera" (1995, 6).

Following the work of Steven Feld and his colleagues in ethnomusicology and anthropology, we explore the connections between a singing voice and place, class, ethnicity, and identity (2004, 321), documenting relationships between in-public and in-private lives, and, as relevant for many but not all of these singers, onstage personae. None of the women are overtly playing a role defined through conventions of performance, as is the case with opera divas and theatrical singers: they are not "protected" by a character, with explicit representational qualities, narratives, and a make-believe framework. For most, their contexts of singing frame their action with a perceived sense of the personal and the "real," as connections are created through repertoire, vocal aesthetics, and language. Issues of authenticity are prevalent, particularly in relation to those singers who also create the songs they sing. Many chapters invoke the sound of the singing voice, some using descriptions given by the singers themselves, while others are provided by the authors as listeners, some of whom are also singers. Deploying adjectives to talk about singing voices and music can be problematical, for, as Barthes observed, the adjective is "the poorest of linguistic categories . . . the adjective is inevitable: this music is *this*, this execution is *that*" (1977, 179). However, descriptions do provide evidence of voice as identity and vocal aspirations, invoking women who come to understanding a sense of self through their own singing voices. We invite you to hear these women's voices on the accompanying website and through the many websites and recordings detailed in this volume.[3]

Combining Literal and Metaphorical Voices:
Agency, Power, and Subjectivities

Literal singing voices form one vital feature in this volume. So too the concept of voice as metaphor is central, with all chapters engaging this theme in one form or another, touching on issues concerned with each woman's individual subjectivities, agency, representation, interpersonal relationships, and choices. The trope of "voice," derived from the idea of voice of the people, indicating a wish, choice, and right of expression, and often associated with the terms envoicing and envoicement, has been a frequently deployed metaphor. As ethnomusicologist Eileen Hayes has observed, "in the late 1980s and early 1990s scholars from across disciplines invoked 'voice' as a metaphor for vocality, cultural agency, political autonomy, and both individual and collective power" (2006, 72). As a metaphor, voice has been a particular feature of feminist movements to express notions of empowerment. In feminist music criticism, "voice" became an essential term to reference women's articulations and communications, as exemplified by Susan McClary in her seminal 1991 study, *Feminine Endings*: "This book bears the traces of countless voices— voices distinctly or only half remembered" (vii). These "voices" are women's opinions and expressions in articles, letters, dinner conversations, and debates in the classroom. Although McClary does indeed touch on individual women vocalists, the singing voice is mostly absent. In other scholarly work concerning music, voice has been referenced in titles such as *Women's Voices across Musical Worlds*, Jane Bernstein's 2003 collection examining roles of women as performers and creators, and the representation of women in a range of musical genres, including some vocal examples.

While drawing on these and other rich scholarly antecedents examining issues of women and music, we present a unique departure: in each chapter we offer narratives that invoke the interface of the literal singing voice and the metaphorical voice, exploring relationships between a singing voice and voice as agency and examining how a singing voice enables voice as power to be enacted. As such we call attention to contexts and concepts of difference and diversity that are deeply concerned with power relations and status, discussing shifting and dynamic sociocultural contexts in which the existence of multiple sets of power relations are inevitable. As subjectivity is an effect of relations of power, so issues concerning the subjective experiences of each woman form an essential element, discussed through personal expressions documented in interviews and other personal communications. Perspectives provided by the women themselves are often framed in terms of decisions, choices, feelings, beliefs, desires, and perceptions. We are not propounding the notion that women's subjectivities have any unifying features, nor are we positing a thesis of equality or even seeking to highlight oppositions positioning women and men as categories in simple binary constructs of comparative or unequal power relations. Notably, however, binaries do emerge in the course of the narratives as woman/man pairings are referenced by many of the women in this collection. Issues of patriarchal power are apparent, engaging the term *patriarchal* to designate multiple forms of received and hegemonic power relations and structures, rather than as an essentialist term.

We address many of the areas and questions posited in previous research concerning women and music-making, identifying "gender and its ideology" in order to formulate "questions about musical activity, works, culture, and experience," as articulated by Susan Cook and Judy Tsou in their volume examining feminist perspectives on gender and music (1994b, 2). Following Cook and Tsou, here we acknowledge "the limitations, subtle and overt, familial and societal, contestable and insurmountable, that women, often regardless of race, class, geographic location, or historical time, faced as performers, as creators, and even as listeners because of the ideology of gender" (ibid., 8). However, unlike much of the previous scholarship, which has focused on restrictions—and indeed, issues of victimhood were predominantly common in second-wave feminism and music scholarship (see Citron 2004)—the narratives in this volume often involve success, accomplishment, and pleasure. Inspired by Ellen Koskoff's seminal volume, we examine "resulting gender-related behaviors and relation to musical thought and practice," and discuss the division of musical roles and responsibilities as conceptually linked to other culture-specific, gender-related domains (1989, 1, 8).[4] We consider "the premises of inherited conventions" (McClary 1991, 19) and matters that "enabled and restricted the careers of some of the women" (McClary 1994, x). Developing ideas from Mavis Bayton's study of women and popular music, we ask "what were their experiences in playing music and how did their careers work?" (1998, vi).

In Whiteley's study of women singer-songwriters and musicians in the United Kingdom in the last decades of twentieth century, she observed that in the 1970s an identification of the separation of the domestic and public sphere was the most significant boundary in society, reflecting the conventional split between career and family and acknowledging that the "traditional tug between domestic/public, passive/active that characterized gendered identity continued to create a conflict of interest for women performers, and this was exacerbated by the continuing emphasis on women as homemakers within the so-called progressive counter culture [of the 1960s]" (2000, 10). Drawing on Jane Sugarman's detailed analysis of gender and singing in the context of weddings in Albania, we inquire: "How do individuals within a community come to regard themselves as gendered beings, and to appraise certain qualities and activities in gendered terms? How is power exerted and experienced in gender relations? How are asymmetrical power relations, as gender relations often are, reproduced from one generation to the next, even with the willing complicity of those who are subordinate? How is it possible for individuals to challenge or renegotiate the terms of such relations? What role does musical performance play in each of these processes?" (1997, 31).

Respect for the Individual: Encompassing the Global

Ellen Koskoff has reminded us of the need to focus on distinct people so that we create "respect for the individual, and respect for the process of life" in ways that help us to "put real people and the truth of their musical lives back into the picture" (2005, 98). Responding to Koskoff, a central premise of this collection is that one named and unique individual human being forms the focus for each chapter. Our approach in this collection draws attention to epistemological issues concerning knowledge bases and subjectivities, closely connecting personal, political, and representational processes. Writing in the journal *Women and Music*, and summarizing Koskoff's ideas, Judy Lockhead has noted "that the destabilization of modern epistemological categories that is the hallmark of postmodern theory often results in abstractions that make individuals—and women in particular—disappear. The particularities of lived experience are subsumed into abstractions and generalities in a conceptual move that replicates the universalizing tendencies of modern thought" (2007, 112). When the specificity of individual lives is subsumed into collectivities, there is a tendency to read one woman's experience as representative of other women, hence references to women's music-making, women's experiences, and women's rituals. Following the "self-reflexive turn" in anthropology in the early 1990s, which led in some quarters to renewed interest in subjective experience, we develop one recent trend in ethnomusicology towards the ethnographic study of the individual (Stock 2001). We engage with a trajectory of scholarship, drawn from feminist, historiographical, and postmodern concerns, which recognizes the value and significance of a single life, not in order to make generalizations about other lives or about a broader context, or indeed to further a comparative approach, but solely in terms of that one person, regardless of status and recognition.[5]

In musicology and popular music studies a specific person has commonly been a principal focus. However, these individuals have most often been high-profile musicians, or, since the development of feminist music criticism in the 1990s, women whose lives and work were not part of the accepted musicohistorical canon of great work, forming what have come to be known as compensatory histories. In Whiteley's work on women musicians in popular music the documented individuals were selected on the basis that they were "familiar both because of their artistic and commercial success, their relevance to debates on feminism and sexuality, and their challenge and transformation of gender-related boundaries" (2000, 9). Although some of the women in this collection fit with these descriptions, all the singers have been selected through each author's personal contact and interest in the person, regardless of perceived appropriateness in relation to exploring certain issues and paramenters. Self- and societal-designation as "woman" was sufficient for inclusion. Together with the focus on a unique woman, a cohering stylistic element aims to maintain the attention on individual experience. By drawing on verbatim material from interviews and personal narrative from conversations, the use of *I* within many chapters provides each individual woman's perspective.

Interfacing with the focus on individuals and specific lives, we invoke *global* as an indication of the relationship between the micro and the macro, between centers and peripheries, and the importance, place, and space of individuals in all their uniqueness and diversity, expressed through distinct subjectivities. Many of these women are engaged with, and participate in global movements, mass culture, and commercialism. Although "researching the globalization of musics through commodification, mass media, local, national, and global politics" (Koskoff 2005, 97) has been seen as problematic because it removes focus from individuals, here we embrace and engage this concept in order to draw attention to individual impact and flow. These narratives give evidence of individual women who seek out their own relationship with processes of globalization. In totality this volume is truly global, for a mapping exercise would reveal the considerable range of places and peoples touched by the singers in this volume, actioned through the multiple journeys of the women themselves, and through their singing voices conveyed and broadcast by radio, television, audio recordings, video recordings, and the internet.

We also invoke global as a reference to flows of power and politics in national, inter- and transnational contexts. Each woman is situated in her own profoundly personal and localized situation, yet she is inherently part of much wider political contexts. Glimpses of each woman's own interface with political activity are evident, to a greater or lesser extent, encompassing major world events, revolutions, social and racial movements, and transformations from communist to democratic states: Amelia lived through Castro's socialist regime in Cuba; Ayben grew up within Turkey's paradoxical society of tension between old and new; Ixya lives with the legacy of the post-1960s Chicano movement in the United States of America and was touched by the 1994 economic meltdown in Mexico; Kyriakou Pelagia's life was profoundly affected by the independence and division of Cyprus; Lexine's life is entrenched in Indigenous politics of Torres Strait Islanders on mainland Australia; Marysia in Poland lived through the transformation from socialist to democratic state; Sathima witnessed and lived through the South African transition to apartheid and its demise; Sima was involved with the Islamic revolution in Iran 1979; and Zainab was caught up in the 1978 Marxist coup d'etat and civil unrest in Afghanistan.

People versus Ideas:
Generalizations, Theorizations, and Contextualizations

Issues of individual subjectivities and global environments lead to questions concerning what is necessary in terms of both theorization and contextualization. Again, Koskoff has touched on this important area: "theory versus experience (ideas versus people), provides a different kind of tension, that between ideas *about* people and the real experiences *of* people and which of these to privilege in our work. Finding a balance between these tensions will, no doubt, be the challenge of the future" (2005, 98). This is indeed a challenge, and in creating this volume each author has struggled in her or his endeavors to realize this balance. One author, in the process of her writing, expressed significant points that this tension creates:

> [W]hen I tried to incorporate more theory into my chapter, I got the sense that Pelagia was turning into a caricature of herself, that I was moving from the living, breathing individual that I know Pelagia to be towards an abstract theoretical entity. This was something that I profoundly disliked and therefore avoided. What I tried to do in my chapter instead was to combine biographical writing with ethnography, to provide a good narrative with the context for the readers to interpret what they read. I hope that you will find this approach appropriate for the purposes of this volume (Nicoletta Demetriou, pers. comm. 2010).[6]

We invite readers to make their own individual responses in relation to how far each author has created a narrative that balances the tension between ideas and people. As evident from Nicoletta's comments above, a major element concerns theorizing an individual person. Part of the dilemma involves balancing the woman's narrative and the author's narrative, for any commentary by the author has a tendency to remove agency from the subject, rendering the individual woman an object. As cultural and music analysts we are more comfortable engaging a theorizing and generalizing model with groups and collectivities. In this volume authors do engage theoretical insights and frameworks to a greater or lesser extent, but there is more of an emphasis on the practice of lived experiences and decision-making. There are also connections here with issues of feminist theoretical models, according to particular areas of music scholarship. Tolbert observed that "ethnomusicologists must struggle . . . to sidestep the ethnocentrism of feminist theory" (2003, 77), and Margaret Sarkissian noted that feminist theoretical models are "oddly absent" from ethnomusicology, "an indication perhaps that ethnomusicologists are less inclined than historical musicologists to search for theoretical generalizations. For the more culturally relativistic ethnomusicologist, the attempt to understand other cultures from their own (rather than a Western-centric) perspective makes generalization, critique, and the construction of theory difficult" (1999, 17).

Along with theorization and generalization, the issue of contextualization is a matter that has been addressed by each author. Each woman is inherently in interrelation with a musical (and cultural, political, and ideological) context or tradition(s)—with what has come before and what exists in the present, each with its own aesthetics, roles, and expectations. A central element of this volume concerns how each individual woman interfaces and interacts with her context and tradition, in terms of goals, risks, and desires. Although this is not a comparative, survey-based, or area-studies volume, details of genres, events, repertoires, and performance contexts are included. These should be treated as frames in a film, fragments in a mosaic, and threads in a tapestry, all of which are important and rich in their own right, and yet are embedded in much larger and more complex soundscapes and environments.

Life Cycles and Biography

As biography refers to life and the course of living, so biographical writing often purports or attempts to capture the entirety of one life, constructing grand narratives, and establishing and verifying so-called "important factual details" (such as date of birth, marriage, death). In this volume we focus on themes and activities, catching glimpses of lives, and accepting that these accounts are necessarily fragmentary, countering the fallacy that our lives are joined-up coherent experiences. Some authors have chosen to focus on salient moments and events of transformation and shift; others map many phases and experiences; yet others take in evocative descriptors of vocality.

All provide some chronological sense and include aspects of childhood and adulthood. Two chapters encapsulate and encompass full life cycles, for two singers are no longer living—Amelia and Zainab. Ages, stages, and phases in life vary: Ixya is thirty and Kyriakou nearly eighty, yet both have had a public life as singers for twenty years. Ayben is near the beginning of her career; Sathima has accomplished a fifty-year career. References to birth and death are present in many chapters, and some include references to motherhood (Marysia, Sathima, Sima, and Zainab). One noteworthy common element is the inclusion of authors' descriptions of their own experiences hearing the singer sing, encompassing moments of connection and profound exhilaration, and emphasizing both the nature of the personal interaction between author and singer and also a fundamental theme: the power of a singing voice.

Frameworks, Feminisms, and Postfeminisms

As this volume specifically focuses on the designation "women" and is concerned with agency, power-relations, individuals, lived experiences, and subjectivity, we acknowledge and engage a variety of feminist perspectives, concerns, frameworks, and theories, particularly aligning with agendas encompassing diversity in terms of relations of gender, intersecting with race, class, ethnicity, sexuality, nationality, ability, age, and other differences. A notion of postfeminisms is also apt, connecting with a regard for multiplicity and focusing on difference and plurality as opposed to equality. As feminist positions have dramatically shifted over the decades, it is worth recalling a linguistic and ideological modification that concerned the movement in the United Kingdom and the United States of America; as Sheila Whiteley notes, in her study of women and popular music, the terminology of *women's liberation* was gradually dropped in favor of "feminists." The ideal of liberation shifted to an agenda of equality because "as Germaine Greer observes, what none of us noticed was that the ideal of liberation was fading out with the word. We were settling for equality. Liberation struggles are not about assimilation but about asserting difference, endowing difference with dignity and prestige, and insisting on it as a condition of self-definition and self-determination" (2000, 31, citing Greer 1999, 1). In the twenty-first century, feminist positions are thoroughly engaged with notions of diversity, difference, and empowerment, rather than (simply) equality.

Within music studies, ethnomusicologically framed research has engaged with the politics of difference for a considerable length of time, usually in relation to key societal divisions (race, ethnicity, religion, gender). In this volume we continue the focus on a politics of difference, and also of self-definition and self-determination, associating with Elizabeth Tolbert's observations that "much of ethnomusicological work that draws on feminist theory is not presented exclusively in these terms but rather is embedded in other paradigms of difference, such as race, ethnicity, and sociocultural identity" (2003, 77).

Invoking feminisms and feminist movements and scholarship engages sets of politics and poetics that may be connected with particular groups of people and specific local and national agendas and contexts. Although many of the women who are the focus of the volume are engaged with processes and issues that cohere with many feminist frameworks, because the majority do not (did not) identify with a named movement of feminism and do not (did not) articulate their lives in these terms, it would be inappropriate to transpose and impose this terminology onto these women and societies (and therefore the authors do not do so in the narratives).

Woman and Gender: Dichotomies, Complexities, and Normativity

All ten people at the core of this volume have engaged singing as a major element in their life. In addition to this, what is it that makes these disparate people into a grouping or cluster? One response is that they are all identified as "woman" by society and self. Woman, as a principal axis of identity, encompasses selfhood and representation, and, as an ontological activity, is principally activated through the binary of woman/man. In this volume the essays narrate how the category woman plays out in a range of lives, locations, and contexts, exploring the question: how is this person, identified as "woman," constructed, shaped, created, received, crafted, and constrained? Partnered with the term *woman* is *gender*; however, there are difficulties with "essentialized terms such as woman and gender," as Tolbert has observed (2003, 77). In 1989 Koskoff noted that "The separation of men and women into two gender categories has profound implications for music thought and behavior" (8), later expanding on this by observing that "Notions of man, woman, gender, sex, and culture as static, bounded constructs, are giving way to process-oriented paradigms favoring chaos, negotiation over time, shifting realities and identities" (2005, 98).

A concept of shifting realities and identities is indeed a useful framework for considering the great diversity and complexity of the lives of the individuals in this volume. Therefore, we offer a brief discussion of the terms *woman* and *gender* in order to open up the themes and threads covered in this collection, drawing on philosophical, music-related, and feminist scholarship. Referencing ideas from, and critiques of, feminist movements and scholarship enables us to highlight some of the principal complexities and dichotomies. As such, this brief overview of salient issues provides a double interface: first, drawing attention to scholarly and political problematics; and second, emphasizing the lived shaping and constraining elements experienced by the individual women, all of which weave their way through the narratives.

Philosopher Mari Mikkola's summary of usage in feminist identity politics offers a valuable framework: "In order to distinguish biological differences from social/psychological ones and to talk about the latter, feminists appropriated the term 'gender'. . . . ('sex' denotes human females and males depending on biological features [chromosomes, sex organs, hormones and other physical features]; 'gender' denotes women and men depending on social factors [social role, position, behaviour or identity]). . . . This enabled them to argue that many differences between women and men were socially produced and, therefore, changeable. . . . So, this group of feminist arguments against biological determinism suggested that gender differences result from cultural practices and social expectations. Gender is socially constructed" (2008). Judith Butler's seminal, and subsequently much critiqued principle still affords an important paradigm: "Gender is not something one is, it is something one does; it is a sequence of acts, a doing rather than a being. Gender is really performative. [It is not] a stable identity or locus of agency from which various acts follow; rather, gender is . . . instituted . . . through a stylized repetition of [habitual] acts" (1999 [1990], 179), which include gender-coded ways of walking, dressing, and singing. Repeatedly engaging in "feminizing" and "masculinizing" acts conceals gender thereby making people falsely think of gender as something they naturally are (1990, 278–79). Locating these gender-concepts within one framework of current feminist identity politics reveals some of the issues at stake. Again, Mikkola provides a good summary: "genders (women and men) and gendered traits (like being nurturing or ambitious) are the 'intended or unintended product[s] of a social practice' (Haslanger 1995, 97). But which social practices construct gender, what social construction is, and what being of a certain gender amounts to are major feminist controversies. There is no consensus on these issues. Gender—or what it is to be a woman or a man—is still very much a live issue" (2008).

We deem each individual to be a polysemic woman, for "if masculine and feminine are defined on the basis of their difference from each other, then woman can only be constructed as opposite, as 'other.' . . . If, however, feminism accepts the diversity of women's experience as process, it becomes evident that different cultures fill 'masculine' and 'feminine' with a variety of characteristics and, as such, the who 'I am' as a woman addresses a multiplicity of subject positions, a 'diversity and specificity of women rather than any notional woman'" (Whiteley 2000, 96, citing Gunew 1990, 29). Drawing on Butler's work, we should understand *woman* as open-ended and "a term in process, a becoming, a constructing that cannot rightfully be said to originate or end . . . it is open to intervention and resignification" (1999, 43). The classification "woman" creates expectations, constraints, and opportunities, for a normativity argument posits a normative idea of womanhood, and "[i]dentity categories [like that of women] are never merely descriptive, but always normative, and as such, exclusionary" (Butler 1991, 160). Issues of normativity and exclusion are, of course, dealt with in this volume. So, even as we focus this collection around the designation *woman* we acknowledge that critiques of the sex/gender distinction have called into question the viability of the category "woman," recognizing that the profoundly political area of this distinction is constantly debated.[7]

Multiplicity, Identities, and Multivocality

When hearing a singing voice, the initial interpretative association of identity often relates to a woman/man axis; however, many other facets of identity come into play for both singer and listener. Although for this volume we are prioritizing woman as a cohering thread of identity, this is not necessarily the axis that predominates in each individual's life. Multiple alignments, including racial, ethnic, cultural, linguistic, class, religious, sexual, and age differences, are all present in this collection. According to Mikkola, "gender realists mistakenly assume that gender is constructed independently of race, class, ethnicity and nationality. If gender were separable from, for example, race and class in this manner, all women would experience womanhood in the same way" (2008). Butler urged that we should recognize "the multiplicity of cultural, social, and political intersections in which the concrete array of 'women' are constructed" (1999, 19–20). Rather than perpetuate the essentialist claim that encompasses "the understanding of the subject that characterizes a single axis of identity as discrete and taking priority in representing the self," here succinctly explained by feminist philosopher Cressida Heyes (2000), we specifically deal with multiplicity, complexity, and shifting identities.

As with the exclusionary and constraining effects of gender noted earlier, so too with other axes of identity and normativity. As Heyes explains, "to the extent that identity politics urges mobilization around a single axis, it will put pressure on participants to identify that axis as their defining feature, when in fact they may well understand themselves as integrated selves who cannot be represented so selectively or even reductively . . . [and] generalizations made about particular social groups in the context of identity politics may come to have a disciplinary function within the group, not just describing but also dictating the self-understanding that its members should have" (2009). Such constraints of self-understanding also relate to societal controls, particularly discussed here in terms of choices concerning repertoire, vocality, venue, professional status, and genre.

In this volume some of the multiple affiliations of identity include: sexuality for Amelia as a lesbian and Santería priestess in Cuba; age for Ayben, who at seventeen began her career as a rapper in Turkey; ethnicity for Ixya as a Mexican or Chicana in the United States of America; age for Kyriakou Pelagia, who began public singing in Cyprus in her midfifties; indigeneity for Lexine, who identifies as an Indigenous Torres Strait Islander, rather than Aboriginal in Australia; ethnicity and nationality for Marysia, whose identity as ethnic Górale and Polish both played out in her migration to Canada; race/ethnicity and nationality for Sathima as a black South African; local Mazanderani ethnicity and class for Sima in Iran; and class issues for Zainab, who was given a designation of belonging to the lower echelons of society in Afghanistan. In each case, these women make vocal choices in relation to their compound affiliations, often engaging in multivocal parameters, enabling them to fit with or resist conventions as they choose. Despite the brevity of these chapters that capture fragments of these women's lives, we encourage readers to notice the diversity of identity formations and connections and the ways in which singing voices shape and are shaped by such multiplicity.

Authors and Singers, Relationships and Writing

As we invite you to engage with a diversity of singers and singing voices, so too we encompass an array of authors and authorial voices—individuals at various stages and phases of their lives and careers, in diverse geographical locations. Authors include senior scholars and newer academics who have recently completed their doctoral studies. Genderwise, nine are women, and one is a man. Work and home locations take in Australia, Canada, Cyprus, Japan, Norway, the United Kingdom, and the United States of America, and many have personal connections to the countries and contexts of their singers. Many are singers themselves, some overtly carrying on the tradition of the singer and others engaging in the same repertoire.

An individual and biographical approach implies a personal association, and indeed each author and singer engaged in a face-to-face relationship. Fieldwork was the common methodological process, encompassing

personal interviews and participant observation.[8] Aware of power differ-
entials but actively seeking ways of connecting with each other, authors
engaged in research projects that embraced a collaborative, people-centered
approach; a concern for the lived experience; and ethical, responsible, re-
ciprocal models of relationships. The personal connection between the
singer and author ranged from brief (one interview) to long-term, some
enduring over many years, and many still ongoing. Several relationships
have moved beyond data collection, with involvement in various recipro-
cal contexts, including actively participating in university teaching and
mounting collaborative performance events. As two singers are no longer
living, although the personal relationship was necessarily ended, the music-
making that led to the research relationship continues with the authors (as
detailed later and in the relevant chapters).

Crafting texts from individual lives, experiences, and memories presents opportunities and dilemmas. The poetic and the political are inseparable, and as
academic and literary genres interpenetrate, an authorial voice transforms and
mediates meaning, translating spoken words, facial expressions, atmospheres,
and sensations. There have been many models for ethnographic biography
and for ethnography in general, including Judith Vander's *Songprints* (1996)—
which included transcriptions of taped conversations with individual Shoshone
women singers—and the life story of Texan-Mexican singer Lydia Mendoza,
which was presented as a narrative transcript of interviews (Broylez-González
2001).[9] In this volume the ten authors incorporate a selection of structural and
organizational graphing processes. Each chapter draws heavily on the one-to-
one relationship, writing from the perspective of "being there." Most chapters
make use of first-person verbatim speech—the literal words of each woman.
Deploying *I* engages a literary mode of connection that is less-heavily mediated than transforming the personal pronoun to *she*. The author is still acting
as presenter, interpreter, and translator, and yet writes knowing the context of
the spoken words, feeling the emotion, and seeing the facial and bodily expressions. Verbatim text ranges from larger transcribed sections (Shino Arisawa,
Kate Barney, Ruth Hellier, Carol Muller, Thomas Solomon), to fewer inclusions
(Nicoletta Demetriou, Amanda Villepastour), to just a handful of words (Gay
Breyley, Veronica Doubleday, Louise Wrazen).

Part Two: Personal Encounters

With the focus upon specificity, individuals, and relationships, this second part
is dedicated to introducing and presenting aspects of the singers and authors
as a prelude to the chapters themselves. It is divided into two sections: *She and*

I: Meet the Singers and Authors, followed by *Threads, Themes, Connections, and Clusters.* In the first we offer a précis of each woman's life paired with a contextual glimpse of the relationship between author and singer; authors briefly explain their own circumstances, thereby placing the emphasis on individuals writing from their own situatedness. In this section, as in the volume as a whole, order has been undertaken on a simple alphabetical level, using the first name of each singer as the principal letter.[10] In the second section I separate out some of the themes, threads, and clusters to enable an overview of predominant coherencies and connections. This section is extended in the Appendix, where details relating to each singer are presented.

She and I: Meet the Singers and Authors

Akiko Fujii was born into a prestigious musical family in Japan in the 1960s, having both a mother and grandmother who were renowned singers of *jiuta*, an inherited male-dominated vocal tradition. Throughout childhood Akiko was apprenticed to her mother and expected to inherit her music school; however, when Akiko was in her forties, her brother became the head of the school forcing her towards major life decisions, which included a career as a professional jiuta performer, rather than as a teacher. Following a path of independence, passion, and inspiration, she chose to break new ground by adapting her performance style to draw in audiences and create intimacy, resisting criticism of an older generation and risking disapproval of her mother, even as she nursed her through illness. Within a traditional context of profound family pressure, Akiko has created a singing career for herself through perseverance and determination.

    Shino Arisawa: "I have known Akiko since 2003 when I began conducting field research in Japan concerning musical transmission within the *jiuta* tradition. As Akiko came from one of the representative families of the tradition, I decided to investigate her lineage through Akiko as she was a younger member and also looked like a friendly and approachable person. When I first visited her concert where her family members, including her mother and brother, performed together, I initially felt they were a happy family with smiles on their faces. However, as my field research progressed, Akiko gradually revealed her complex feeling towards her family and her musical career. In my research, therefore, I also aimed to investigate emotional aspects in musical transmission where tradition is handed down from father to son, from mother to daughter, or from grandparents to grandchildren, who are family members, but are also masters and disciples. I looked at musical transmission as an emotional act, which is a blend of love and hatred, faith

and betrayal, and many other complicated feelings. Akiko's mother, who was also her master, passed away while I was conducting field research. Akiko initially did not talk much about her feelings, but later expressed how much her mother's death had impacted on her emotional transformation, as I describe in my chapter."

. . .

Amelia Pedroso was a renowned Cuban ritual singer and priestess in the Santería tradition, who generated remarkable achievements in men-dominated and heterosexual contexts, openly creating a lesbian and gay-friendly ritual house in Havana and, in the early 1990s when she was in her forties, moving into a drumming domain that specifically prohibited Cuban women—although paradoxically non-Cuban women were taught in Cuba. Pedroso formed an all-women ensemble and toured and ran workshops in the United States of America and Europe. She attracted women to her, acquiring a role as an iconic activist, developing a network of students and religious godchildren, and leaving a remarkable transnational legacy following her death in 2000.

    Amanda Villepastour: "While undertaking my masters research, I first saw Amelia Pedroso perform in March 1998 in Havana but did not have the opportunity to meet her or the other musicians in her group, Ibbu Okun. In the following year when Pedroso toured the United Kingdom, I assisted with the workshops and concerts led by Pedroso in London and Manchester, filmed her performances, and conducted a formal interview along with several informal conversations, leading to two journalistic articles in *Straight No Chaser* and *Glendora*. As the U.K. orisha religious community was and is small, and I had been studying Cuban and Nigerian batá drumming since 1996, Pedroso took an interest in my work and experience. Our new friendship was fleeting due to geographical distance and Pedroso's death soon after her U.K. visit."

. . .

Ayben Özçalkan made her mark as a seventeen-year-old, rapping on her older brother's CD recording in Istanbul, Turkey, in 1990. She developed her own style and technique as a young rap artist, even though she risked bringing disapproval to her family by performing in a male-dominated genre. After putting her career on hold as she cared for her dying mother, she then relaunched herself as a rapper, with multiple appearances on TV, to become the personality that she is today. She overtly tackles women's issues in her performances through her lyrics that deal explicitly with the treatment of women in Turkey.

Thomas Solomon: "I first heard of Ayben shortly after I began doing research on Turkish rap in 2000, while living and working in Istanbul. I didn't hear much about Ayben in the following few years, but I took note when she resumed recording and entered the public arena again during 2004. By this time I was living and working in Norway, so I mostly followed her career 'from afar,' though I was also able to get updates 'on the ground' and occasionally see her perform live during my regular short visits to Istanbul every summer. I was finally formally introduced to Ayben for the first time at a hip-hop party in late summer 2006, and we agreed to do a formal interview later that fall when I would be in Istanbul for an extended period of fieldwork. Ayben's schedule was quite full at that time, since she was busy in the recording studio working on her first full album, as well as shooting a video clip, having live performances (including trips abroad), and doing interviews with journalists. But we eventually were able to do the interview one afternoon in November. I had to listen to her very carefully during the interview, since Ayben speaks very fast (at least that was my impression), though I also noticed that despite the speed with which she spoke, her pronunciation was always very clear, with consonants and vowels carefully articulated, and without ever slurring over syllables—the same qualities that characterize her rapping style. I noted during the interview that the rhythmic quality of her speaking voice, and her generally fast speech, made it sometimes seem like she was spontaneously rapping, even when she was just engaging in normal conversation."

• • •

Ixya Herrera debuted at the age of twelve, dueting with her idol Linda Ronstadt in front of a crowd of thousands at the Tuscon Mariachi Conference 1992 in Arizona. Growing up in California, in the supportive environment of a musical family, and with the legacy of Chicano cultural politics, she has developed a solo career engaging a repertoire of diverse Mexican genres. In her self-crafting processes she aspires to enchant audiences with the thrill of her singing voice, negotiating stereotypes and placing satisfaction before commercial gain. She continues to push forward with recordings and concert appearances, engaging a form of subtle activism, and demonstrating self-determination and self-definition.

Ruth Hellier: "Ixya and I met for the first time in Santa Barbara, California, in 2008. Following years of living in the United Kingdom and Mexico, I began a process of migrating to California, to join my husband.[11] Having experienced Mexicanness in Mexico I was interested in developing an understanding from the perspective of 'el norte' (the north). I therefore sought out a singer in southern California with Mexican connections, and began a research relationship with Ixya. I remember meeting Ixya for the first time, a young woman who was the vision of grace and charm, both offstage and on. Although our schedules and life events have often prevented us from meeting as often as we would have liked in the last three years, with my migration now permanent, Ixya and I are planning opportunities for performance and pedagogical collaborations over the coming years."

• • •

Kyriakou Pelagia passed her childhood and much of her adult life undertaking women's roles of village domesticity in Cyprus, as homemaker and cultivator of produce, caring for her husband, and raising a family. Singing was important to her as child, but she had no public outlet. Life changed in the 1990s with the introduction of private radio stations. Pelagia made frequent auditory appearances, resulting in an invitation to perform with a local music ensemble and record a CD, which subsequently led to national fame. With a singing career that began as an older woman in her fifties, her social role and offstage life as a housewife and grandmother is integral to her vocal performances.

Nicoletta Demetriou: "I was born and raised in Nicosia, Cyprus. My maternal family hails from Paralimni, Kyriakou Pelagia's village. Pelagia and her husband, Giorgos, remember my grandparents, especially my grandfather Nicolas (nicknamed Koustros), working in the fields of the village, before leaving with my grandmother to live in the nearby town (Famagusta). In Paralimni's close-knit, family-oriented community, the fact that I was 'Koustros's granddaughter' (named after him, too—Nicoletta) not only helped to secure me an interview with Pelagia, but also immediately established a sense of familiarity and continuity. I've been singing Cypriot folksongs since childhood. As a child, I was part of a number of music and dance groups in Nicosia, and the singer of my school's folk dance group. As a secondary school student in Nicosia in the 1990s, I witnessed the rise of private radio stations as well as Pelagia's rise to fame.

Next to folk singing I also studied classical singing for many years. After completing my secondary school education in Cyprus, I moved to Thessaloniki, Greece, where I completed a BA in Music Studies and continued my vocal training. Singing took me to Vienna next, where I had further vocal training. There I also studied Ethnomusicology at the Institute for Musicology of the University of Vienna, and decided to once again turn my attention to Cypriot folk music. In 2003 I rejoined a folk music group in Cyprus and began touring the island for performances in the summer months. In 2004 I moved to London to do a PhD in Ethnomusicology. During my fieldwork, in 2005–6, I continued singing throughout Cyprus with the group I was affiliated to. Back then I also met and interviewed a number of folk musicians. I did my first interview with Pelagia in May 2006, as part of my PhD research. I returned to Paralimni in October 2008 for further fieldwork and interviews with Pelagia for this volume."

• • •

Lexine Solomon released her first solo album in 2002 when in her midforties, celebrating her own identity as an Indigenous Torres Strait Islander woman living in mainland Australia. She engages her singing voice and her lyrics to articulate and express agency, empowerment, and celebration. With a combination of newly self-composed songs and covers, she is specifically involved with reclaiming and documenting the women in her family, and with encouraging and enabling women in positions of marginality, particularly Torres Strait Islander and Aboriginal women. As singer, facilitator, manager, and producer, her multifaceted vocal career involves touring nationally and internationally to perform and run workshops.

    Katelyn Barney: "I first met Torres Strait Islander performer Lexine Solomon in 2004 while undertaking research for my PhD on the contemporary music performance practices of Indigenous Australian women. After I completed my thesis in 2006, Lexine asked me if I would collaborate on a project with her. We decided to focus on the experiences of Lexine's fellow Torres Strait Islander women musicians and were successful in securing funding together. Over the last seven years, we have travelled across Australia together interviewing performers, presenting at conferences and writing articles. Our research relationship has grown into a strong friendship. We share a love of good food, music and laughter. My chapter draws on our experiences together as well as interviews undertaken with Lexine over the last seven years."

• • •

Marysia Mąka spent her childhood and early adulthood in the Podhale region in the Tatra Mountains of southern Poland as a Górale or Highlander, singing with local groups. In 1992, at age twenty-nine, she migrated to Toronto, Canada, where singing enabled her to sustain and renew her sense of personal identity in relation to motherhood (as mother of twelve children) and ethnicity.

    Within a framework of dislocation, local contexts, and a happy marriage and family life, Marysia creates community through her singing and compositions, using her voice to maintain connections to landscape, people, a sense of home, and language.

Louise Wrazen: "I first met Marysia in 1985. I lived with her sister and her family in the small village of Rogożnik when I first arrived in Podhale, and we often visited Marysia and her family in the neighbouring village of Stare Bystre. I spent a fair bit of time with Marysia at her home or accompanying her to various rehearsals, either at the church or at the local community hall where she led the local ensemble with her husband. I heard her sing for the first time at an ensemble rehearsal, and recorded her there as well as in her home. She has always been warm and welcoming, extending an unquali-fied generosity and openness—even though the times we see each other are often separated by months or years. I also lived with her for a short time in Podhale (in 1989). There were few formal interviews during this period; rather, there were many conversations and a lot of listening and observing. I helped with chores, hung around the kitchen, spent time attending to a variety of errands and activities with Marysia, and learned some repertoire from her and her husband.

I didn't see Marysia for several years after she came to Canada, yet when we met again I was relieved to find an older connection sustained. We now required a different schedule of arranged meetings and more focused conver-sations due at least in part to Marysia's hectic life as a mother of a very large family. Seeing her now both at her home as well as at various performances and in the community always with her children, I began to think differently about Marysia's singing as more firmly contextualized within her roles as mother and wife."

• • •

Sathima Bea Benjamin grew up in Cape Town, South Africa, during the transition to apartheid in the 1940s. Taking melodies she heard on her grand-mother's radio, she developed her own jazz singing voice, weaving in her own compositions. With a life embedded in an awareness of race and gender, she left for Europe in 1962. Her migratory lifestyle took her through tours in Europe, supporting her husband musician and caring for her daughters, to her own career development in New York City as a jazz singer with her own trio—a woman in a man's world—where she continues to record, create, and perform. Her vocality and life-stories reveal risks, freedoms, and creative processes as she creates a counternarrative to the discourses of masculinity in jazz.

Carol Muller: "Sathima and I both spent our childhoods in Cape Town, South Africa and yet, despite a common point of origin our engagement with Cape Town was fundamentally different. Sathima was born in 1936, twelve years before what became known as the apartheid government, came to power. 1936 was the same year that my parents were born. I was born in Cape Town in 1963, just shy of three years after the infamous Sharpeville Massacre, and a year after Sathima left for Europe. We met in New York City in 1989 when I was a graduate student at New York University, and Sathima and her husband, jazz pianist Abdullah Ibrahim, were living in exile from South Africa. I had called to speak to Abdullah Ibrahim but he was not home. Sathima and I talked and agreed to meet to discuss her own life and music. We would do this many times, mostly with a recording device between us. In the mid 1990s we decided to write a book together, and so I began to do oral history research amongst family members and musicians involved with South African jazz, particularly as it happened in Cape Town in the 1950s and early 1960s.

The piece of Sathima's life that was the most challenging to reconstruct, however, was her time as a jazz migrant in Europe from the early 1960s through 1977, when she and Abdullah decided to base themselves in New York City at the famous Chelsea Hotel until South Africa was liberated. In 2006 I discovered a CIA archive about African musicians, writers and artists in England and Europe in the 1960s. Contained inside the archive of London's Transcription Center—the place poorly funded by the CIA—were letters and other documents by and about Sathima and Abdullah. While Sathima has focused on performing and recording, I have done the interviewing, archival work, and writing. We hope that our co-authored, experimental book about her life and our working relationship will inform many about Sathima's extraordinary life and artistry, but also enable some to rethink the contours of thinking about jazz, diaspora, song, creativity, and South Africa's place in the story."[12]

. . .

Sima Shokrani, an Iranian singer specializing in Mazanderani repertoire and language, was profoundly influenced by the work songs of her grandmother, demonstrating an engagement with political and ideological issues from childhood, as she challenged linguistic constraints and participated in the revolution of 1979 as a university student of twenty-one. She has shaped her career as woman singer within the well-known constraints in Iran, as restrictions are placed around women singers by law. Making choices to sing songs that articulate women's agency in romantic and other relationships, she negotiates her multiple identities in private and public singing contexts. Supported by her husband, and despite the painful migration of her daughters to Germany, Sima chooses to remain in Iran, where she fulfills a role as a senior woman.

Gay Breyley: "Since 2005 I have conducted regular fieldwork in the northern Iranian province of Mazanderan, where I met Sima and a range of other singers and musicians, professional and non-professional. I have spent a lot of time as a guest and friend of Sima and her musician friends, listening to Sima sing in social contexts and watching her teach young women, as well as conducting interviews with Sima about her life and opinions. I'd like to say that she's the most generous person in every way—with her music and hospitality."

• • •

Zainab Herawi began her singing career as a child apprentice in the Herat region of Afghanistan in the 1940s, within the context of a class-based society, where singing by women was considered to be morally questionable. Zainab's is a story of unfulfilled fame because, although she was invited to sing for Kabul Radio when twenty-seven, family and background pressures and constraints led to her returning home, where she continued to sing for wedding celebrations. As a series of choices and struggles involving the interfacing domains of family, location, religion, and vocality, her life as a local singer with a large family was one of frequent anguish and frustration; yet her songs live on in the narratives and performances of musician and scholar Veronica Doubleday.

Veronica Doubleday: "During the 1970s I undertook fieldwork in the city of Herat, in Afghanistan. There I studied singing and learned to perform Afghan music, working principally with Zainab Herawi. For some ten months, until my departure in 1977, I concentrated on working with Zainab to research women's music and the position of female singers in the local community. We formed a close relationship and Zainab taught me many songs. Also, on occasion I performed as a member of Zainab's band. Since that time I have continued to perform the music I learned in Herat, and I regularly give concerts with my husband John Baily and noted Afghan musicians. Within Afghanistan and the transnational Afghan community I am acknowledged as an accomplished singer with an authentic repertoire of Heratu folk material."

• • •

Threads, Themes, Connections, and Clusters

In creating this collection we are relating to, and building on, deep foundations laid by earlier research on music, gender, and women, published as edited collections, monographs, and essays, and we acknowledge this prior scholarship.[13] Many of the issues and themes touched upon and discussed in preceding studies recur as motifs in this volume. Here, in this final section of the introductory chapter, I provide an outline of conspicuous clusters and connections, and of predominant threads and themes that interlace through the narratives. These emerge and emanate from aspects that the women themselves regard as important, rather than being imposed by the authors. It is important to note that we are not attempting to engage generalizations and broad theorizations in relation to these unique women. Given the focus upon individual lives and specificity, such an undertaking would be problematic and would undermine the thrust of the project. Nevertheless, because these are biographical narratives of women singers there are obviously commonalities and recurrent strands, even as the diversity documented within these threads, themes, connections, and clusters serves to emphasize individual experiences.

Two overarching and interlocked motifs are present throughout: discussion of the literal singing voice and the metaphorical voice. While the first encompasses vocal aesthetics, repertoire, and attributes directly concerned with singing and vocality, the second is a broader concept relating to self-determination, self-definition, agency, and the power to choose—which therefore takes in choices about the literal singing voice. By focusing on processes of decision-making and choices, we move away from the notion of "constraints" towards "tensions" and "opportunities." Pertinent questions should therefore be posited by readers in relation to each action: "What is the choice?" followed by "How, why, and with what consequences did she make this decision?" These relate to all matters, including, for example, vocal aesthetics, repertoire, bearing a child, marrying, caring for a family member, recording a song, and moving to another country.

Although the notion of tension might be seen negatively as a strained state or a condition resulting from forces acting in opposition to each other (for example, a binary of family/career), this is obviously not inherently pessimistic but rather implies ideas of change and transformation, with the possibility of strengthening and enhancement. Given the framework of multiplicity, complexity, and dichotomy, this idea of tension derives from being stretched, encompassing a relationship between elements and qualities with differing demands or implications. We therefore consider themes as tensions, each presenting possibilities with a range of consequences. Decisions should not be regarded as being obvious and straightforward. Some of the concerns exemplified in other studies as problematic are also seen to be less clear-cut in the positive/negative binary. For example, although a role of wife and homemaker has often been regarded as challenging for a career singer, for Kyriakou Pelagia this has been an advantage.

There are numerous threads and subjects that create obvious connections between particular chapters (for example, geopolitical issues; age-related matters; and family-background themes). Beyond the very overt associations and general themes, the specificity of the experiences varies widely; therefore, grouping together surface similarities would simply emphasize the drawbacks of generalizing. For example, there are parallels and apparent comparisons between Ayben and Ixya in terms of their supportive and traditional families, yet Ixya is drawn to an aesthetic of hyperfemininity and Ayben to a masculinist terrain of hip-hop. In another example, Sima in Iran, and Zainab in Afghanistan were both immersed in local music traditions with Islamic restrictions, and both were given the opportunity to record on national radio, yet Sima's context of an encouraging and happy marriage contrasts with that of Zainab, who experienced an uncooperative and difficult married environment, each generating very different situations for the singing life of these two women. One further illustration: because this collection is specifically woman-centered there may be expectations that each chapter includes discussions of motherhood in relation to each woman; however, only five narratives include references to bearing and raising children.

Finally, given the multifariousness and diversity of the material, creating order is challenging because issues are shared, overlapping, and interfacing. One issue might be mentioned under a subheading, but could equally fit with another. We trust that readers will encounter the connections and specificities as they engage with each chapter. If readers desire a comparative overview, brief outlines as they relate to each singer are given in the Appendix. The threads, themes, connections, and clusters are grouped together under eight subheadings:

> Repertoire and Function: "Sing what?" and "Why sing?"
> Vocal Aesthetics and Self-Crafting: "Sing how?"
> Bodies and Clothes: "What to wear?" and "How to move?"
> Childhood, Families, and "Home"
> Journeys and Migration
> Risk, Tensions, Opportunities, and Activism
> Recording and Broadcast Technologies
> Legacies

REPERTOIRE AND FUNCTION: "SING WHAT?" AND "WHY SING?"   Choices and issues regarding engagement with a musical repertoire, tradition, and genre show widely differing experiences. In most cases, certain expectations exist (expectations of family and of audience) relating to gender, age, ethnicity, religion, and class. Some women display a desire for change and transformation, challenging and taking on men's prerogatives. Others reveal an aspiration for immersion in cultural heritage. In noting such choices it is apparent that there is no simple equation. Newer radical forms, such as rap, for example, do not necessarily equal activism, and traditional forms do not necessarily equal stasis and reticence. There are some commonalities: Akiko, Amelia, and Ayben all demonstrate appropriation of men's prerogatives and traditions. Ayben, Kyriakou, Sima, and Zainab all faced restrictions of cultural conservatism and religion, invoking stereotypes of the iniquity of women's vocality.

Across the ten individuals many motivations and rewards for singing are evident, including emotional, musical, financial, religious, familial, and political. These women sing to enable belonging and identity (of self and others), to celebrate personal and cultural heritage, to empower, to give pleasure, to cause an emotional response, to entertain, and to make money. Some women specifically engage song lyrics as a strategic element of their agency—documenting family history, telling a woman's story and experiences, expressing sentiments, and enabling reflection. Significantly many of these women also teach singing and facilitate workshops. Embedded within each of these functions and roles is the notion of connection: each woman sings to connect with people. One conspicuous facet is that all the narratives encompass notions of pleasure and of the need to sing for "self" to create self-identity and to enable a sense of self-belonging.

VOCAL AESTHETICS AND SELF-CRAFTING: "SING HOW?" Embedded in all the chapters are overt and subtle references to vocal aesthetics, encompassing the sound of a singing voice, vocal gendering, and embodied aspects of singing. Each woman crafts her own voice within and beyond expected frameworks, demonstrating a profound musical and embodied knowledge. Aesthetics include falsetto and purity (Ixya), a hearty and resonant chest timbre (Marysia), vibratoless and nasal (Kyriakou), a low register (Sima), and power and strength (Lexine). One recurrent theme is that strength is necessary to achieve a delicate expression. Some accounts provide an insight into self-crafting processes, referring specifically to individuals cultivating their own style, with descriptions of the relationships between listening, copying, practicing, and creating a distinctive voice. Ayben taught herself at home and crafted her rapping voice; Ixya and Sathima began singing at home through listening to recordings and copying; Amelia, Kyriakou, Lexine, Marysia, and Sima all learned within familial and community environments, singing along with others and developing their individual voices.

BODIES AND CLOTHES: "WHAT TO WEAR?" AND "HOW TO MOVE?" Although the principal focus is on the aurality of voice, most of the women sing for an audience or aural community of hearers who not only listen but also look, and in some cases deliberately gaze. Choices about body-use, body-form, and body-covering therefore form a vital element in the reception of their voices. References to body-use include "sitting down" (Zainab), jabbing and chopping (Ayben), and smooth and graceful legato gestures (Ixya). Discussions of corporeality include a so-called "normal" body (Kyriakou, Sathima, Sima), a youthful and graceful body (Ixya), a body transformed by multiple pregnancies (Zainab), and an aging body (Kyriakou). Sartorial and costume elements encompass deliberately everyday clothes (Ayben, Kyriakou, Sathima); the transformation of the quotidian (Ixya); and a fully covered body and face, creating an "erotic voice" (Zainab).

CHILDHOOD, FAMILIES, AND "HOME"   Childhood experiences are invoked in all chapters, with a conspicuous coherency demonstrating how these are indeed formative years when ideas and practices concerning singing are molded and shaped. All the women began singing as children, some formally as an apprentice, others for pleasure within community settings. Familial contexts and the import of the role of family in each singer's life are also predominant, with experiences ranging from wholly supportive and indeed crucial in enabling the singer to shape her singing and career (Ayben, Ixya, Marysia), to obstructive and restrictive, preventing a singer from moving in directions that she desired to go (Akiko, Zainab). Negotiating between the public and private spheres and between real-life and performing personae are also associated with the familial domain. Blood relationships are referred to, as are relationships that are undertaken through choice, such as life-partner and husband, with some explicit references to love and romance (Sathima, Sima). It is worth noting that the absence of such narratives is not necessarily an indicator of diminished importance, but it may denote disinclination in sharing such elements because they are too distressing.

For some of the women issues of identity and choices are overtly tied up with motherhood (Marysia, Sathima, Sima, Zainab). A role as homemaker, housewife, and grandmother is central to the reputation of one singer (Kyriakou). Family members and families take on many functions in the narratives, including agent, producer, fellow musician, famous musical predecessor and teacher, musical role model, and decision-maker. A notion of "home" is also recurrent, with accounts of the family home as a pedagogical space, blurring musical apprenticeship with family life (Akiko, Zainab), and references to the role of intimate, personal, and private spaces for shaping and developing vocal practices (such as a bedroom (Ayben), kitchen (Marysia, Sathima, Sima), living room (Ixya), and home studio (Lexine)).

JOURNEYS AND MIGRATION   Stories of journeys, travel, and migration are invoked in several chapters, forming a significant element for many of the women. Each life can, of course, be understood as a journey, as we all make temporal progressions that are marked along the way with both momentous and subtle actions. Here, however, the focus is on literal travel and migration, including long-distance and permanent moves from one continent to another for career and life purposes (Marysia, Sathima); disinclination to travel far for concerts (Kyriakou); cross-border journeys for recordings and events (Ixya); national excursions to capital cities for radio recordings (Sima and Zainab); and international visits for workshops and concerts (Amelia, Lexine, Sima).

RISK, TENSIONS, OPPORTUNITIES, AND ACTIVISM   Although a broad grouping, the cluster of risk, tensions, opportunities, and activism brings together major issues and moments of these women's lives that encompasses a diverse range of facets. Such diversity is to be expected, given the various affiliations of identity beyond gender, comprising race, ethnicity, social class, religion, family, and age. Some accounts invoke marginalized identities, concerning disenfranchisement and opportunities, and powerful stories of perseverance and also failure. It is striking that the issue of risk appears in many chapters—risk that is specifically associated with the activity of singing. Perhaps the most extreme and overt negative consequence of singing included in this volume concerns the legal threat of imprisonment, which relates to women performing onstage and to solo female singing in Muslim and Muslim-influenced societies, therefore affecting Zainab in Afghanistan, Sima in Iran. Correlated to this is the strong condemnation of women who sing in public, a prohibition that impinged on Kyriakou in Cyprus. Many subtler and less-public forms are also referred to, most specifically rejection, disapproval, and shame associated with family and fellow community members. In most cases the singers are subject to the risk of failing as a singer and being considered mediocre or simply not very good.

Taking a risk also facilitates many positive outcomes, not least of which is to enable confidence. Within the narratives are various examples of the "I'll never forget" moments of opportunity and self-confidence (Ayben, Ixya, Kyriakou). Similarly there are many references to activism, from overt rebellion and resistance (Amelia, Ayben, Sima) to subtle and nonsubversive tactics. Some chapters deal with blatantly political, religious, and ideological agency (Amelia, Ayben, Kyriakou, Lexine, Sima), whereas others are far from controversial. Some narratives concern overcoming challenges and obstacles (Akiko, Ayben, Lexine, Zainab), whereas others are more related to gently shaping pathways (Ixya, Marysia).

RECORDING AND BROADCAST TECHNOLOGIES   Observing the role of re-cording and broadcast technologies in the lives of the singers may be an obvious thread, yet it is one that captures aspects of the interface of self-definition, self-crafting, and vocal production with a virtual world of global flows. Through the facilitatory role of technology, singing voices circulate as unseen waves of immense sonic significance. Many accounts refer to the direct influence of hearing recordings of other singers and of learning repertoire through recorded media—including LPs, cassettes, and CDs—and on the radio (Akiko, Ayben, Ixya, Sathima, Sima, Zainab). Most of the women also record their own singing voices, employing audio technology to disseminate their voices beyond live contexts.

LEGACIES   Finally and fittingly, each woman in this volume creates a lega-cy—ripples of influence that extend from her singing voice and life of sing-ing. Again, given the scope of personal contexts, such legacies cover a wide spectrum of facets, including gender, age, politics, genre, nationality, ethnicity, sexuality, and religion. Influences range from the subtle and hidden joy in a home, a private gathering, or a local setting, to the transnational posthumous life effects of a major figure (Amelia). Through their singing lives these women have established seniority as a positive asset (Kyriakou, Sathima, Sima); cre-ated role models for career women (Akiko, Lexine, Sathima); opened up singing in public to women in local settings (Kyriakou); enabled diasporic generations to connect with their homeland (Ixya, Lexine, Marysia, Sathima, Sima); empowered women to reflect on their indigenous status, encouraging them to become activists (Lexine); challenged men's actions towards women (Ayben, Sima); played with stereotypical constraints and engaged stereotypi-cal attributes as resistance (Akiko, Amelia, Ayben, Ixya, Kyriakou, Sima); and given thousands of listeners huge pleasure, often with numerous recordings resounding with their voices.

Amelia Pedroso and Zainab Herawi are no longer living, and here we acknowledge and cherish the lives of these two women.

• • •

On Listening and Connecting

A singer implies a listener—a person who pays attention to a singing voice, deriving pleasure, stimulation, and inspiration from listening. Singers enable listeners to enter into community with other listeners and to be transported to private and intimate spaces, places, and memories. We call you to become part of the network and to find connections with your own lives and voices, both literal and metaphorical. Within these narratives these women express a sense of generosity, a need to sing, to reach out, to give pleasure and touch others with their voice. Now we invite you to know something of the lives and voices of these ten women: Akiko, Amelia, Ayben, Ixya, Kyriakou, Lexine, Marysia, Sathima, Sima, and Zainab.[14]

Figure 0.1. Ixya Herrera and Ruth Hellier, Santa Barbara, California, 2008. © Ruth Hellier and Ixya Herrera.

Notes

1. In Christopher Small's work *Musicking: The Meanings of Performing and Listening*, the verb "musicking" encompasses all musical activity, including listening, performing, and composing.

2. For example, ethnomusicologist Zoe Sherinian has discussed the pitching of church music for voices associated with men, rather than women, in the context of South India (2005).

3. A companion website provides examples of these women singing, and, where relevant, updated information concerning ongoing recordings, concerts, and comments. I acknowledge the support of the University of California, Santa Barbara, in hosting this website and the Interdisciplinary Humanities Center for providing funds. With grateful thanks to website project managers: Linda Shaver-Gleason and George Blake, both doctoral students at UCSB. www.music.ucsb.edu/projects/womensingers.

4. I am immensely grateful to Ellen Koskoff for contributing an insightful and weighty Afterword to this volume. Here I acknowledge her influence in providing inspiration to so many scholars and students in the study of women and music-making.

5. It might appear that we are engaging a contradictory element in citing postmodern theories to be problematic in relation to universalizing tendencies, even as they are useful in rendering an individual life to be of value. Such contradictions and dichotomies are accepted and welcomed.

6. Used with permission of Nicoletta Demetriou.

7. Developing some of the issues further, the matter of how a "unified women's category could be articulated for feminist political purposes . . . illustrated (at least) two things. First, that gender—or *what it is to be* a woman or a man—is still very much a live issue. Second, that feminists have not entirely given up the view that gender is about *social* factors and that it is (in some sense) distinct from biological sex. The jury is still out on what the best, the most useful or (even) the correct definition of gender is. And some contemporary feminists still find there to be value in the original 1960s sex/gender distinction. . . . The various critiques of the sex/gender distinction have called into question the viability of the category *women*. . . . Linda Alcoff holds that feminism faces an identity crisis: the category of women is feminism's starting point, but various critiques about gender have fragmented the category and it is not clear how feminists should understand what it is to be a woman (2006). . . . Feminism is the movement to end the oppression women as a group face. But, how should the category of women be understood if feminists accept the above arguments that gender construction is not uniform, that a sharp distinction between biological sex and social gender is false or (at least) not useful, and that various features associated with women play a role in what it is to be a woman, none of which are individually necessary and jointly sufficient (like a variety of social roles, positions, behaviours, traits, bodily features and experiences)? Feminists must be able to address cultural and social differences in gender construction if feminism is to be a genuinely inclusive movement and be careful not to posit commonalities that mask important ways in which women *qua* women differ. These concerns (among others) have generated a situation where (as Linda Alcoff puts it) feminists aim to speak and make political demands in the name of women, at the same time rejecting the idea that there is a unified category

of women (2006, 152). If feminist critiques of the category *women* are successful, then what (if anything) binds women together, what is it to be a woman, and what kinds of demands can feminists make on behalf of women?" (Mikkola 2008).

8. See Barz and Cooley 2008 regarding fieldwork ethics, and Sherinian 2005 for a discussion concerning a feminist position.

9. See Hellier 2001 for a review of Broylez-González's publication. One of the seminal ethnographic models is Lila Abu-Lughod's *Writing Women's Worlds: Bedouin Stories* (2008 [1993]), "a book about women and an experiment in feminist ethnography," using narratives, arguments, and everyday lives of some individual families. With this publication Abu-Lughod notes that she aimed to do three things: "to confront my discipline of anthropology with the ways it has tended to typify cultural groups, to challenge public discourse about women of the Muslim Middle East, and to show Western feminists that defining patriarchy is not at all a simple matter." See Bowers 2000 for a discussion of writing a biography of a woman blues singer.

10. Although Kyriakou Pelagia is usually known by her surname, for the purposes of creating order her first name has been used to cohere with the format.

11. I would like to thank Tim Cooley, my wonderful husband, for his invaluable feedback and support.

12. *Musical Echoes: South African Women Thinking in Jazz.*

13. Edited collections have been particularly important and influential, including Bowers and Tick 1986, Koskoff 1989, Herndon and Ziegler 1990, Dunn and Jones, 1994a, Cook and Tsou 1994a, Cooper 1995, Whiteley 1997, Moisala and Diamond 2000, Bernstein 2003, and Magrini 2003. Significant work focusing on individual women singers includes: three women in Afghanistan (Doubleday 1988); five native American singers (Vander 1988 [1996]); Egyptian singer, Umm Kulthum (Danielson 1997); Gertrude "Ma" Rainey, Bessie Smith, and Billie Holiday (Davis 1999); Texan-Mexican singer Lydia Mendoza (Broylez-González 2001); three sisters in jazz (Hassinger 1989); Bessie Smith (Yurchenco 1990); Bessie Smith and Sophie Tucker (Antelyes 1994); Madonna (Vickers 1994); Macedonian singing star Esma Redzepova (Silverman 2003); pop music stars, Sinèad O'Connor, and k.d. lang (in Whiteley 1997); Umm Kulthum, Joan Baez, Mercedes Sosa, and Tori Amos (in Bernstein 2003); Tina Turner, Pat Benatar, Cyndi Lauper, and Madonna (Lewis 1990).

In her influential feminist work of 1991 Susan McClary included brief analysis of three contemporary women singers and musicians—Diamanda Galas, Laurie Anderson, and Madonna; Burns and Lafrance (2001) focused on four female musicians—Tori Amos, Courtney Love, Me'Shell Ndegeocello, and P. J. Harvey; and Hudson (2007) engaged narratives, interviews, conversations, and directly reported dialogue in her publication on thirty-four women in Texas music. *The World of Music* dedicated one volume to "Ethnomusicology and the Individual," which included Qureshi's article on singer Begum Akhtar (2001). Other publications focusing on individual women musicians have included Kaeppler (1990), Kimberlin (1990), Whiteley (2000), Moisala (2000), Reynolds and Press (1996), and Seroussi (2003). Further noteworthy studies include Sugarman's work on women, singing, and subjectivity in Albania (1997); Bayton's sociological analysis of women in contemporary popular music in the United Kingdom (1998); O'Brien's survey of women in rock, pop, and soul (2002); and Weidman's writing on gender and the politics of voice in South India (2003).

14. This volume had a long gestation period. Initially the idea came out of my own research working with Taidemar Perez, a wonderful young Venezuelan singer working in London, who sang with a Colombian ensemble (Hellier-Tinoco 2005), which influenced my decision to convene the conference on "Gender and Sexuality in Performance, Fieldwork, and Representation" for the British Forum for Ethnomusicology 2006, held at the University of Winchester, U.K. This led to a panel at the ICTM Conference 2007 entitled "Perspectives on the Female Voice: Identity, Representation and Control," comprising Drs. Laudan Nooshin and Katherine Schofield and myself (see Hellier-Tinoco 2007). This was followed by an international call for proposals for this current volume. Due to time constraints Drs. Nooshin and Schofield were not able to contribute to this volume; however, I wish to acknowledge their hard work and support in the developmental stages. I also wish to acknowledge the support of the Special Initiative Fund, University of Winchester, under the directorship of Professor Elizabeth Stuart.

I also thank graduate students taking Professor Tim Cooley's course on Studies in Ethnomusicology, at the University of California, Santa Barbara, for their useful comments. Finally, I thank Anne Rasmussen and an anonymous reviewer for their insightful feedback, and Laurie Matheson, Editor-in-Chief, University of Illinois Press, for her tremendous support for this project.

Website: www.music.ucsb.edu/projects/womensingers.

References

Abu-Lughod, Lila. 2008 [1993]. *Writing Women's Worlds: Bedouin Stories*. Berkeley: University of California Press.

Alcoff, Linda. 2006. *Visible Identities*. Oxford: Oxford University Press.

Antelyes, Peter. 1994. "Red Hot Mamas: Bessie Smith, Sophie Tucker, and the Ethnic Maternal Voice in American Popular Song." In *Embodied Voices: Representing Female Vocality in Western Culture*, eds. Leslie C. Dunn and Nancy A. Jones, 212–29. Cambridge: Cambridge University Press.

Barthes, Roland. 1977. *Image, Music, Text*. London: Fontana Press.

Barz, Gregory, and Timothy Cooley, eds. 2008. *Shadows in the Field: New Perspectives for Fieldwork in Ethnomusicology*. New York: Oxford University Press.

Bayton, Mavis. 1998. *Frock Rock: Women Performing Popular Music*. Oxford: Oxford University Press.

Bernstein, Jane A, ed. 2003. *Women's Voices across Musical Worlds*. Boston: Northeastern University Press.

Bowers, Jane. 2000. "Writing the Biography of a Black Woman Blues Singer." In *Music and Gender*, eds. Pirkko Moisala and Beverley Diamond, 140–65. Urbana: University of Illinois Press.

Bowers, Jane, and Judith Tick, eds. 1986. *Women Making Music: The Western Art Tradition, 1150–1950*. Urbana: University of Illinois Press.

Broylez-González, Yolanda. 2001. *Lydia Mendoza's Life in Music/La Historia de Lydia Mendoza*. New York: Oxford University Press.

Burns, Lori, and Melisse Lafrance. 2001. *Disruptive Divas: Feminism, Identity and Popular Music*. London: Routledge.

Butler, Judith. 1990. "Performative Acts and Gender Constitution: An Essay in Phenomenology and Feminist Theory." In *Performing Feminisms: Feminist Critical Theory and Theatre*, ed. Sue-Ellen Case, 270–83. Baltimore: John Hopkins University Press.

———. 1991. "Contingent Foundations: Feminism and the Question of 'Postmodernism.'" *Praxis International* 11:150–65.

———. 1999 [1990]. *Gender Trouble: Feminism and the Subversion of Identity*. London: Routledge.

Citron, Marcia J. 2004. "Feminist Waves and Classical Music: Pedagogy, Performance, Research." *Women and Music* 8:47–60.

Cook, Susan C., and Judy S. Tsou, eds. 1994a. *Cecilia Reclaimed: Feminist Perspectives on Gender and Music*. Urbana: University of Illinois Press.

———. 1994b. "Introduction: 'Bright Cecilia.'" In *Cecilia Reclaimed: Feminist Perspectives on Gender and Music*, eds. Susan C. Cook and Judy S. Tsou, 1–14. Urbana: University of Illinois Press.

Cooper, Sarah, ed. 1995. *Girls! Girls! Girls! Essays on Women and Music*. London: Cassell.

Danielson, Virginia. 1997. *The Voice of Egypt: Umm Kulthum, Arabic Song, and Egyptian Society in the Twentieth Century*. Chicago: University of Chicago Press.

Davis, Angela Y. 1999. *Blues Legacies and Black Feminism: Gertrude "Ma" Rainey, Bessie Smith, and Billie Holiday*. New York: Vintage Books.

Doubleday, Veronica. 1988. *Three Women of Herat*. Austin: University of Texas Press.

Dunn, Leslie C., and Nancy A. Jones, eds. 1994a. *Embodied Voices: Representing Female Vocality in Western Culture*. Cambridge: Cambridge University Press.

———. 1994b. Introduction. In *Embodied Voices: Representing Female Vocality in Western Culture*, eds. Leslie C. Dunn and Nancy A. Jones, 1–13. Cambridge: Cambridge University Press.

Feld, Steven, Aaron A. Fox, Thomas Porcello, and David Samuels. 2004. "Vocal Anthropology: From the Music of Language to the Language of Song." In *A Companion to Linguistic Anthropology*, ed. Alessandro Duranti, 321–45. Oxford: Blackwell Publishing.

Frith, Simon. 1995. "The Body Electric." *Critical Quarterly* 37(2):1–10.

Greer, Germaine. 1999. *the whole woman*. London: Doubleday.

Gunew, Sneja, ed. 1990. *Feminist Knowledge, Critique and Construct*. London: Routledge.

Haslanger, S. 1995. "Ontology and Social Construction." *Philosophical Topics* 23:95–125.

Hassinger, Jane. 1989. "Close Harmony: Early Jazz Styles in the Music of the New Orleans Boswell Sisters." In *Women and Music in Cross-Cultural Perspective*, ed. Ellen Koskoff, 195–201. Urbana: University of Illinois Press.

Hayes, Eileen. 2006. "Theorizing Gender, Culture, and Music." *Women and Music* 10:71–79.

Hellier, Ruth. 2001. "Review of Y. Broyles-González's *Lydia Mendoza's Life in Music/La Historia de Lydia Mendoza*." *British Journal of Ethnomusicology* 10(2):126–28.

Hellier-Tinoco, Ruth. 2005. "Embodied Voices in Cross-Cultural Contexts." Paper given at the conference of the *British Forum for Ethnomusicology and AHRB Centre for Cross-Cultural Music and Dance Performance*, University of London.

———. 2007. "Politics, Aesthetics and Constraints of an Embodied 'Latina' Voice in Britain." Paper given at the *39th World Conference of the ICTM (International Council for Traditional Music)*. University of Music and Performing Arts, Vienna, Austria.

Herndon, Marcia, and Susanne Ziegler, eds. 1990. *Music, Gender and Culture.* West Germany: Florian Noetzel Verlag.

Heyes, Cressida. 2000. *Line Drawings.* Ithaca: Cornell University Press.

———. 2009. "Identity Politics." In *The Stanford Encyclopedia of Philosophy (Spring 2009 Edition)*, ed. Edward N. Zalta. http://plato.stanford.edu/archives/spr2009/entries/identity-politics/ (accessed March 2012).

Hudson, Kathleen. 2007. *Women in Texas Music: Stories and Songs.* Austin: University of Texas Press.

Kaeppler, Adrienne. 1990. "The Production and Reproduction of Social and Cultural Values in the Compositions of Queen Sālote of Tonga." In *Music, Gender and Culture,* eds. Marcia Herndon and Susanne Ziegler, 191–220. New York: C F Peters.

Kimberlin, Cynthia Tse. 1990. "'And are you pretty?' Choice, Perception, and Reality in Pursuit of Happiness." In *Music, Gender and Culture,* eds. Marcia Herndon and Susanne Ziegler, 221–40. New York: C F Peters.

Koskoff, Ellen, ed. 1989. *Women and Music in Cross-Cultural Perspective.* Urbana: University of Illinois Press.

———. 2005. "(Left *Out in*) *Left* (the *Field*): The Effects of Post-postmodern Scholarship on Feminist and Gender Studies in Musicology and Ethnomusicology, 1990–2000." *Women and Music* 9:90–98.

Lewis, Lisa. 1990. *Gender Politics and MTV: Voicing the Difference.* Philadelphia: Temple University Press.

Lockhead, Judy. 2007. "Review of *Beyond Structural Listening?* Postmodern Modes of Hearing." *Women and Music* 11:111–24.

Magrini, Tullia, ed. 2003. *Music and Gender: Perspectives from the Mediterranean.* Chicago: Chicago University Press.

McClary, Susan. 1991. *Feminine Endings: Music, Gender, and Sexuality.* Minneapolis: University of Minnesota Press.

———. 1994. "Forward: Ode to Cecilia." In *Cecilia Reclaimed: Feminist Perspectives on Gender and Music,* eds. Susan C. Cook and Judy S. Tsou, iv–xii. Urbana: University of Illinois Press.

Mikkola, Mari. 2008. "Feminist Perspectives on Sex and Gender." In *The Stanford Encyclopedia of Philosophy (Fall 2008 Edition)*, ed. Edward N. Zalta. http://plato.stanford.edu/archives/fall2008/entries/feminism-gender/ (accessed March 2012).

Moisala, Pirkko. 2000. "Gender Negotiation of the Composer Kaija Saariaho in Finland: The Woman Composer as Nomadic Subject." In *Music and Gender,* eds. Pirkko Moisala and Beverley Diamond, 166–88. Urbana: University of Illinois Press.

Moisala, Pirkko, and Beverley Diamond, eds. 2000. *Music and Gender.* Urbana: University of Illinois Press.

O'Brien, Lucy. 2002. *She Bop: The Definitive History of Women in Rock, Pop and Soul.* London: Continuum.

Peraino, Judith. 2007. "Listening to Gender: A Response to Judith Halberstam." *Women and Music* 11:59–63.

Qureshi, Regula Burckhardt. 2001. "In Search of Begum Akhtar: Patriarchy, Poetry, and Twentieth-century Indian Music." *World of Music* 43(1):97–137.

Reynolds, Simon, and Joy Press. 1996. *The Sex Revolts: Gender, Rebellion, and Rock 'n' Roll*. Cambridge: Harvard University Press.

Sarkissian, Margaret. 1999. "Thoughts on the Study of Gender in Ethnomusicology: A Pedagogical Perspective." *Women and Music* 3: 17–27.

Seroussi, Edwin. 2003. "Archivists of Memory: Written Folksong Collections of the Twentieth-Century Sephardic Women." In *Music and Gender: Perspectives from the Mediterranean*, ed. Tullia Magrini, 195–213. Chicago: Chicago University Press.

Sherinian, Zoe C. 2005. "Re-presenting Dalit Feminist Politics through Dialogical Musical Ethnography." *Women and Music* 9:1–12.

Silverman, Carol. 2003. "The Gender of the Profession: Music, Dance and Reputation among Balkan Muslim Rom Women." In *Music and Gender: Perspectives From the Mediterranean*, ed. Tullia Magrini, 119–45. Chicago: University of Chicago Press.

Stock, Jonathan. 2001. "Toward an Ethnomusicology of the Individual, or Biographical Writing in Ethnomusicology." *World of Music* 43(1):5–19.

Stokes, Martin. 1995–96. "'Alaturka Fantasies': Deceit, The Voice, and the Arabesk Stage in Turkey." *New Formations* 27:42–58.

Sugarman, Jane C. 1997. *Engendering Song: Singing and Subjectivity at Prespa Albanian Weddings*. Chicago: University of Chicago Press.

Tolbert, Elizabeth. 2003. "Review: Music and Gender." *Women and Music* 7:76–82.

Vander, Judith. 1996 [1988]. *Songprints: The Musical Experience of Five Shoshone Women*. Urbana: University of Illinois Press.

Vickers, Nancy J. 1994. "Maternalism and the Material Girl." In *Embodied Voices: Representing Female Vocality in Western Culture*, eds. Leslie C. Dunn and Nancy A. Jones, 230–46. Cambridge: Cambridge University Press.

Weidman, Amanda. 2003. "Gender and the Politics of Voice: Colonial Modernity and Classical Music in South India." *Cultural Anthropology* 18(2):194–232.

Whiteley, Sheila, ed. 1997. *Sexing the Groove: Popular Music and Gender*. London: Routledge.

———. 2000. *Women and Popular Music: Sexuality, Identity, and Subjectivity*. London: Routledge

Yurchenco, Henrietta. 1990. "Mean Mama Blues: Bessie Smith and the Vaudeville Era." In *Music, Gender and Culture*, eds. Marcia Herndon and Susanne Ziegler, 241–51. New York: C F Peters.

1. Akiko Fujii

Telling the Musical Life Stories
of a Hereditary Jiuta *Singer of Japan*

SHINO ARISAWA

Whereas my brother has said that he wants to be a distinguished teacher of the school, I told him my goal is to save jiuta for the Japanese people.

Born into a prestigious musical family in 1963, Akiko Fujii has lived through many professional and personal changes, culminating in a career in her chosen art form of traditional classical singing. Her life experiences have cultivated and sculpted her as a musician, a woman, a wife, a daughter, a granddaughter, and a sister. When training in jiuta song she struggled to locate her own musical identity in relation to two senior women within her family—her mother and grandmother. Following in the footsteps of these two rather contradictory role models, Akiko's exploration into her own aesthetics of singing and performance successfully rekindled the essence of jiuta music and represented the passion of women for contemporary listeners. Furthermore, Akiko's dictatorial father and her difficult rivalry with her brother both had a great impact on her determination as a single woman pursuing her musical career. These two men heavily influenced the young Akiko's sense of gender roles within the family and broader society as she sought a way to become a professional singer. Families hold a crucial responsibility for lifelong psychological development, and it was through her family that Akiko negotiated those gender identities that would later condition her aesthetics in the art of singing.

Akiko comes from a long line of jiuta players. *Jiuta* is a secular Japanese vocal music accompanied by the three-string *shamisen* lute. Unlike other vocal traditions of Japan in which singers and shamisen players have separate roles, a jiuta singer sings to his/her own shamisen accompaniment. A musician, therefore, often appears on stage alone, and that creates a solitary atmosphere for the performer, having nobody around him/her to seek help. Among other vocal traditions of Japan, jiuta also has a distinctive style of singing originally developed by blind male musicians between the seventeenth and nineteenth centuries. Although authorized transmission was exclusively restricted to those blind men, jiuta also became an important repertory for geisha, who sang and played shamisen to entertain male customers in the pleasure quarters. After the modernization of Japan in the late nineteenth century, sighted people, including women, started performing jiuta as professionals, and the performance context of jiuta shifted from indoor private entertainment to a staged classical art. There are several Japanese vocal genres accompanied by shamisen, but jiuta's distinctive feature lies in its lyrics: they depict intricate emotions of women who endure suffering for their loved ones, who feel strongly for falling flowers, and who shed tears—ultimately these are women who follow their passion and their belief in love.

In reworking the performance context of jiuta Akiko sought to gain a more intimate atmosphere with her audience by incorporating speech, another significant element of her performance. She spent time at concerts detailing her personal relationships with her family. As a result, listeners could witness the creative process of an isolated but determined woman striving for a musical career through her jiuta training and her family relations. Akiko's jiuta performance came to embody her whole life and emotional experiences. For her these were fully integrated into her artistic world, presenting the compelling drama of an independent woman.

Material for this chapter is drawn from my research conducted between 2003 and 2009.[1] During this time I was associated with Akiko as a researcher, her jiuta student, a friend, and a colleague in the art world. In our formal interviews as well as informal conversations, Akiko expressed her complex feelings experienced from her childhood to the present day, including key events that took place in her youth, within her marriage, her divorce, and ultimately her mother's death. Musical life stories can reveal our desires and the self that we wish to realize in relation to our music. They can be seen as constructions or fantasies of the world, created by the person telling the story, in which one's individuality is negotiated in relation to the surrounding society (Diamond 2000, 131). For Akiko, the telling of her musical life story was a way of reexamining her own life experiences. Thus she reconstructed her identity to reflect her desire to pursue a career as an independent singer. Many of the stories Akiko told me included details of her relationship with her audience, which was a crucial aspect for her constructions of self images, including her presentation as a woman singer. Although these stories may not be precisely accurate records of the events, it is possible to examine, through these selected incidents, the performer's views of herself as a performer (Sawin, 2002, 49–50). These subjective views about Akiko's relationship with her audience can indicate crucial aspects for her as a singer.

Akiko's desire and the realization of self in her stories are further enriched by images of women in the lyrics of jiuta. Akiko expressed strong empathy with these images. Singing songs can often be an act of reflecting on self-image (Price 1983, 1985), and it can also "serve to re-enforce and define gender identity" (Koskoff 1989, 9). In this chapter, I examine how Akiko constructed her gender identities in relation to the emotions of women in jiuta. In their teachings of jiuta, Akiko's grandmother and mother handed down their own images of women and gender roles. I look closely at how Akiko further developed her own views about women in jiuta, in particular how she portrayed the emotions of these women as reflections of her own aesthetic experiences.

Born into a Prestigious Musical Family

I had been trained to become the heir [of the school] until my brother entered the Tokyo University of Fine Arts and Music.[2] So for my childhood I was like an uchi-deshi ("internal apprentice") for my mother, despite the fact that we were actual mother and daughter. From my earliest recollections, I felt that my mother was observing me all the time, and I also felt that I was controlled by the family, or in other words, by my mother.

Akiko was born into an extremely prestigious musical family. Her grandmother Keiko and mother Kunie were both prominent jiuta singers of their times. When Akiko was a child, her mother was already involved in performing concerts, as well as playing for radio and television. In addition she had a heavy load of responsibilities as the *iemoto* (house-head) of her *ryûha* (school). Within the spheres of Japan's *dentô geinô* (traditional performing arts), such as the tea ceremony, flower arrangement, music, and theatre, the iemoto is a powerful figure who authorizes the transmission of her or his art by issuing certificates, licensing teachers, and controlling detailed artistic matters such as performance styles. The iemoto also manages financial and social matters, such as the setting of tuition fees, and controls their members' performance activities—for instance deciding where and who should perform a certain musical piece. Akiko's mother inherited the position of iemoto from her mother, and thus was a representative of the school.

An *uchi-deshi* (internal apprentice) is a student who lives with his or her teacher and carries out various kinds of work, including housework, preparing meals, cleaning, and other routine chores. Such internal apprenticeships used to be quite common in the traditional Japanese performing arts, whereby students who wished to become professional artists were expected to faithfully follow their master's instructions and share in their daily life. It was thought that this would enable them to forge a stronger bond with their master.

Although Akiko's mother held a respected position within her school and musical spheres, as the wife of a businessman she had another important role within the home—that of managing housework and looking after her husband and two children. Akiko's mother may have thought that having an internal apprentice at home would threaten her husband's authority, and so instead she gave extra duties to her daughter. Akiko was caught in a trap, under enormous pressure from two directions. She not only had plenty of extra housework as an internal apprentice, but was also under psychological pressure from being heir to the school.

My mother was extremely busy, but when she was at home she totally dedicated herself to her husband [Akiko's father], who was an autocrat. Perhaps it was a reaction to stress, but she was always irritated and snappy. The brunt of her irritation was borne by her children. My brother turned his aggression on me and bullied me when I was a child. Because there was no uchi-deshi at that time, I did everything—such as housework, including looking after my father—and when I graduated from school, I picked up my mother from work and was a kaban-mochi ("bag carrier"). I couldn't bear it psychologically, and I ended up all skin and bones. I often caught a cold, had anemia, and had to stay in bed because of stomach-aches caused by kidney disease. I also refused to go to school and often stayed indoors all day.

Being a *kaban-mochi* (bag carrier) symbolizes Akiko's suppressed status. The term describes a person who serves a superior—colloquially, this might be called "a dogsbody"—the image is of a person struggling beneath a heavy load and accompanying their superior everywhere. Akiko had complex feelings about her parents' relationship as well as her own situation, which she felt her mother forced her into. She described how her mother had been always preoccupied with her responsibilities, and consequently how she would run out of patience:

I couldn't love my mother. She was extremely bitter, strict, and abusive. I even hated her. Because of that, I couldn't concentrate on my training and spent everyday with zero energy. It was a kind of depression. It was around the time when my brother entered the Tokyo University of Fine Arts and Music, and people around me began to think that he would inherit our school. I wondered whether I should look for a different career, but I couldn't think about it, and just closed my mind. My parents accused me of being lazy. Every day was hell, and I often thought about committing suicide.

Akiko had ambivalent feelings about jiuta. She followed the art with no other options because she knew that she was *"born into the family of jiuta."* However, it was jiuta that deprived Akiko of a "normal" relationship with her mother. For Akiko, professional and family life had coexisted within the home since her childhood. Although Akiko saw her mother as a role model in terms of her being a jiuta musician, as a mother she was far less of a role model. This woman had no need to earn a living because her husband was wealthy. So her role within the family was as a full-time housewife supporting her husband. Akiko's father failed to respect her mother's musical career. Her mother carefully monitored his moods and dedicated herself fully to serving him as a housewife. There was much tension between them, and Akiko felt her parents' relationship was one of "pretending" to be a couple.

Within postwar Japanese society many women began to engage in highly respected professions, becoming doctors, lawyers, and so on, but at the same time they were faced with the difficulties and expectations of fulfilling multiple roles inside and outside their homes. In general, society still considered marriage and motherhood to be the primary roles of women. If a woman tried to pursue her own career, this was regarded as inappropriate. Due to a strong cultural tradition that demanded that women dedicate themselves to their homes and families, those who chose to be career women and have families at the same time had to deal with the social stigma of displaying "aberrant behavior" in terms of neglecting their husbands and children (Dilatush 1977, 191–203; Hendry 1981, 28; Iwao 1993). Looking at her mother struggling with her two roles within the family—master of an art and full-time housewife—Akiko developed a complex feeling toward gender roles. While she was encouraged to follow in her mother's footsteps as a career woman, she saw the reality of its consequence: a suppressed position in relation to the husband who had no respect for her career.

In addition to this, sibling rivalry arose between her and her brother. Akiko had been regarded as the next to inherit the school when she was a child. This was due to the fact that her brother, who was also learning jiuta, had expressed no intention of pursuing a career in music, but instead wanted to study science at university. Although he began learning jiuta at a very early age from his grandmother and mother, this was simply because he grew up in an environment where the people around him were musicians. However, when he was a high school student he had an accident that hospitalized him for a while and subsequently gave him the chance to reconsider his career. He then began to take seriously the training from his grandmother and mother and eventually entered the Tokyo University of Fine Arts and Music. Akiko, on the other hand, gave up attending the university due to illness. Getting into the Tokyo University of Fine Arts and Music is part of the standard career progression of children from hereditary musical families, and so for Akiko, her own failure and her brother's success at the university meant that she was put into second place for succession to their musical lineage. As expected, Akiko's mother announced, at a 2006 recital, that she had handed over her position as head of the school to her son, who would now be responsible for continuing the school.

In many musical families, a male child is seen as the legitimate heir of the lineage, whereas female children are expected to play supporting roles and often remain dilettantes in spite of their skills. Although many women musicians have played a leading role and achieved success as iemoto, within traditional music the majority of female musicians are still given supporting parts. Within the circle of jiuta, many school members tend to be women but the iemoto are very often men. It is generally the case that a male child succeeds to his parent's position, and a female becomes head only if the incumbent head does not have a son, or if the son chooses a different profession. Akiko's grandmother was the exceptional woman—she broke free and established herself as iemoto of her own school by becoming independent from her teacher, despite the fact that her teacher was strongly offended by her decision. The school founded by Akiko's grandmother was handed down to her mother, the family's only child.

Akiko described how she had believed that inheriting the art of jiuta from these women was her fate. Akiko, seeing herself as responsible for these two senior women's heritage of art, felt she had lost her own place in the family. Her stress and depression became even deeper when her brother entered university and stood, ahead of her, as a rival. While struggling to find a direction, she sought a new way of life in marriage. "*My desire for marriage, which I had since childhood, was a dream of escaping from home,*" said Akiko. Her marriage, however, was not a happy one. "*It was,*" Akiko said, "*the wrong marriage from the beginning,*" and broke down very quickly. Her husband was a *sarari-man* (salaried man), and an office worker. "*He was not a musician,*" said Akiko, and so failed to understand her career as an artist. Like her father, who had no connection with the art world, Akiko found her husband had no respect or support for his wife's profession. These stories suggest that Akiko had an idea that marriage would bring her a better place to live and a home where she would be loved, cared for, and most importantly, encouraged to pursue her musical career. Akiko had a desire to find a husband who found values in art and showed his sympathy with her passion as a musician. She dreamed of a true partner, the kind of person her mother could not have had.

In Pursuit of a Professional Career

I thought that if I didn't commit myself and work hard in life, then people would end up regarding my art as a mere "ojosan-gei" (a hobby of upper class daughters).[3]

Knowing her brother would inherit the school, Akiko had to take a different path and pursue her own musical career. Most amateur players of jiuta are women, often wives and daughters from wealthy families who can afford to spend money on entertainment. Akiko wanted to distance herself from such an image and show the public that she was an independent, professional musician. Having made up her mind to divorce, Akiko began saving money to survive alone. Although the divorce rate in Japan continues to increase, it remains a social stigma. Those who choose to divorce are largely women with higher levels of education, earning a stable income from their jobs (Tanaka 1995, 52). Giving up university, Akiko had no legitimate qualification that would support her in society. The only thing she could rely on was the art form she had inherited from her grandmother and mother. "*In order to live alone forever as a single woman, there is only one way for me—that is to achieve the art myself,*" said Akiko. However, she faced the problem of a significant decline in the popularity of traditional music in present-day Japan, due to the relentless development of popular music and other modern genres. This was an issue not encountered by her grandmother's and mother's generations. So it was far from easy for Akiko to pursue a career as a jiuta singer. Meanwhile her brother had inherited the school and eventually gained the right to receive all the benefits from running the school, not to mention the prestige of being the iemoto. Akiko, on the other hand, had to find a way to survive both financially and socially as an independent woman.

Determined to pursue her career, Akiko embarked on a demanding journey, pushing herself to carry out challenging engagements in order to establish herself as a professional jiuta singer. Due to the rapid decline in the popularity of jiuta, it was almost impossible to attract large audiences to concerts. Currently most jiuta musicians secure finances through tuition fees and membership fees from their amateur students, not from performing concerts. As Akiko did not inherit the school, she had no financial foundation to rely on. Giving concerts without sponsorship would therefore result in a deficit because there would not be enough tickets sold to cover the costs of organizing the event. In 2001 she started giving a recital every two months in an informal setting for small audiences of around fifty people. The venue was a small space adjacent to an Italian restaurant, Taberuna [Taverna], in Shinjuku, central Tokyo. I began attending these Taberuna concerts, and after being present at several of these, I was struck by how different they were from the usual jiuta event. Not only was the setting surprising, but also the sense of intimacy created between the performer and audience due to the restricted space—listeners sitting in the front row were close enough to touch Akiko, and everyone present could see the sweat running down her face (figure 1.1).

Before the Meiji Restoration and the consequent Westernization of Japan in the late nineteenth century, jiuta was performed as entertainment in private households, as well as in the pleasure quarters. In this context, performances took place in an intimate environment with no clear boundary between performer and audience. After the development of modern concert halls in the twentieth century, the boundary between stage and audience became obvious. Thus the original context of a jiuta performance, where the performer and the audience interact via music and conversation, was lost. However, the venue in which Akiko chose to perform was originally a karaoke area within an Italian restaurant. The owner had refurbished the karaoke space to make a small concert venue and sought the opinion of Soh

Figure 1.1. Akiko Fujii performing "Kageboshi" ("Shadow") at her recital in the Kioi Hall, Tokyo, October 2008. Photograph by Hideyuki Masuda. © Akiko Fujii.

Fujimoto, director of the Japan Traditional Cultures Foundation,[4] as to how
to use this new space. When Fujimoto asked Akiko if she was interested in
performing regular recitals in this newly refurbished place, at first she was
hesitant. Being born into a prestigious musical family, her audience's expec-
tation would be extremely high, and no mistakes would be allowed for in
her performance. Playing a small venue, where every single breath would
be audible, must have made her hesitant, aware of the pressure she would
be under. However, she was trying to find a new direction, and so after a
while she decided to challenge herself,[5] using the opportunity to explore the
boundaries of her performance aesthetics. She decided to take advantage of
the small venue to create an intimate atmosphere, enhancing it further by
giving informal talks on stage between performances. "*I wanted to give talks
like backstage talks containing things the audience wouldn't be able to know if
they just watch musicians performing on stage,*" said Akiko. However, things
were not easy.

> *My mother objected saying it was foolhardy. I think there were two reasons
> for her objection. First of all, she looked down on informal settings, especially
> the idea of having my own chat. Also, she doubted that I could give concerts so
> frequently because she thought I wasn't good enough.*

Within traditional Japanese music, it is widely accepted that a formal performance should be given on a *himôsen* (a red carpet) with a *kinbyôbu* (a
golden folding screen) because performances without such a stage setting
are considered too informal or lowbrow. In premodern Japan, households
of aristocrats and warlords were furnished with such interiors, especially on
auspicious days or for ceremonies. In present-day Japan, although traditional
households have mostly disappeared, musicians still continue to use this
stage setting for performances in concert halls. In so doing, they wish to
create an image of authentic, sophisticated tradition associated with upper-
class culture. According to Akiko, different performance contexts have been
maintained to the present day. She suggests there were two types of musical lineages in the jiuta tradition: one associated with the *karyûkai* ("flower
and willow world" or the pleasure quarters), and the other a direct lineage
of authorized blind musicians. Before modernization in the late nineteenth
century, authorized transmission of jiuta could be passed down only to blind
male musicians who belonged to the Tôdô guild that was acknowledged by
the Tokugawa shogunate.

Akiko recalls that teachers of the past used to say "Our *gei* (art) is different
from theirs, and we must perform on a red carpet and with a golden folding screen." She believes that such comments were made "*because of their*

self-respect," seeking to distinguish their high-art form from the low-class entertainment offered by geisha in the pleasure quarters. Whereas geisha have been defended by several academics (e.g., Downer 2006; Foreman 2008) as respected artists within their respective circles, they were still looked down upon by a broad spectrum of Japanese society, especially among the older generation. To such people they were viewed as prostitutes or, at best, low-class entertainers, the playthings of men. Singing jiuta in an informal setting and chatting to the audience may have evoked an image of the pleasure quarters and caused Akiko's mother to have reservations about the idea. Akiko's talks, however, were not the kind of banter between geisha and their male customers, creating "undercurrent eroticism" between two genders (Foreman 2008, 114). The style of Akiko's speech was rather a recounting of her memories, often concerning the training with her grandmother and mother, describing the distinctions between these two women:

> *Training from my grandmother was passion itself. During lessons she would become heated and suddenly stand up with a red face, her body shaking with excitement. She taught me jiuta full of passion and energy, and always sang for me as if she was performing for her audience on stage. My mother had a completely different attraction, which was her own style of singing. One could say her singing somehow held some sexiness created by her subtle vocal technique. My mother had taught me these subtleties ever since I was very young.*[6]

On a different occasion, Akiko described how the personalities of these two women were so diverse: her grandmother was a passionate woman, and her mother had a logical mind. While studying closely with these women, Akiko found their performances of jiuta also varied from each other. Comparing them to baseball pitchers, Akiko described her grandmother's voice as "straight" and her mother's as "curving." She had two role models with completely different personalities, which she thought resulted in the different aesthetics of their singing styles. Akiko went on to explain that her grandmother had a "pure art" (*junsui na gei*) thanks to being "clumsy" (*bukiccho*). On the other hand, she saw her mother as a "clever" (*kiyô*) person and associated this personality trait with her highly technical style of singing.

Reflecting on her relationship with both her mother and grandmother, Akiko acknowledged she had been aiming to achieve the singing style of her mother, who she thought had gained an extraordinary vocal technique through hard training. But later Akiko came to appreciate the power of her grandmother's robust voice, even though it did not have as much complexity as her mother's. After recognizing these distinct styles of singing, she became determined to pursue a style borrowing from both of them, in order to create "*something outstanding.*"[7] "*My grandmother and mother were my role models, but just following their footsteps is not enough—it's important to create my own art.*"

Blind men who originally handed down jiuta damaged their voices on purpose so as to obtain a rough sound. This vocal quality became associated with this musical genre, symbolizing the image of blind men. Such voices were sometimes called *hôshi-goe* ("voice of monks"), referring to the tradition whereby musicians originally had some connection to Buddhist temples. They also wore costumes similar to monks' robes. However, following modernization in the late nineteenth century, sighted people including women also began performing jiuta professionally. Eventually, the gritty "voice of monks" disappeared, and musicians sought to develop new vocal aesthetics for this genre.

Akiko's grandmother was an emerging woman musician who established a place for women jiuta singers. She had a robust sound quality that could be compared to the virile image of male musicians. However, she polished her sound somewhat to accommodate contemporary aesthetics. Akiko's mother explored a different style, developing a much more delicate, ornamented method, integrating other vocal genres such as *nagauta* from the Kabuki theatre and the recent *yamatogaku* developed in the early twentieth century, together with an influence from Western classical singing. Due to her graceful style of singing and elaborate ornamentation, her voice was often characterized as "feminine" by her contemporary audiences and held up in contrast to the previously prevalent gamut of harsh, earthy sounds.

Akiko had been highly praised by her audiences for her warm, delicate voice and her refined style, comparable to her mother's singing, and Akiko acknowledged this herself. But she was searching for a more robust style that would enhance the power in her voice. This fundamental vocal shift occurred after Akiko listened repeatedly to her grandmother's tape recordings in order to learn a particular piece. Akiko found a "*strength*" in her voice, "*through the use of the entire body.*" She had not fully realized this physical power when learning with her grandmother while she was still alive: "*I realized I had to break new ground in my singing, otherwise I thought that I wouldn't be able to fully acquire the piece.*" Akiko expressed her view of performance aesthetics as follows:

> Whether you are man or woman, strength is necessary. If you don't have the strength, delicate expression can't be achieved. If strength is considered to be masculine, then my singing has recently become slightly more masculine. . . . But perhaps it means the range of my expression has become wider. In general men

are thought to be courageous. Also, in terms of musical expression, to be steadfast is considered as manly. But that kind of description just deals with the surface.[8]

By seeking strength, Akiko was exploring a way to enrich her musical expressiveness. She used this notion of strength to convey the musical drama of a couple in love. The piece in question was "Nureôgi," or "Wet Fan," which she had chosen to perform in concert for the first time. This is a highly dramatic piece: it depicts a couple walking hand in hand to a river on their way to commit double-suicide. As the couple walk by the river on a rainy, autumnal night, everything they see and hear—autumn leaves, chrysanthemum flowers, cries of birds, and sounds of the river—touches the couple's hearts as they know they will never come back to "this world." They swear to remain committed as a couple to their everlasting love, and to fall together as passionate flowers. Akiko had never before performed a piece from the *shigetayû* repertory, to which "Wet Fan" belongs. This genre was once extremely popular, mainly in entertainment districts. However, the subject matter of tragic love and double-suicide came to be seen in more modern times as immoral, and it eventually fell out of fashion. Akiko described the reception of her first performance of "Wet Fan":

When the music finished, there was a kind of roar of excitement in the audience. I was also excited. There was silence at first, and then huge applause exploded across the hall.[9]

She felt her exploration of vocal aesthetics was highly valued by her audience. The earthy, robust style of singing inspired by her grandmother created a great impact both on Akiko and her listeners—she had managed to bring back the dramatic power of the music for a contemporary audience. As she described the evening, I heard her express desire and determination to expand the musical frontiers.

Between performances, Akiko also talked about her thoughts on each piece, and her feelings about learning and playing. At a performance of "Kurokami" ("Black Hair"), she described how the lyrics illustrated the passionate feeling of a woman waiting for her lover's visit, and she went on to express her thought about the metaphor of the word "unity," suggesting the intimate relationship between the couple:

The next piece I will perform is "Kurokami,"[10] *which is a piece often played by beginners to learn basic techniques. I started learning the shamisen at the age of eight, and also learnt this song at about that age. So, I was singing "musubore taru omoi [feeling of unity]" even before I was ten years old. I didn't know what it meant. But it's a secret when I found out its meaning.*[11]

By explaining the lyrics, Akiko believes that those in the audience unfamiliar with jiuta can increase their knowledge of the music, for one of the difficulties for contemporary listeners is understanding the lyrics, which are written in classical Japanese. However, Akiko's talk about lyrics is not just intended to make traditional music comprehensible for a present-day audience. More significantly, it personalizes her performance by sharing her emotions arising from the world depicted in those lyrics. Such lyrics explore passionate feelings of women toward their love, and frequently an unrequited love. Women depicted in jiuta were mostly idealistic images created by male poets between the seventeenth and the nineteenth centuries. Consciously or unconsciously, Akiko manipulates these images of femininity, reinterprets them, and portrays herself as representing women's voices through her speech and singing. Turning her thoughts toward people in the past, about whom the lyrics of jiuta spoke, Akiko finds the strong bonds between the people of that time especially moving:

I think people in the past had a strong faith not only between couples, but also between mothers and their children, masters and their disciples, and in many other people's relationships.

For Akiko, such relationships can be described as "for one's dear life," and she feels "people's strength" in them. Jiuta has always conveyed strong, faithful, and passionate relationships, expressed via women's voices. As someone who has negotiated an emotional minefield with regard to her family and her jiuta training, Akiko has at last found her own meanings in her performance of this art form.

Akiko's complex feelings toward her mother were particularly in transformation due to her mother's illness at that time. This significant episode changed their relationship dramatically. Akiko realized that, before her death, her mother felt compelled to teach Akiko the repertories and performance techniques she had not yet passed on. In spite of her ambivalent feeling about her mother's appointment of her brother as successor, Akiko understood her mother had been seriously considering Akiko's life and future, if not quite in the same way that she had taken care of her son.

When I divorced, I was at my wits end because I didn't have much income to survive on. But the divorce enabled me to nurse my mother, and I practiced jiuta day and night. In every way, the divorce made me commit to that art for life. It has become a treasure that I could spend intimate time with my mother due to the divorce. . . . My mother, who lived only for the pursuit of her art, was perhaps not such a good mother, but she made me follow her art. At the time of her death, I felt deeply content that we had come to love each other and could finally become real mother and daughter, as well as real master and disciple. If I hadn't pursued my artform seriously, I wouldn't have been able to understand my mother and appreciate her. My mother taught me jiuta for life, and so I am determined to take on her teaching for life.

Self-Realization

The experience of Akiko is both inspirational and poignant on many levels. This is because Akiko describes a variety of aspects of women's lives, struggles, and achievements, which many women can relate to. In Akiko's generation, more and more women who pursue professional careers choose to remain single so that they can avoid taking double roles: career woman and full-time housewife. Although she once hoped to establish a family with an ideal husband, happy to encourage her enthusiastic pursuit of an artistic career, Akiko faced a reality in which her husband showed little respect for her artistic interests. Akiko therefore chose to become single, though she knew that the decision would cause financial difficulties as well as social disapproval of a single woman without a legitimate job.

Akiko's feelings toward her brother also involved delicate issues. Although he inherited the school, according to Akiko, "various problems" arose among the members, who still maintained a great admiration for their previous head. When Akiko and her brother talked about their future, her brother told her that he wanted to be a distinguished *shidôsha* (teacher) of their school. Akiko replied that her goal was to save the tradition of jiuta for the Japanese people. Saving the tradition of jiuta means continuing the heritage that Akiko's grandmother and mother left for her. Singing jiuta, for Akiko, is to trace the musical lives of these individuals who taught her about the emotions of women in such different ways.

Her mother's death had a significant impact on Akiko: the loss of her mother was also the loss of her master whose art she had followed. "*I can't understand why she is no longer here,*" Akiko lamented. Singing jiuta meant following in the footsteps of the two senior women in her family, who were pioneers in cultivating the position of women within the traditional music of Japan. However, since childhood Akiko had watched these professional women struggle to negotiate their gendered identity as wives and mothers within their families, despite the great successes they had achieved in society.

Akiko's fundamental desire is not to become a teacher, but to continue to be a *hyôgensha* (artist), who inspires present-day people through her art form. Voice is a fundamental device of human beings used to differentiate one from another and express identities, articulated as "giving voice" and "having voice" (Feld et al. 2004, 341–42). In her own musical life stories, Akiko portrays her self-conception as an independent woman singer, triumphing over adversity in her youth, and embarking on an uneasy journey in pursuit of her musical career. Whereas Akiko revealed to me her emotional struggles with regard to her family, in her concert talks she never expresses negative feelings about her family members, but rather she portrays them as a strongly bonded family and precious musical colleagues who played crucial roles in the creation of Akiko as a singer. Akiko continues to negotiate her identities through the voices of women in jiuta—not only the reflections of her two women role models, but also the images of her own self-realization. Thus she continues to encourage her contemporaries and inspire still more women in the future to express their passionate selves.

Acknowledgments

I would like to express gratitude to Akiko Fujii, who kindly assisted with this research and disclosed her life story, allowing me to write about it in this chapter. I also owe a lot to Soh Fujimoto, Andrea Hector-Watkins, Clive Bell, and Christie Goodall for their helpful suggestions.

Notes

1. All translations from Japanese to English, including quotations from literature and interviews, are the author's own, unless otherwise stated. All interviews with Akiko Fujii were conducted in October 2008, unless otherwise stated.

2. Tokyo University of Fine Arts and Music is the English description of Tokyo geijuts daigaku.

3. Akiko Fujii quoted in "Close Up." *Hogaku Journal* 2005, 219:2.

4. Japan Traditional Cultures Foundation is the English description of Nihon dentô bunka shinkô zaidan.

5. Interview with Soh Fujimoto, October 2008.

6. Taken from Akiko Fujii's talk at her concert on June 15, 2009.

7. Interview with Akiko Fujii, September 2009.

8. Ibid.

9. Ibid.

10. The "black hair" referred to in this piece describes the sadness of a woman with black hair, who is unhappily sleeping alone. In Akiko Fujii's commentary, she refers to the beginning of the lyrics "*kurokami no musubore taru omoi oba*," which means "the feeling of unity, like my black hair, is tied up."

11. Taken from Akiko Fujii's talk at her concert on June 20, 2005.

References

"Close Up." 2005. *Hogaku Journal* 219:2.

Diamond, Beverley. 2000. "Gender in Musical Life Stories." In *Music and Gender*, eds. Beverley Diamond and Pirkko Moisala, 99–139. Champaign: University of Illinois Press.

Dilatush, Lois. 1977. "Women in the Professions." In *Women in Changing Japan*, eds. Joyce Lebra, Joy Paulson, and Elizabeth Powers, 191–208. Boulder: Westview Press.

Downer, Lesley. 2006. "The City Geisha and Their Role in Modern Japan." In *The Courtesan's Arts: Cross-Cultural Perspectives*, eds. Marcha Feldman and Bonnie Gordon, 223–42. Oxford: Oxford University Press.

Feld, Steven, Aaron A. Fox, Thomas Porcello, and David Samuels. 2004. "Vocal Anthropology: From the Music of Language to the Language of Song." In *A Companion to Linguistic Anthropology*, ed. Alessandro Duranti, 321–45. Oxford: Blackwell Publishing.

Foreman, Kelly M. 2008. *The Gei of Geisha: Music, Identity and Meaning*. Hampshire: Ashgate.

Hendry, Joy. 1981. *Marriage in Changing Japan*. London: Croom Helm.

Iwao, Sumiko. 1993. *The Japanese Woman: Traditional Image and Changing Reality*. New York: Free Press.

Koskoff, Ellen. 1989. "An Introduction to Women, Music and Culture." In *Women and Music in Cross-Cultural Perspective*, ed. Ellen Koskoff, 1–23. Urbana: University of Illinois Press.

Price, Sally. 1983. "Sexism and the Construction of Reality: An Afro-American Example." *American Ethnologist* 10(3):460–76.

———. 1985. *Co-wives and Calabashes*. Ann Arbor: University of Michigan Press.

Sawin, Patricia E. 2002. "Performance at the Nexus of Gender, Power, and Desire: Reconsidering Bauman's Verbal Art from the Perspective of Gendered Subjectivity as Performance." *Journal of American Folklore* 115(455):28–61.

Tanaka, Yukiko. 1995. *Contemporary Portraits of Japanese Women*. Westport: Praeger Publishers.

2. Amelia Pedroso

The Voice of a Cuban Priestess Leading from the Inside

AMANDA VILLEPASTOUR

1st April 1998: I am in Havana on my first field trip to Cuba, day four. I arrive at UNEAC (Unión de Escritores y Artistas de Cuba) [Union of Writers and Artists] for an outdoor performance. I hear batá drums as I make my way through the crowd and approach the stage. I feel excited by the sound of the drums. As the performers come into view, I am astounded to see that the three drummers are women. I hear a soaring voice leading the performance. I look for the lead singer, who would usually be standing beside the drummers. There isn't one. After a couple of minutes of scanning the performance space, I realize one of the drummers is leading the song. Everything is new and different.

Amelia Pedroso (1946–2000) was an esteemed, yet controversial, ritual singer or *akpón* in an Afro-Cuban spiritual tradition popularly known as Santería, or to the devotees themselves, Regla de Ocha or simply Ocha. Pedroso's voice—literal and metaphoric—continues to posthumously shape issues of gender in the music-making of Santería.[1] While the overwhelming majority of ritual singers in the tradition are men, there is no religious discourse that narrates why this should be so, as there is in Afro-Cuban drumming traditions. However, it is not Pedroso's status as a leading woman akpón that created controversy. Using one kind of power, as a priestess (*santera*) and akpón, Pedroso appropriated another form that had previously been prohibited for Cuban women. She was almost certainly the first Cuban woman to cross a traditional gender line and perform publicly with her own all-women group on the drums, the batá, which accompanied her vocal performances. Pedroso died in 2000 before she could fulfill her deeper, far more radical mission: to own and play her own consecrated batá drums, which Cuban practitioners call *fundamento*.[2] Through her resistant actions and radical ideology, Pedroso's influence has spread beyond the shores of Cuba and the bounds of her own lifetime, leaving a network of students and religious godchildren who have inherited her legacy.[3]

The phrase "leading from the inside" refers both to the way Pedroso led her all-female ensemble Ibbu Okun musically, and to the manner in which she led what has now become an international female batá drumming movement, with Pedroso as its iconic symbol. As the prestigious Cuban priestess and musician within a movement that was partly initiated and primarily enacted by non-Cuban women, Pedroso "led from the inside" culturally, religiously, and musically. I propose that Pedroso created "power loops" in two respects. The first—at the micro level—was a musical power cycle, as Pedroso directed her ensemble by leading vocally—the true seat of power in batá performance. But Pedroso was unusual because she led vocally while simultaneously playing one of the drums, though typically not the lead drum. This musical loop provides a useful metaphor for the second, macro power loop between Pedroso, an iconic Santería religious and musical insider, and non-Cuban women, who were in fact first to cross the gender boundary and play the batá drums.

By playing the batá, I propose that Pedroso used one form of power—as priestess and akpón—to lever another, as a female batá drummer, for which no word traditionally exists. (The traditional word for batá drummer is the masculine *batálero*, though the term *batálera* is now creeping into the vocabulary of women, and sometimes men, to designate female batá drummers.)[4] In this chapter, I argue that it was Pedroso's high status as a ritual singer and priestess that empowered her radical resistance to the preexisting gender boundaries in the music of Santería. Although there are stringent prohibitions against homosexuals and women in several forms of Afro-Cuban drumming, the wider Santería community is accepting and welcoming of homosexuals, providing a degree of refuge from a historically homophobic political and social environment. Indeed, key Santería priesthoods are routinely occupied by gay men and women. With this intrareligious tension in view, it is of great interest that Pedroso was a lesbian.

Briefly revisiting the well-trodden ground of issues related to "insider" and "outsider," Santería and batá drumming are becoming increasingly globalized (see Olupona and Rey 2008) and the boundaries between insider and outsider are becoming ever more porous at the transnational level. However, my study not only examines the reconfiguration of internal gender boundaries among devotees across national and cultural borders but proposes a nebulous boundary perceivable only to practitioners themselves: this world and the "other world." Within a belief system where the living "pass to the ancestors" and transform into a kind of spirit called "Egun," Pedroso remains present in the lives of people she influenced. While she instigated objective change in women's access to both singing and batá drumming during her lifetime, Amelia Pedroso maintains her power as an icon, and to some, an Egun, by continuing to guide and inspire those who share her vision.

Mapping Pedroso's Life in Music

Amelia Pedroso Acosta was born into a musical family in 1946. Although it is relatively common for children to be initiated into the path of Santería priesthood in Cuba, Pedroso was taken through the ceremony at the particularly young age of three. Knowledge of the Santería song repertoire is important for any devotee, but as a child, Pedroso studied the songs with her uncle, Lázaro Pedroso, who is a renowned akpón and has produced a manuscript about Santería songs (n.d.). Amelia Pedroso also studied the Santería song liturgy with her grandmother in her childhood but became a serious student of Santería music and sacred music performance around the age of twenty, evolving into a respected priestess and akpón in the religious community. She also became a well-known stage performer, initially with the internationally recognized *rumba*[5] group Clave y Guaguancó which she joined in 1985 and with whom she made a recording titled *Songs and Dances* in 1994. Two further recordings featuring Pedroso were soon to follow: *Grupo Ilú Añá Sacred Rhythms* (1995) and Emilio Barreto's *Santisimo* (1996). Pedroso also performed with two of the major Cuban state-funded groups, Danza Nacional de Cuba and Danza Contemporánea. In a daring break from tradition, Pedroso formed her own group, Ibbu Okun, a mostly female ensemble (including a male dancer) that employed three women batá players—herself and two other musicians. Over the years that followed, Amelia Pedroso and Ibbu Okun became the symbolic nexus of an international network of female batá drummers.

Pedroso left Cuba for the first time in December 1993, touring the United States with the best-known and foremost akpón in Cuba throughout the 1990s, Lázaro Ros. On this trip, Pedroso began to make an impression on U.S. American women, occasionally playing the batá at parties with her male colleagues. In September of the same year, Pedroso traveled to Canada to be an instructor at Afrocubanismo, a ten-day festival at the Banff Centre for the Arts, Alberta. While there, she made a recording with Havana master drummers Regino Jiménez, Fermín Nani, and José Pilar at the Banff Centre, released as *Grupo Ilú Añá Sacred Rhythms* two years later. In April 1995, Pedroso toured the United States again, this time with her own group Ibbu Okun. The tour was primarily organized by U.S. American women. According to one female participant (who asked not to be named), some New York male batá teachers (both Cuban exiles and locals) told their students not to attend Pedroso's workshops. These teachers disapproved of Pedroso's controversial stance and urged their female students not to support her. A cluster of male batá players who attended one of Pedroso's workshops in New York created tension by standing outside the door where she was teaching, at no point entering the space. In Philadelphia, male drummers also discouraged students and friends (of both sexes) from attending Ibbu Okun's week of events, though the event was well-attended by men and women (Elizabeth Sayre, pers. comm.).

In 1999 Pedroso toured the United Kingdom. Traveling on her own, she collaborated with U.K.-based musicians and dancers and performed concerts and conducted song workshops in London and Manchester (figure 2.1). Unlike her trip to the United States with Ibbu Okun, Pedroso's trip to the United

Figure 2.1. Amelia Pedroso, Manchester, U.K., March, 27, 1999. Photograph by Amanda Villepastour.

Kingdom was less politically charged. With only a fledgling Santería religious community at that point and as yet no significant community of female batá players, Pedroso's presence did not mobilize a vanguard of female musicians (at least at that time) as it had in the United States. In the same year, another recording featuring Pedroso's singing voice was released. *Blues for Yemayá* is a musical fusion produced by German-born jazz flautist and composer Mark Alban Lotz (recorded in Havana in 1997 and released in 1998).

Pedroso made two more international trips. In August 1999 she traveled to New York with her partner Alina Valera. While there, they attended the Catskill Women's World Drum & Percussion Happen'n (cofounded by percussionist Ubaka Hill) near Woodstock, New York. Pedroso's last trip to the United States was in 2000. After a battle against cancer, she had a relapse while abroad and returned urgently to Cuba, where she died just weeks later on May 24, 2000.

Sadly, negative stories persist concerning Pedroso's death. Narrow-minded, fundamentalist Santería practitioners in the United States have been heard saying that Pedroso died because she played the batá. One woman I spoke with (who wishes not to be named) said that she received divination and was told not to play the batá as Pedroso "may have died" because she did. Other unsubstantiated stories circulate that Pedroso did in fact play a fundamento while in New York and then became ill, while others say that she was killed by magic. What can be said is that Amelia Pedroso's cancer had been poorly treated in 1998 when she was first diagnosed in Cuba, an all-too-common situation due to the economic blockade that deprives Cuban citizens of essential medicines.

In terms of Pedroso's private life and family situation, she was a lesbian and did not marry or give birth, although she did raise a close relative as her own daughter and was with her longtime partner, Alina, at the time of her death. Historically, Cuban culture is not conducive to living an openly gay or lesbian lifestyle partly due to oppressive pre- and postrevolutionary policies. Yet Pedroso created her own family within her ritual house—known in the Santería tradition as an *ilé*—in Havana and a transnational network of religious godchildren. Several of Pedroso's U.S. American students and godchildren had helped to fund her medical care and attended her funeral and three-month commemoration ceremony (a Santería rite) in Havana.

The Voice of Resistance

The spiritual tradition Santería has developed in Cuba over the past two centuries, beginning among slave communities. Now commonly referred to as a religion, Santería's strongest cultural influence came from the people now collectively known as Yorùbá in southwest Nigeria and southeast Republic of Bénin, where a contemporary, parallel set of spiritual and musical practices exist. The main spiritual beings in Santería in Cuba are called *orichas*[6] and *eguns* (ancestral spirits). Central to the religious practice on both sides of the Atlantic is the batá drum (Yorùbá: *bàtá*).

In Cuba it is strictly taboo for women to play the consecrated batá, known as *fundamento*, as opposed to a batá that is not consecrated, referred to as *aberinkulá*. As in Nigeria, the batá is more than a musical instrument. It is a sacred vessel in which the oricha of drumming, Añá, is ritually constructed in material form and placed inside the batá; this is a complicated and expensive one-week ritual procedure conducted exclusively by male, heterosexual priests who form a brotherhood. When a set of fundamento is consecrated, Cuban priests say "a set of drums is born" (*nacido*). The taboos against female involvement with Añá (and therefore the batá) revolve primarily around menstruation. It is believed that menstrual blood has the capacity to diminish the efficacy of the oricha medicine inside the drum. Conversely, Añá is believed to have the potential to harm women, although postmenopausal women in Cuba are not relieved from menstrual taboos in the Añá cult.

Pedroso questioned and resisted the Añá taboo against female contact. In my limited time discussing the matter with Pedroso, I noticed that her logic revolved around two ideas. The first was that Cuban men had appropriated menstruation as a way of marginalizing women. The second idea was based on Pedroso's peripheral knowledge of the Àyán cult in Nigeria, from which Añá in Cuba largely derives.[7]

Pedroso stated, *"For me, I understand that all of the things in Africa, the root of the religion in Cuba, the root of the oricha, the root of everything, the main base is there, it is possible for women to be initiated but it is not possible in Cuba. Why is it not so in Cuba? It must be for the simple reason that men have taken control of this whole power, and why would that be? It must be because of menstruation."*

Appearing to accept the taboo, she reiterated a commonly held belief among Santería devotees: *"Menstruation debilitates Añá. It puts me in a weak position toward the saint.*[8] *The problem is that when a woman has menstruation, she can't touch the drum so she can't have any contact with Añá."*

In response, I probed, "We know that, but why are they saying that? What is it about the actual menstruation?"

"That's their way of keeping women apart."

It is possible that the male hegemony of akpónes partly derives from the anxiety around proximity of the female body to the Añá within the batá drums (see Schweitzer 2003, 41–46; Vincent [Villepastour] 2006, 144–45).

The Musical Voice

Pedroso was considered to have an ideal voice for percussion-led Afro-Cuban music.[9] Fitting with the general vocal aesthetics of Santería vocal music, her delivery was very direct, with little or no audible vibrato and minimal use of melisma. The melodic range of oricha songs typically sits within a major ninth, and Pedroso always sang in a chest voice in a range that is quite low for a female. Based on analysis of two recordings,[10] her range was from E♭ below middle C to B♭ above middle C (figure 2.2).

Hearing Pedroso sing acoustically in a ceremony with three batá drums in London in 1999, it struck me that her voice cut *through* the drums rather than *above* them in terms of either pitch or amplitude. In the absence of a technical vocabulary to scientifically describe *what* sound she produced or *how* she produced it, I noted at the time that Pedroso employed a cutting, "edgy" timbre that easily distinguished her voice acoustically from the more rounded sonority of the hand-struck *enús* (larger skins) in particular. If a feminine vocal aesthetic is encapsulated with adjectives such as "sweet," "decorated," "delicate," or "high," and descriptions such as "penetrating," "driving," "direct," "low," or "deep" evoke a more stereotypically masculine aesthetic, then Pedroso's voice was, at the very least, androgynous or ambiguously gendered. In listening to the recording *Santisimo* on which Pedroso recorded alongside male akpón Emelio Barreto, it is striking that they placed their voices in a similar range. Barreto also sings in a chest voice but in a high range for a man (generally speaking, though not high for a male in this tradition) while Pedroso sings low for a woman, (again, generally) and in fact lower at the bottom of her range than Barreto. Looking at the enú tunings on *Ilú Añá*[11] and *Santisimo*, it is evident that both the male and female voices stay close to the pitch ranges of the drum tunings on these two recordings (see figure 2.2). Commercial recordings aside, the audibility and clarity of the akpón through vocal power and manipulation of timbre become central in the course of a ceremony.

Figure 2.2. An analysis of two of Pedroso's recordings, "Ilú Añá" and "Santisimo."

The Spiritual Voice

In Santería ceremonies where the batá is used, called *bembés, güemileres*, or *toques*, there are several voices: that of the akpón, the vocal chorus created by congregants, the "voices" of the three batá drums that create musical conversations (*conversaciones*), and the voice of one or more orichas who possess their congregants. Depending on the phase of the ceremony, the musical "chain of command" changes. Of the four main performance segments, it is in the third that the akpón steps into the firm lead and becomes the most powerful and crucial musical force in the room.[12] This section, known as the *wemilere* or *iban balo*, is freer and it is in this "party" (Spanish: *fiesta*) phase where spirit possession is most likely to occur. During the wemilere, the akpón is not restricted to a set liturgy as in other sections but rather responds to the social and spiritual needs of the congregants. Beyond musical abilities and mechanical ritual knowledge, an additional component for the akpón and drummers is *aché* (Yorùbá: *àṣẹ*). This is variously translated as "vital power," "life force," "sacred potential" (Verger 1963, 13); "power, authority, command" (Abraham 1958, 71); "a coming to pass [. . .] effect; imprecation" (Crowther 1852, 47); an equivalent of "amen," "a secret and sacred power" (McKenzie 1976, 191); "vital force, energy, mystical power and potential which is present in all life in varying amounts and differing manifestations" (Drewal 1974, 26); "authority, command, life force, spiritual vitality" (Gleason 1973, 66); and "the power of transformation" (Drewal 1992, 27). Hallgren (1995) undertook an excellent study of understandings and interpretations of *àṣẹ* from the nineteenth century to postcolonial Nigeria. He argues that *àṣẹ* is traditionally associated with the authority and power ensconced in utterances, whereas the contemporary interpretation is more associated with vital force, life force, and transformative power. Bringing it back to contemporary Cuban practices and drawing on Hallgren, aché presides fundamentally in human utterances. This understanding of aché places the akpón irrefutably in the ritual seat of power, above and beyond the batá drummers.

Pedroso was renowned for her aché, which was unleashed during ritual performances. According to Carolyn Brandy, who was the last person to be initiated into the oricha priesthood by Pedroso in the final months of her life, her godmother's aché was so powerful that devotees would sometimes be "dropping" into trance as soon as she began to sing. The mere sound of Pedroso's voice could facilitate altered states. It is believed that akpónes communicate very closely with the orichas in Santería music-making by unleashing their most powerful musical canon just moments before possession occurs. This canon is the closely guarded oricha *tratados* (sung prayers dedicated to specific orichas). The akpón's utterances—the confluence of sung incantations and aché—bring the orichas into the ritual space through the bodies of devotees.

The Voice of the Drum

In the traditional configuration, encompassing an akpón and three drummers plus a vocal chorus performed by the congregants, the akpón is in command and leads for most of the ceremony in terms of the time distribution. He or she traditionally fulfills a dedicated role and stands beside the drummers, who are always men and conventionally do not simultaneously sing the lead and play in ceremonial contexts (although this is common in folkloric performances and is becoming increasingly common in Cuba perhaps due to economic constraints).

In yet another break from tradition, within Ibbu Okun (at both stage performances and ceremonies) Pedroso led vocally while simultaneously playing the second drum, the *itótele*, which follows the *iyá* lead drum.[13] She simultaneously led and followed within a cyclic chain of command that is not traditionally part of the musical or social power structure. One might think of it as a "short circuit" whereby the "current" travels along a different path from the one intended or expected. If utterances are at the core of aché, the transformative power within Santería practice, then Pedroso was at the nexus of power before she ever picked up a drum. Given that it is extremely challenging to simultaneously play the batá and sing a virtuosic lead awash with aché, and that Pedroso experienced some religious marginalization due to her controversial desire to perform on the batá, one is compelled to ask: Did Pedroso forego the full force of power she had as a dedicated akpón by leading her ensemble from inside on the itótele?

When taking into account the fact that the akpón is a recognized hub of spiritual and social power, and that Cuba generally and the Santería tradition specifically is awash with forms of *machismo* or masculinist prowess, it comes as no surprise that the overwhelming majority of akpónes are male, which adds emphasis to Pedroso's remarkable achievements as a singer. Although there is no religious discourse that states why the akpón should be male (as in drumming), the gender asymmetry among ritual singers is overwhelmingly in favor of males (Moore and Sayre 2006). It may be that the kind of timbre required for a soloist to cut through the batá drums (described above) is more common in male voices than female voices, partly accounting for the predominance of male soloists in this tradition. Yet that alone cannot explain the extreme asymmetry. Regardless of how this male hegemony developed, Pedroso ascended to the top of a bastion of male power by emerging as one of the most renowned akpónes of her time. In view of her uncontested power as a singer, it is interesting to consider the motivations behind Pedroso's decision to play the batá. When I interviewed Pedroso in 1999, I asked her how she began playing the batá and she answered,

> *I have been singing for the batá for thirty-one years and the sound and rhythms of the batá always called me and moved me, and I thought, "Oh, if only I could play!" [. . .] Yes, there were many obstacles. I never thought that women could play the batá.*

Pedroso's response explicitly suggests that her initial drive toward learning the batá was aesthetic rather than ideological and political. Such musical drive and passion is genderless. Yet although Pedroso's initial motivation for drumming may not have been political, her action of playing the batá *became* a political statement. Whereas Cuban women had not played aberinkulá (the unconsecrated batá) until the early 1990s, foreign women visiting Cuba had been playing the drum under the gaze of Cuban women for a decade. The boundary was no longer man/woman, but had become an issue of non-Cuban woman/Cuban woman.

While the prohibition against women playing the fundamento is reasonably well documented (e.g., Pryor 1999; Sayre 2000; Hagedorn 2001, 20–21, 89–97), little has been written about the controversy around women playing the aberinkulá. Although aberinkulá had been in use since the early 1900s in Cuba (Ortiz 1955, 381–85, sv "panderetas lucumí"), no woman played them prior to the early 1980s. European women were in fact the first to play aberinkulá in Cuba around 1982 at a Havana workshop led by members of the *Conjunto Folklórico de Cuba*.[14]

Pedroso became increasingly frustrated by the explicit discrepancy between the treatment of Cuban and foreign women in her hometown. In response to the marginalization she experienced as a Cuban woman, Pedroso stated,

> *In Cuba, for many years now, the men still do not want their Cuban women to be playing drums, but a foreigner arrives and they teach them. [. . .] They are not a threat because they leave. If more and more women get together, and more and more women are playing, they will be the ones who are pushed aside.*

Using her knowledge and authority as an oricha priestess and ritual singer, in the early 1990s Pedroso, who was by then well into her forties, proceeded to teach herself the batá repertoire playing aberinkulá and proceeded to disseminate her newly acquired skills. Largely through her international travels, Pedroso quickly developed an iconic status. Women saw her play and were inspired to learn the batá and travel to Cuba to study with her. As a Portland-based Cuban-American musician and goddaughter of Pedroso, Virginia Lopez stated, "Before seeing Amelia, I would never have *dared* play the batá."

Pedroso's international reputation grew alongside the Cuban government's instigation of the *periodo especial económico* (special economic period) in 1991, which brought a new set of government policies. Introduced after the collapse of the Soviet Union in 1990 and its withdrawal of economic support to Cuba, then president Fidel Castro opened the nation to mass tourism in order to attract much needed revenue into the country. The Cuban constitution was amended in 1992 and citizens were guaranteed nondiscrimination based on religious belief and for the first time people with religious beliefs were allowed to join the Communist Party. The Pope's visit to Cuba in 1998 also led to further relaxing of religious oppression. In this newly constructed environment, the government selectively condoned religious tourism, which became known as *ochatur* or *santurismo* (see Hagedorn 2001, 9), and appropriated religious music forms as tourist attractions. Pedroso's unusual credentials did not escape the gaze of Cuban authorities. A Havana-based government organization, Asociación Yoruba de Cuba, organized Ibbu Okun workshops in December 1998 and January 2000, which were attended exclusively by foreign women.

While most of Pedroso's batá students in the United States were also women, some men did attend her workshops. I spoke with an accomplished male Añá drummer, Orlando Fiol, who attended one of Ibbu Okun's workshops in New York City. He said that Pedroso and her iyá player, Aleida Nani, were unsure of several rhythms. In response to one particular rhythm Ibbu Okun performed, Fiol said to the women, "That is not how it goes, but I can teach you." The three Cuban women responded positively to Fiol's offer and accepted the opportunity to learn from him.[15] This account, along with other criticisms about Pedroso's technique (Elizabeth Sayre, pers. comm.) suggests that Pedroso was a better singer than she was drummer, which is not surprising given that she lacked an environment where she could learn drumming in community (routinely available to Cuban men). Furthermore, she had been drumming for a far shorter time than she had been singing. Fiol's anecdote, along with my observations of Pedroso in the United Kingdom, indicate that she did not self-segregate and was open to engaging with and learning from men. Her segregation came from the outside.

A Transnational Sisterhood

Pedroso and the non-Cuban network of women playing the batá needed one another in several respects. Because both groups of women had limited opportunities to share information and play publicly in their home communities, forming mutual bonds was advantageous in a range of ways. Although many non-Cuban women were getting what they needed in terms of musical instruction from male Cuban teachers (both with master drummers in their home countries and in Cuba), it was, nevertheless, much harder for women to gain musical knowledge and performance opportunities, which were routinely offered to men. Pedroso's emergence as a visible, authoritative, and resistant Cuban woman gave license to non-Cuban women to start questioning the musical gender boundaries in their own environments. At the same time, many non-Cuban women were and remain uncomfortable with the discrepancy between themselves and Cuban women. Rather than envying or resenting what she perceived as the favoritism shown to foreign women, Pedroso metaphorically joined hands with them, forming bonds of sisterhood, family, and godchildren. There were several likely explanations for this.

Figure 2.3. Susan Matthews's painting "Amelia" captures Pedroso's iconic status. The California organization Women Drummers International commissioned the artwork for the 2007 Born to Drum women's drum camp. Artist and photographer, Susan Matthews. © SM, www .SusanMatthewsGallery.com (accessed February 2012).

For reasons that need further investigation, my fieldwork and research has shown that a disproportionate number of women batá players are lesbian or bisexual. Although gay women are marginalized to varying degrees around the world, their marginalization in Cuba has been particularly harsh (see Lumsden 1996).[16] Given that gay Cubans have been especially persecuted in the twentieth century, relative to, say, gay people in the United States, it is arguable that, as a Cuban lesbian, Pedroso had less at stake in defying the patriarchy around singing and drumming than heterosexual women. My female research participants have repeatedly said that heterosexual women who uphold musical gender boundaries are frequently concerned about "looking good" in front of the men.

As in music, gay Cubans have formed religious alliances. Within Santería, networks of religious lineages are formed through initiation (as in the Añá drumming cult). With the globalization of orisha religion generally, and with Santería specifically, it is financially attractive for Cubans to have foreign god-children, and also immensely socially prestigious. Many transnational religious networks that have developed over the last four decades have been led by musicians (men and women), because under former President Fidel Castro's policies, musicians were among an elite group (which also included visual artists and sportsmen and women) who were granted permission to leave and return to Cuba. Through Pedroso's own travels and the networks that developed, she acquired numerous European and North American godchildren.[17] Many of the aspiring akpónes and women batá players I interviewed in the United States have ritual affiliations with Pedroso. It was her interlinked musical and religious activities at home and abroad that instigated a "sisterhood" in opposition to the Añá brotherhood, the male-only drumming cult. Within her circle of musicians and religious devotees, Pedroso stated her mission in no uncertain terms. Less than two years before her death, she privately said to me, "*Women will play Añá*," meaning that women will, one day, be able to play the consecrated batá drums, which is currently taboo. On her last trip to the United States in March 2000, two months to the day before her death, Pedroso uttered it publicly in a song workshop in the presence of twenty to thirty participants (Elizabeth Sayre, pers. comm.). But Amelia's vision did not stop there. Carolyn Brandy maintains that Pedroso had explicitly declared her mission to *own* a fundamento one day.

While the majority of women Santería devotees regard the religion's prescribed gender divisions and taboos as uncontestable tradition, Pedroso viewed women's musical gendering as an asymmetry that needed reform. Yet given that Pedroso was already remarkably powerful as a priestess and akpón and could authoritatively lead an all-male ensemble of drummers and transform gatherings of devotees, why was she so concerned with appropriating another form of power and overturning a religious taboo that excluded women from playing the fundamento? While her choices might seem a logical progression, women singers who were her contemporaries and predecessors had not followed the same path but rather accepted the religious drumming taboos as a given and hence maintained their religious status. In an environment where ceremonies are poorly paid and competition is high, Pedroso could little afford to dent her social and religious status. Since she has died, Pedroso's full motivation remains speculative. One simplistic proposition might be that she was influenced by the actions of foreign women. Another (though not mutually exclusive) explanation is that she perceived a gender asymmetry that she regarded to be unfair and decided to take the lead simply because as a reputable priestess and musician, she felt she could. Or perhaps she decided to do so because she simply loved the sound of the drum. While all of these reasons are probably relevant, Brandy added,

> Amelia was very devout and believed that she was spiritually destined to play the drums. She was called to play the drums and she had enough courage not to back down. We foreigners only gave her that moment in time to walk through that door. Ame felt that her playing batá and fundamento was natural, and in the natural order of her spiritual progression and destiny. Just because some of her male peers told her "no" was not good enough for Amelia, especially when all the evidence proved them wrong *and* they could sell it for money.

As a gay Cuban woman, another of Pedroso's motivations that I look at below is that she felt oppressed in other arenas of her life.

Sexuality in Santería Music and Religion

In the course of my research in Cuba and the Cuban diaspora in the United States and Europe, it became evident that a disproportionate percentage of the international network of women batá players is lesbian (though frequently not openly so). At the heart of this international sisterhood, Pedroso was openly gay. The visibility of lesbian women playing batá is especially interesting in view of issues of attitudes toward sexuality within Santería generally and batá drumming specifically.

While some branches of Afro-Cuban religion provide a refuge for homosexual men and women, for example, in Pedroso's own *ilé* or ritual house, others are aggressively homophobic. Not only are Afro-Cuban ritual practices highly gendered in terms of a binary male/female divide, but there are several initiations, cult memberships, and priesthoods that can be undertaken only by heterosexual men. One such cult practice is the Añá brotherhood, which admits only heterosexual males. While the exclusion of women is primarily argued around the idea of menstruation being harmful to the Añá medicine inside of the drum, it is also argued that Añá is potentially harmful to women, who, it is said, can miscarry or become barren. Prominent batá drummer Felipe García Villamil goes so far as to say, "[T]he spirit that inhabits the drums, desirous of blood, may cause women to bleed to death" (Vélez 2000, 156). Yet no biological argument exists to exclude homosexual men. When questioning Cuban batá masters about the matter, they frequently conflated the homosexual/female argument, though in no coherent way. Homosexuals are frequently viewed as feminized men who take on the most negative stereotypes of women. The late "Cha Chá" Vega explained, "In Abakuá[18] we say that with a skirt, the secret gets out. Men wear trousers, so the secret stays in. Homosexuals are even worse." Furthermore, homosexual males and women are regarded as being more prone to spirit possession, which is regarded as undesirable for drummers. (Equally undesirable is an akpón with a tendency toward spirit possession, which may be a contributing factor in the male hegemony of akpónes.) Considering this dual female/homosexual taboo in relation to Añá, the most excluded group within this patriarchal system is comprised of lesbians, deeming them the most unlikely candidates for Añá initiation.

The bastions of heterosexual male power among Afro-Cuban spiritual practices are the Ifá cult, the Abakuá cult, and the Añá drumming cult. The attitudes toward homosexuals within the Añá cult have likely crossed over from the all-male Abakuá and Ifá cults, both of which have no space in the priesthood for homosexual men. In some ways, Santería exists in opposition to these exclusively heterosexual male cults. In fact, many Santería devotees are gay and indeed can ascend to positions of power such as *oba oriaté* (head divining priest). Some Santería ilés are particularly dominated by gay men and women, and Amelia Pedroso's ilé was one such center. In terms of actual religious practice, Pedroso was also somewhat radical. She conducted a ceremony, the presentation of the "warrior" orichas Echú, Ochossi, Ogún, and Osun (Robin Burdulis, pers. comm.), which most practitioners believe should be conducted only by males.

Although Pedroso led an ilé mostly populated by gay and lesbian devotees, many in her own blood family did not accept her sexuality. When she died in 2000, her longtime partner, Alina, was excluded from some of the family arrangements (Carolyn Brandy, pers. comm.). Pedroso's sexuality both marginalized her in Cuban society and her blood family and connected her to an international religious family and network of activist gay women.

Cierre

The fourth, shortest, and final segment of a bembé (ceremony) is the closing, or *cierre*. The akpón steps aside while the drummers perform rhythms that "salute" the orichas and eguns (ancestors). Falling silent, Pedroso has now become an Egun to be saluted. Given that Havana is home to a vibrant religious and musical culture with many great musicians, what was it that set Amelia Pedroso apart? And why did she emerge as an international figure who continues to be influential after her death? First, Pedroso was enormously skillful and knowledgeable as a singer and aesthetically had the perfect voice for the oricha song repertoire. Second, as a priestess initiated at the age of three in an environment where years of initiation pushes one up the religious hierarchy, Pedroso wielded spiritual authority in Santería and was believed to be endowed with abundant spiritual power, aché. Third, she became internationally mobile in a political climate where foreign, and most particularly U.S. American visas and Cuban permission to travel were, and continue to be difficult to obtain. Pedroso's mobility enabled her to forge a mutually beneficial international network of non-Cuban women who wanted to be led by a cultural insider. Fourth, Pedroso's gender activism drew attention within both local and transnational communities built around Santería and its music. As a gay woman, Pedroso was already considered to be subversive in her own environment, but fitted in quite comfortably with an international network substantially, though not exclusively, populated by lesbian women.

Although Pedroso had acquired significant esteem and power as a ritual singer within Cuba before she began drumming in the early 1990s, it was her decision to perform on the batá drums that made her a transnational cultural icon. Levering the situation with her position of power as a senior priestess and musician, Pedroso mobilized first her own musicians at the local level, and then a transnational network of female batá drummers. It is these loops of power that developed transnationally between women that are spiraling into real social and religious change. Through the attention that her drumming attracted, Pedroso's singing voice became known outside of Cuba, and as her international audience and network of students and religious godchildren grew, her status strengthened at home in Cuba. Although Pedroso became known internationally as a drummer in the latter years of her life, her real mastery was vocal. Her unique timbre, command of the religious repertoire, powerful aché, and virtuosic command of closely guarded texts struck awe in devotees and musicians.

Devotees and aficionados have been left with several significant commercial recordings of Pedroso's vocal performances. Moreover, within a tradition where ancestors are remembered, invoked, worshipped, petitioned, and contacted through routine spiritual practices, Amelia Pedroso's name is frequently uttered in prayer and ritual and thus her voice remains audible among contemporary devotees and musicians. Just as she led from the inside, she now leads from the other side.

Glossary

Aché: spiritual power believe to reside primarily in human utterances.
Akpón: ritual singer in Afrocuban musical traditions.
Bembé: a Santería ceremony in which batá drums are used.
Itótele: the middle-sized drum in the batá ensemble.
Iyá: the leading and largest drum in the batá ensemble.
Okónkolo: the accompanying and smallest drum in the batá ensemble.
Santería: an Afrocuban spiritual tradition deriving from the Yorùbá people in West Africa.
Santero/a: initiated oricha devotee.

Notes

1. This article draws from research conducted during a fellowship at the Latino Centre, The Smithsonian Institution in 2008. I am grateful to the many people interviewed at that time though special mention is due to Elizabeth Sayre and Carolyn Brandy who not only shared their knowledge of Pedroso and the events during her U.S. visits, but suggested revisions in the final stages of preparing this chapter.

2. The word *fundamento* is also used for other religious objects in Santería.

3. With the breakup of family lineages under slavery, ritual lineages took precedence. *Santeros* (priests) form ritual relationships with *ahijados* (godchildren) through initiation ceremonies and are themselves referred to as the *padrino* (godfather) or *madrina* (godmother).

4. A closed Facebook group called Bataleras was instigated by New York percussionist Lisette Santiago on November 2, 2010.

5. *Rumba* is a Cuban secular drum and dance form that has developed into a folkloric and concert genre alongside community performance.

6. Spelled òrìṣà in Yorùbá and orisha in English when referring to transnational traditions.

7. Pedroso did not have the opportunity to travel to Africa and had limited contact with Nigerians, whose insider knowledge of Yorùbá drumming cults may have been limited. She claimed to glean some of her information from a book she saw in France while traveling, but could not remember the title or author. She also referred to "a Nigerian man" as the source of her information. Pedroso is correct that women are initiated into the Àyàn cult in Nigeria. However, there is a set of loosely related menstruation taboos. See Vincent [Villepastour] 2006, 161–66.

8. Santeros use the words *santo* (saint) and oricha interchangeably.

9. I am grateful to Katherine Meizel for both sharing her insights on Pedroso's recorded voice and being a helpful sounding board as I searched for descriptive language to explain vocal technique and timbre.

10. Emilio Barreto (1996) *Santisimo* and Grupo Ilú Añá (1995) *Sacred Rhythms.*

11. The *enú* (large head) of the *okónkolo* (small accompanying drum) evidently changed during the recording session as it is A on some tracks and B♭ on others.

12. There are four main segments. The first is the *oro seco* (literally "dry ceremony," and also called *oro igbodú*) and is performed without vocals, so it is the iyá drummer who leads musically. The second segment is the *oro cantado* (also known as the *oro eyá aranla*), which is led by the akpón and is comprised of a sung liturgy with *batá* accompaniment. The third segment is the *wemilere* or *iban balo*, and the final relatively short section is the closing sequence, known as the *cierre.*

13. Although Pedroso played the iyá in earlier years, she became best known as an itótele player.

14. I have heard two accounts of this occasion from Michael Spiro (pers. comm.) and Carlos Gómez (mult. comm.).

15. Fiol said that he had already noted the group's musical limitations after hearing them perform, but he attended the workshop because he wanted to give them some money and because he was curious about Fermín Nani's style and hoped to learn about it from his daughter Aleida, who performed in the group (pers. comm., email, November 27, 2008).

16. Since Pedroso's death in 2000, there has been a significant shift in social attitudes toward homosexuality in Cuba, largely due to the efforts of Raul Castro's daughter Mariela, who has campaigned against homophobia and oppression of gays.

17. At the time of her death, Pedroso had thirteen godchildren who had been through the full initiation ceremony and an undetermined number who had received more rudimentary initiations. Pedroso had a modest number of godchildren relative to other internationally connected Cuban priests and musicians who initiate godchildren into the hundreds.

18. Abakuá is a ritual brotherhood deriving peoples from contemporary eastern Nigeria. Most Cuban batá drummers are also initiated into the Abakuá cult.

References

Abraham, R. C. 1958. *Dictionary of Modern Yorùbá.* London: University of London Press.

Crowther, Samuel. 1852. *A Vocabulary of the Yorùbá Language.* London: Seeleys.

Drewal, Henry John. 1974. "Efe: Voiced Power and Pageantry." *African Arts* 7(2):26–29, 58–66, 82–83.

Drewal, Margaret Thompson. 1992. *Yorùbá Ritual: Performers, Play, Agency.* Bloomington: Indiana University Press.

Gleason, Judith, with Awotunde Aworinde and John Olaniyi Ogundipe. 1973. *A Recitation of Ifa, Oracle of the Yoruba.* New York: Grossman Publishers.

Hagedorn, Katherine J. 2001. *Divine Utterances: The Performance of Afro-Cuban Santería.* Washington, D.C.: Smithsonian Institution Press.

Hallgren, Roland. 1995. *The Vital Force: A Study of Àṣẹ in the Traditional and Neo-Traditional Culture of the Yorùbá People.* Lund Studies in African and Asian Religions, Volume 10, ed. Tord Olsson Lund. Lund, Sweden: Department of History.

Lumsden, Ian. 1996. *Machos, Maricones, and Gays: Cuba and Homosexuality.* Philadelphia: Temple University Press.

McKenzie, Peter. 1976. "Yorùbá Òrìṣà Cults: Some Marginal Notes Concerning Their Cosmology and Concept of Deity." *Journal of Religion in Africa* 8:189–207.

Moore, Robin, and Elizabeth Sayre. 2006. "An Afro-Cuban Bata Piece for Obatala, King of the White Cloth." In *Analytical Studies in World Music*, ed. Michael Tenzer, 120–62. Oxford: Oxford University Press.

Olupona, Jacob J., and Terry Rey, eds. 2008. *Òrìṣà Devotion as World Religion: The Globalization of Yorùbá Religious Culture*. Wisconsin: University of Wisconsin Press.

Ortiz, Fernando. 1955. *Los instrumentos de la música Afrocubana*. Havana: Editoriales Cárdenas Y Cía.

Pedroso, Lázaro "Ogun Tola." n.d. *Obbedi Cantos a los Orishas: Traducción e Historia*. Unpublished manuscript.

Pryor, Andrea. 1999. "The House of Añá: Women and Batá." *CBMR Digest* 12(2):6–8.

Sayre, Elizabeth. 2000. "Cuban Batá Drumming and Women Musicians: An Open Question." *Center from Black Music Research Digest* 13.1: n.a. http.//www.cbmr.org/pubs/131/kalinda131.htm (accessed March 2012).

Schweitzer, Kenneth. 2003. *Afro-Cuban Batá Drum Aesthetics: Developing Individual and Group Technique, Sound and Identity*. DMA dissertation, Provine School of Music, University of Maryland

Vélez, María Teresa. 2000. *Drumming for the Gods: The Life and Times of Felipe García Villamil, Santero, Palero, and Abakuá*. Philadelphia: Temple University Press.

Verger, Fátúmbí Pierre. 1963. "Trance States in Orisha Worship." *Odu* 9:13–20.

Vincent [Villepastour], Amanda. 2006. *Bata Conversations: Guardianship and Entitlement Narratives about the Bata in Nigeria and Cuba*. PhD thesis, School of Oriental and African Studies, University of London.

Discography

Clave y Guaguancó. 1994. *Songs and Dances*. Xenophile CD 4023.

Emilio Barreto. 1996. *Santisimo*. Luz Productions CD LUZ0002.

Grupo Ilú Añá. 1995. *Sacred Rhythms*. Fundamento Productions 6120.

Grupo Ilú Añá. 2001. [reissue] *Sacred Rhythms*. Bembe CD 2055828.

Lotz of Music in Havana. 1998. *Blues for Yemayá*. Via Records CD 9920592.

Personal Communications

Carolyn Brandy, Oakland, July 28, 2008, email June 3, 2011.

Robin Burdulis, telephone interview, July 8, 2008.

Orlando Fiol, Philadelphia, June 10, 2008.

Regino Jiménez, Havana, April 8, 2004.

Virginia Lopez, telephone interview, April 26, 2008.

Amelia Pedroso, Manchester, March 27, 1999.

Elizabeth Sayre, multiple communications since 1999.

Michael Spiro, Humboldt, July 25, 2008.

Estéban "Cha Chá" Vega, Matanzas, April 5, 2004.

3. Ayben

"The Girl's Voice in Turkish Rap"

THOMAS SOLOMON

It is a warm, muggy evening in late May 2004 in the northern Istanbul district of Maslak, where an outdoor hip-hop festival is taking place.[1] Since midafternoon various Turkish hip-hop acts have taken the stage, including well-coordinated rap groups, charismatic solo performers, and enigmatic DJs holding court from behind their setups of turntables and mixers. A variety of rap styles—pop rap, hardcore rap, oriental rap—are represented, and the performers have all been men. In the late evening the much-anticipated headliner from New York takes the stage with his crew, and the crowd rushes forward to catch a view of him. RZA, from the renowned rap group Wu-Tang Clan, has brought with him an international roster of performers, including Netherlands-based rappers Cilvaringz and Salah Edin, both of Moroccan descent, as well as Wu-Tang Clan's DJ Sueside. The languages of the raps are now English and Arabic, but the performance of hypermasculinity emanating from the stage continues in the vein established by the Turkish rappers earlier in the day.

About midway through the set, RZA stops and gestures to stage left, where a young woman has been standing in the wings, watching the performance intensely, obviously enthralled. Cilvaringz escorts the young woman, recognizable to many in the crowd as the Turkish rapper Ayben, to center stage, and she is given a microphone. She is wearing a tank top and the baggy, low-slung pants of hip-hop fashion. The DJ starts the music, and Ayben begins rapping, somewhat hesitantly at first. After a few lines, she stops and looks over to RZA, who shouts encouragement to her and motions to continue. She hesitates again a bit while waiting for the right moment to enter in the cyclical rhythmic structure of the music and then launches again into her rap. This time she is confident, animated, vigorous—in the zone—as she delivers a series of fast, staccato rhymes, chopping and jabbing at the air with her hand to punctuate the complex, syncopated structure of her lines. The crowd roars in approval. After she has finished her verse, RZA indicates to her to hand off the microphone, and Salah Edin takes over the rapping as Ayben exits to stage right, having spent barely two minutes onstage.[2]

Ayben would later characterize this brief performance as one of the highlights of her career as a rapper. She described how when she was younger she listened to Wu-Tang Clan, had posters of RZA and the group on her bedroom wall, and carried a picture of RZA with her in her wallet. She was a tremendous fan of RZA, but he seemed to her to be so far away and unapproachable. Then here he was in Istanbul, actually inviting her to join him onstage. In the days after the festival an interview with RZA was broadcast on the Turkish music channel Dream TV, and RZA commented specifically on Ayben's performance, saying that she rapped very fast and was really good. Ayben described how, while sitting at home and watching this interview in which RZA praised her rapping, she felt the pride well up inside her and she began to cry tears of joy. Someone whom she idolized had given her the chance to make her *voice* heard and had taken her—and her rapping—seriously.

• • •

In their introduction to *Embodied Voices: Representing Female Vocality in Western Culture*, Leslie Dunn and Nancy Jones note how, in feminist discourse, "'voice' has become a metaphor for textual authority, and alludes to the efforts of women to reclaim their own experience through writing ('having a voice') or to the specific qualities of their literary and cultural self-expression ('in a different voice')" (1994, 1). As Bernstein explains in *Women's Voices across Musical Worlds*, such metaphors are meant to "express autonomy, authority, and agency that have been denied to women" (Bernstein 2004, 4). Dunn and Jones argue that it is necessary to go beyond this metaphorical use of "voice" and return to "the concrete physical dimensions of the female voice upon which this metaphor was based" (1994, 1).

Writing from the interstices of ethnomusicology and linguistic anthropology, Steven Feld and Aaron Fox also emphasize the connection between empirical and metaphorical evocations of voice and vocality (2000, 161). Voice is both "the embodied locus of spoken and sung performance" and "a metaphor for difference, a key representational trope for identity, power, conflict, social position, and agency" (ibid.). Feld and Fox argue that

> The connection between these empirical and metaphorical invocations of voice indexes a broader . . . project . . . that means to link embodied expression with social agency. This connection explores how vocality is a social practice that is locally understood as a conventional index of authority, evidence, and experi-

ential truth. As such, voice and vocality is a particularly significant site for the
articulation of opposition and difference. . . . [V]ocality has become the site
where linguistic and musical anthropology most strikingly conjoin a poetics
and politics of culture. (ibid.; see also Feld et al. 2004, 341–42)

In this chapter I explore how one Turkish rapper has developed her own voice,
both literally and metaphorically. In more literal terms, the rapper Ayben has
worked over the last decade to develop her technique in composing rap texts
and performing them, gradually finding her own rapping voice. In more metaphorical terms, her increasing self-confidence in her own rapping ability, and
her growing sense of the potential of her rap performances to become a vehicle
for reclaiming the everyday experiences of Turkish women, have led her to use
her rapping to express the agency she feels has been denied women in urban
Turkish society, giving a voice to Turkish women whose interests and concerns
she perceives have been underrepresented in Turkish popular culture. Ayben is
a young woman in a historically patriarchal society (Kandiyoti 1995) who has
chosen to work in a musical genre also dominated by an overtly masculinist
orientation—both in its place of origin in the United States of America and as
re-emplaced in Turkey. Ayben has thus had to negotiate a particularly complex
gendered subject position through her self-penned song texts and in the way
she deploys her voice in her personal rapping style. I explore here Ayben's voice
and subject position through a combination of analysis of rap songs from different periods in Ayben's career and discussion of excerpts from an interview
I conducted with her in 2006. I think it is important to not just try to recover
Ayben's voice and agency through analysis of her songs, but to also take seriously her explanations, in her own words, of her life and her artistic project.

Background and Early Career

Ayben Özçalkan was born in 1982 in the Istanbul district of Üsküdar, on the
Asian side of this city divided by the Bosphorus Strait. By her early teens she
had become familiar with rap music through listening to U.S.A. rap groups
such as the Wu-Tang Clan, but also especially through following the activities
of her elder brother Bilgin, who would later become the well-known Turkish
rapper known as Ceza ("Punishment").

Ayben is not the first woman Turkish rapper. Two other rappers, both
from the Turkish diaspora, preceded her in constructing Turkish female
subjectivities through rap music performance. Both Aziza-A from Berlin,
and Sultana, who was based in New York when her first album came out
in 2000, had already released albums before Ayben began her professional
career in earnest. But Ayben is the first "home-grown" female rapper—i.e.,

not from the diaspora—to gain any significant media attention in Turkey. Much of the attention she has received has thus focused on the novelty of her being a woman rapper in Turkey and on her family relation to her older brother Ceza, himself the first full-blown homegrown Turkish rap star.

Ayben comes from what she herself describes as a "traditional" Turkish family from a traditionally oriented neighborhood in Üsküdar, a district popularly known for having a large religiously conservative Muslim population. During our interview[3] she talked about how the values of her parents and her local community place certain expectations on her as a young woman and how this could potentially have constrained her choice to be a rapper and performing artist. She also talked about how the fact that her older brother had already achieved substantial success as a performer by the time she started working seriously on her own career was an advantage to her because her family—particularly her father—had learned with Ceza's success that one could actually make a viable career as a rapper in Turkey.

> In the structure of the Turkish family, daughters are special, the jewel of the home. But at the same time, the family expects things of them. Schooling is always very important. Maybe there are families in Anatolia that don't send their daughters to school, but I'm talking here about Istanbul. My family is conservative. They might think it's wrong for a girl to go out at night. Or in that culture, adults might disapprove of a girl performing onstage. I'm actually from a family that is committed to those traditions.
>
> On the other hand, it has been a big advantage for us that my father listens to music,[4] that in his youth he was from the generation of '68, that he is a man who has seen and experienced a lot. Of course, everything is not how it looks. Since the beginning [of her brother's rap career] there have been times when my father supported it and when he didn't support it, but I didn't experience that. After he saw my brother's success, it was more a question of "What will the neighbors say?" In the end, our mother and father are from the same culture since they were children.
>
> We grew up in Üsküdar, they are also from Üsküdar, etc. There's a certain attitude in the neighborhood we live in. . . . In the traditions and customs of the Turkish family, respect and love are of course very important. Besides that, they can regard as strange the idea of going onstage to perform. There are some Turks who think this is wrong. There are those who think that people who perform onstage are a little weird. . . . In regard to the traditions and customs of the Turkish family, I come from a family with strong family ties. Our family ties are very strong, we are bound to each other.
>
> Besides that, relations with our neighbors are very important. I'm still Ayben the girl from the neighborhood. Along with that, at the same time I'm still the

Ayben who cooks at home, who does the dishes, who washes the clothes, who cleans house, who cleans the windows. That continues along with this [her musical career], I'm carrying on with both of them together. Of course I don't know how long it can continue like this. I don't know how long I will carry on with both of them without them getting in the way of each other.[5]

Ayben's comments about the conservative disapproval of women performing onstage deserve further explication. As in many other Muslim and Muslim-influenced societies (Doubleday 1999, 2006 [1988]; Jones 1987; Naroditskaya 2000; van Nieuwkerk 1995; Olsen 2002; Sakata 1987) in Turkey there has historically been an attitude of disapproval against Muslim women (often in contrast with women from non-Muslim minorities, such as Greeks, Armenians and Jews) performing publicly onstage—what Atamert refers to as a "taboo on dancing and singing Muslim women" (2001, 12) and what O'Connell pithily calls the "male preference for female invisibility in the public domain" (2006, 287). The assumption is that women who, as performers onstage, willingly make themselves available to the gaze of the male spectator must be of questionable morals, and such performers may often be assumed to be promiscuous (Bryant 2005, 232; Greve 2003, 123; O'Connell 2006). This is not to imply that there is a dearth of prominent successful female performing artists in Turkey today—they are legion, especially in the various subgenres that collectively make up Turkish pop. The point, rather, is that within the more conservative segment of urban Turkish society that Ayben's family inhabits, it is one thing for some other (family's) woman to make a career as a performing artist, but it is an altogether different matter for a local "neighborhood girl" to enter this suspect profession. Ayben's emphasis on her strong family bonds and her assertion that she is still the "girl from the neighborhood" who takes care of the household chores can be understood as a strategy for insulating herself from potential accusations that, as a performing artist, she is somehow being drawn into what is perceived as the degenerate lifestyle of pop stars as constantly reported in the tabloid press and on television magazine programs. Ayben thus engages in a delicate negotiation with what Dunn and Jones refer to as "patriarchal constructions of the feminine" (1994, 3), accepting some aspects of the constraints her family and neighborhood obligations place on her, while also challenging other aspects as she pursues her chosen career as a performer.

Ayben's first recorded appearance as a rapper was in a guest appearance on one song on the first album by the Istanbul rap group Nefret ("Hate"), consisting of her brother Ceza and his friend Dr. Fuchs.[6] The song, "Yüz Yüze" ("Face to Face"), was recorded in 1999, when Ayben was seventeen years old, and released the following year. During our interview, my question about Ayben's interest in other branches of hip-hop such as graffiti or break-dance led to her recalling how her brother invited her to do the guest spot on the song.

When I was a kid, of course I had a yen to do graffiti. But I don't have a talent for drawing at all. I wanted to dance, but I don't have a talent for it. It wasn't something I could do. It wasn't something I would stick with. I always had rap in my heart. I had never imagined you can rap in Turkish, but I learned from my brother that it is possible. I saw with my brother that it can also be done in Turkish, and I decided to try it too, and he gave me a chance on the song "Yüz Yüze" on Nefret's album. He said, "OK, you can do it" and I did it. I was writing [lyrics] before that, but for some reason I somehow couldn't make them [other rappers] like me. That was the first album [of Nefret]. When he said "Come on and rap [on the song]," I got really excited. I'll never forget that day in the studio. We did it, and it came out well.[7]

On this song Ayben shares rapping time with her best friend Elif, who was also Ceza's girlfriend (and later his fiancée). The two girls use the song to introduce themselves as female rappers, a novelty at that time in the very male-dominated world of Turkish hip-hop. Ayben specifically identifies herself in the song as "Ceza's little sister," both indicating her indebtedness to her brother for inviting her to participate on his album, and also establishing a pedigree of sorts, claiming a certain authenticity through her blood relationship to a rapper who was by this time already well-established on the Istanbul hip-hop scene. But rejecting the idea that rapping is for men only, Ayben rhetorically asks "Who said girls can't do this?" and counters with the evocative, antiessentialist line "It's not a matter of bracelets, it's a matter of spirit." The last line of her first verse, "Türkçe rapin kız sesi" ("The girl's voice in Turkish rap"), has, since this song, become a slogan of sorts for Ayben which she has used again in several later songs, and which also has appeared on posters and other promotional material on her various websites.

Ayben's rapping in this song corresponds closely with the fairly simple style of rapping (compared to later developments) now associated with U.S.A. "old-school" or first-generation rap beginning in the 1970s and continuing through the 1980s. The textual lines line up evenly with the metrical units—each new line of text begins exactly on the first beat of a measure, and each textual line is wholly contained within a single measure. The text is delivered with a singsongy intonation, with most textual lines ending predictably with a stressed syllable on the third or fourth sixteenth note subdivision of the last quarter note of the measure. Rhymes are mostly confined to the ends of textual lines, and not much is going on in terms of line-internal rhyming. The eight lines of the verse are easily analyzable as a series of four couplets on the basis of semantic unity and (in the case of couplets 2 and 3) end-rhyme. All of these features are consistent with what Adam Krims, in his book *Rap Music and the Poetics of Identity*, describes as typical of early rapping in the United States of America, which generally featured a fairly predictable "antecedent/consequent couplet and . . . matching-beat-class end-rhyme" structure (2000, 49). Of the eight lines in this verse, all but one have a midline caesura, with the text constructed such that the caesura—an audible pause that breaks up a line—occurs naturally between two distinct phrases or logical word groupings within the line, and thus does not disrupt the semantic flow of the text. The second half-line after the caesura always begins squarely on the downbeat of the third quarter note in the measure, with the result that the relationship between the text setting and the meter is easy to follow. The predictability of the placement of the caesuras and the beginning of each half-line of text, the repeated intonation pattern in which the last, prosodically stressed[8] syllable of each half-line of text usually ends on a higher pitch, and the end-rhyme of couplets 2 and 3 all contribute to creating the singsong, old-school quality of the rapping. The transcription in figure 3.1 represents some aspects of Ayben's rapping style in this verse, focusing particularly on the point of articulation of syllables within the rhythmic structure of each line.[9] Each line across represents one measure in 4/4 meter. The top line of numbers 1–4 represents quarter note values; the second line of numbers represents sixteenth note subdivisions. The syllables of each line are lined up underneath the rhythmic position on which they are articulated. The sign ¶ in the rhythmic transcription represents the beginning of a new textual line; in this song all of these coincide with the beginning of a measure. A forward slash (/) in both the rhythmic transcription and the textual transcription with translation underneath represents the end of the metrical unit (one measure), here always coinciding with the end of a textual line. Rhymes (also all at the end of textual lines) are indicated with underlining.

	1				2				3				4					# of syllables
	1	2	3	4	1	2	3	4	1	2	3	4	1	2	3	4		in line
1	'Dok-		san		do-		kuz		se-	fer	sa-	yı-	lı	u-	çak		/	11
2	'Be-	nim	a-	dım	Ay-		ben		Ce-	za-		nın	kar-		de-	si	/	12
3	'İş-		te	kız	M		C		a-		pay-		rı		bir	ses	/	10
4	'Ge-	li-	yo-	ruz	iş-	te	şim-	di	tan-	ta-	na-	yı	kes				/	13
5	'Kim	de-	miş	kız-			lar		be-	ce-	re-	mez	bu	i-	si		/	12
6	'Bi-	lek	i-	şi	değ-		il		sa-		de-	ce	yü-	rek	i-	si	/	13
7	'Dok-	tor	ve	Ce-	za				kar-	şı-	nız-	da	Nef-		ret		/	11
8	'Ay-	ben	ve	E-			lif		Türk-	çe	ra-	pin	kız		se-	si	/	12

Figure 3.1. Nefret featuring Ayben and Elif, "Yüz Yüze," (2000): Ayben's first verse, articulation of syllables within rhythmic structure of each line. Lyrics by Ayben Özçalkan. © 2000 Hammer Müzik (Turkey). Used by permission.

Doksan dokuz sefer sayılı uçak /	Flight number ninety-nine [i.e., the year 1999]
Benim adım Ayben Ceza'nın kardeşi /	My name is Ayben, Ceza's little sister
İşte kız MC apayrı bir ses /	This is a girl MC, a very different voice
Geliyoruz işte şimdi, tantanayı kes /	We're on our way, so cut the crap
Kim demiş kızlar beceremez bu işi /	Who said girls can't do this?
Bilek işi değil sadece yürek işi /	It's not a matter of bracelets, it's just a matter of spirit
Doktor ve Ceza karşınızda Nefret /	Here's Nefret—the Doctor [rapper Dr. Fuchs] and Ceza
Ayben ve Elif Türkçe rapin kız sesi /	Ayben and Elif, the girl's voice in Turkish rap

Ayben's first recorded rap thus embodies the tension between the patriarchal constraints she works under and what Wayne Koestenbaum would call her "will to be heard" (cited in Dunn and Jones 1994, 6). She both depends on her older brother's patronage ("My name is Ayben, Ceza's little sister") and also claims a position of independence and authority as she affirms her (and Elif's) unique voices as a vehicle for speaking for other girls within the context of Turkish hip-hop ("This is a girl MC, a very different voice"; "the girl's voice in Turkish rap"). But compared to the more complex rapping style she would later develop (see next section), Ayben's voice here can still be heard as tentative, relying as it does on old-school stereotypes of how to embody a message in rhyme, rhythm, and intonation. As she identifies herself in the text, it is the voice of a *girl* (*kız* in Turkish), the voice of one who is just starting out and who, while having discovered her own vocality, has only begun exploring its possibilities.

Career Hiatus and Return to Professional Activity

After "Yüz Yüze" was released in 2000, Ayben took a four-year hiatus from recording. During this period her mother was sick with cancer (and eventually passed away in January 2004). Although she didn't say much about it in the interview with me, in other published interviews Ayben has talked about how she was caregiver for her mother throughout the period her mother was sick, until she passed away. Ayben describes this as a physically and emotionally intense period because she was mostly staying home with her mother taking care of her twenty-four hours a day. In our interview Ayben talked about how she also kept working on her rapping skills during this period, even though her professional career as a performer was on hold and she was mostly at home. She described to me how she learned more about rapping by memorizing other performers' recorded raps and recording herself directly to a computer while rapping along with rap songs on CDs. In this way she internalized ways in which syllables can be put together in a rap text and delivered rhythmically in performance, to create what rappers call a *flow*, or personal rapping style (Rose 1994, 39, Krims 2000, 48–49; Turkish rappers also use this English term).

Actually, I continued writing songs. I took great pains to not stay far away from rap because for me during that period, at that time I—my mother was sick and all. I stayed away from the rap scene for a long time, but I did the best I could to not stay away from rap itself. I was always writing. I even used to do like this at home: I'd play a CD, put a microphone by the CD player and rap along with it and record it like that onto a computer, and I'd copy it to a diskette and have my brother play it for people. I remember the days when I used to say "Brother, will you play it for them?—look how good it turned out, how good I did it." Now when I look back at those times, they were—How can I explain it? It was harder—When I look at it now, I've begun to see things now more in terms of technique. Some things are developing and it means that now that I've started doing this professionally, I'm doing this as a profession, and this is what makes me happiest.[10]

During the period when she did not record professionally or give any concerts, and was mostly at home taking care of her mother, Ayben thus used the resources available to her at home to continue to develop her rapping skills and cultivate her own style. The way in which she learned existing raps by other performers and then recorded herself rapping along with them mirrors the way self-taught musicians in other genres such as rock or jazz long have developed their craft, learning licks by playing along with favorite recordings, eventually synthesizing the different styles of other players and adding their own ideas to develop their own instrumental voice. In Ayben's case, this involved learning the stylistic vocabulary of rap—techniques of rhyme, alliteration, assonance, and consonance, the rhythmic articulation of syllables and their emplacement within a metrical framework, different approaches to intonation and melody— internalizing all these features through repetition, and then moving beyond imitation to develop her own, individual rapping voice.

Several months after her mother passed away, Ayben reappeared on the rap scene with guest spots on two songs ("Sinekler ve Beatler" ["Flies and Beats"] and "Araba" ["Vehicle"]) on her brother Ceza's 2004 album *Rapstar*. With these two songs, recorded some five years after her debut on "Yüz Yüze," Ayben restarted her career with a very different rapping style than that used on the earlier song. In contrast to the singsongy old-school flow of her verses on "Yüz Yüze," on these two songs she delivered her verses with a percussive, aggressive high-speed flow similar to that of her brother. In the song "Araba" Ayben also introduced for the first time a new tagline for which she would become famous—"Benim adım Ayben / Korkun benden!" ("My name is Ayben / Be afraid of me!")—and which she would later reuse in other songs.

Once she returned to performing publicly with her new style—including the onstage appearance with RZA described at the beginning of this article—Ayben also started developing her career through various high-profile appearances, some serendipitous, some strategically planned. She frequently performed brief guest spots at her brother Ceza's concerts. She appears for a short time with her best friend Elif rapping and talking about women rappers in celebrated German-Turkish film director Fatih Akın's 2005 documentary about Turkish popular music, *Crossing the Bridge—The Sound of Istanbul*. Her career especially got a boost with two high-profile guest appearances as rapper on songs by well-established female Turkish rock and pop singers Aylin Aslım in 2005 and Nil in 2006. Both of these singers are well-known for how they play with gendered representations of women in Turkey, in both their music and their visual self-presentation, and Ayben described to me how she carefully chose to do these two duets from among the various duet offers that she received during this period. She joined both these singers for live performances in concerts and on television and went on tour as featured guest artist with Aylin Aslım.

During the period 2005–7, Ayben's professional career and visibility in the Turkish media thus slowly developed through her judicious choice of guest appearances on records with other artists. She also released a few of her own solo songs as "underground" tracks (Solomon 2005b) to selected Turkish hip-hop websites, where they were made available for free download. A number of clips of her in live performance—either filmed on cell phones at her concerts by fans, or recorded off her numerous television appearances—also became available on the internet.

Around this time she additionally began working on her first solo album. One of the new songs on this album, called "Dişi Köpek" ("Female Dog"), is about the sexual harassment women commonly experience in urban Turkey when on the street and not accompanied by a man such as their father, older brother, or husband. Ayben uses the song to vent her anger about how women commonly experience rude comments and wolf whistles when out and about in the city, simply going about their own business. The title of the song, and the first line of the chorus that Ayben herself *sings* after she raps the verses, refer to a well-known Turkish proverb, "Dişi köpek kuyruğunu sallamayınca erkek köpek ardına düşmez," which can be literally translated as "If a female dog does not wiggle her tail, the male dog does not go after her" (Yurtbaşı 1993, 359). The proverb establishes the sexist idea that if a woman acts provocatively, she deserves what she gets—that is, if a woman is bothered in a sexual way by a man, she must have been "asking for it" through her behavior. The proverb in effect discursively institutionalizes and legitimizes this sexist attitude in everyday Turkish life, and Ayben's ironic appropriation of it in this song makes clear her agenda of attacking the status quo of gender relations in Turkey. While the song would not be commercially released on Ayben's album until May 2008, Ayben performed part of it live on Turkish television in 2006 and a clip of the performance was uploaded to YouTube by a fan, so I was able to watch the performance and ask her about the song before it was officially released on her album. In our interview Ayben explained what she was trying to do with this song.

This is something that really bugs me. Things like sexual harassment on the street, men making rude remarks etc. It's like this: you can like somebody, find them attractive. But if it starts to get ugly, if it gets to the point of making improper overtures to a woman and making her feel ill at ease, then that's really bad. It's one thing to say you like somebody, but they make movements with their hands that make women feel uncomfortable on the street, they say offensive words, this happens a lot to women.

This is my biggest complaint—to not be at ease on the street, to not be able to wear what you want to. . . . In fact, men can look disapprovingly on a woman who is just going out in the evening to have fun. Those men making rude remarks, those backward men—they think they're so smart. But to think that indecently assaulting women—those men with the mentality of disapproving of girls who go out to have fun by themselves, I really hate them . . . I'm really against making rude remarks on the street, it really bothers me, and in this way I've expressed it. I mean, I wanted to express something I've experienced.

Anyway rap is for me the art of defending with words. It's a way of explaining everything I want to, from one point of view it's freedom. Maybe the guy who made rude remarks to me on the street will hear my song. He will say, "Wow, she's right. This girl is saying something, and she's right, it really shouldn't be like this." Maybe he'll come to his senses, or maybe he'll just say, "What on earth is she saying?" and close his mind. You can never tell, but I wanted to say it. This is what's on my mind, and I did it [made a song about it].[11]

The transcription of the first verse of "Dişi Köpek" in figure 3.2 shows how extensively Ayben had developed her rapping technique since "Yüz Yüze" was recorded, incorporating a number of techniques generally associated with what is often called "new school" rapping in the United States of America. In contrast to the earlier song, in this rap the textual lines don't line up squarely with metrical units. Measure boundaries occur in the middle of textual lines (and even in the middle of words), and new lines of text start in the middle of measures. While in "Yüz Yüze" every textual line is neatly contained within the boundaries of a single measure, such enjambments occur in eight out of the twelve measures containing the eighteen textual lines in the first verse of

"Dişi Köpek."[12] The rap also gives an impression of being faster—not actually in tempo but because it is more dense in terms of the number of syllables put into each measure. Another technique that adds to the sense of the rap being faster is the use of triplets, thereby getting three syllables within the space of two sixteenth notes. The techniques used here thus represent a move from what Krims (2000, 49–52) calls "sung" rhythmic style in "Yüz Yüze" to "speech-effusive" rhythmic style in "Dişi Köpek." In contrast with the rather rudimentary end-rhymes employed in "Yüz Yüze," here there are also denser rhyme complexes, with many internal rhymes besides rhymes at line ends, as well as the use of alliteration ("Yolda yürüyemez" ["She can't walk on the road"]), assonance (combined with word-final rhyme in "yeter der geçer" ["she says 'enough' and continues on"]), consonance ("zaten itler" ["as a matter of fact the sons-of-bitches"]) and other kinds of play with the sounds of the words. Gone here also is the singsongy quality, as Ayben varies the intonation contours from one line to the next. The use of textual lines of constantly varying length—from two to seven words each—often cutting across measure boundaries, also mitigates against a repetitive singsongy quality and contributes to the move in the direction of "speech-effusive" styling. Three symbols I use in this figure that did not appear in figure 3.1 are parentheses ( ) indicating interjections by another voice (probably the track's producer Roka[13]), not included in the syllable count; vertical bars | | surrounding triplets; and φ between two syllables to indicate an empty second position in a triplet, as in | ♪φ♪ |. In figure 3.1, I use the forward slash (/) to indicate measure boundaries in the rhythmic transcription, in the Turkish text below it, and in the English translation. In figure 3.2, I similarly use the forward slash in the Turkish text below the rhythmic transcription, thus indicating the placement of enjambments. But I do not use it in the English translation since the very different word order of the English equivalent from the original Turkish makes this unworkable.

```
            1                        2                        3                        4             # of syllables
      1     2     3     4      1       2    3     4      1     2     3     4      1     2     3     4      in line

 1  'Yol-  da    |yü-  ru-   ye-|mez        ka-   dın    'Her  a-    dım   da     bir   he-   ce             /   15
 2  laf    a-    tar          'Yal- nız   ol-   mak    'suç  mu    san-  ki     'Bak  ye-   ter             /   14
 3  der    ge-   çer          'Tep- ki-   siz           kal-  mak   ay-   rı     dert  'Ce   vap   ve-       /   14
 4  rir-   sen   it    gü-    ler         'Na-  mus    el-   den   git-  me-    sin   (Ha!)                  /   12
 5  'Kal-  dı-   rım-  da     ve-   sa-   it            bek-  le-   mek   ö-     lüm   ge-   lir   'Ve-       /   15
 6  sa-    it    gel-  me-    den   de    za-   ten    it-   ler   he-   men    |di-  zi-   lir| (Yeh!) 'Ya- /   16
 7  yay-   ken   ay-   rı     dert  '|A-  ra-   ba|    ku-   la-   nır-  ken    ta-   ciz   |e-   di- lir|    /   17
 8  'If-   ti-   ray-  sa     ha-   zır                 'Ha-  tun   |a-   ra-ba| kul-  la-   nır   mı         /   15
 9                '|Hak- φ kı| yok  'Ka-  dın   ge-   ce     so-   kak-  ta    eğ-   le-   nir-  se           /   14
10  |ta- φ ciz|                |hak φ kı|      var    'Ser- best  ser-         |do-  la-   şa-|  'So-        /   12
11  maz                        ka-   dın            'Doğ- ru    ya    so-    kak   se-   nin   ma- lın 'So-  /   13
12  kak    se-   nin          me-   kâ-   nın          (Nah  ha!)                                            /    6
```

Figure 3.2. Ayben, "Dişi Köpek" (2008): first verse, articulation of syllables within rhythmic structure of each line. Lyrics by Ayben Özçalkan. © 2008 Pozitif Edisyon (Turkey). Used by permission.

Yolda yürüyemez kadın	A woman can't walk on the street by herself
Her adımda bir hece / laf atar	He makes rude remarks—a syllable matches her every step
Yalnız olmak suç mu sanki	As if it were a crime to be by herself
Bak yet<u>er</u> / d<u>er</u> ge<u>çer</u>	She says "Enough!" and continues on
Tepkisiz kalmak ayrı dert	If she doesn't react, it's one kind of grief
Cevap ve/rirsen it gül<u>er</u>	If she responds, the son-of-a-bitch laughs
Namus elden gitmesin /	"Don't let her lose her honor"
Kaldırımda vesait beklemek ölüm ge<u>lir</u>	Waiting on the sidewalk for a ride is pure torture
Ve/sait gelmeden de zaten it<u>ler</u> hemen dizi<u>lir</u>	And while she's waiting the sons-of-bitches line right up [to harass her]
Ya/yayken ayrı dert	When she's a pedestrian it's another kind of grief
Araba kullanırken taciz edi<u>lir</u> /	When she's driving a car she's harassed
İftiraysa haz<u>ır</u>	He's always ready with slander
"Hatun araba kullan<u>ır</u> mı? /	"Can a woman drive a car?
Hakkı yok"	She doesn't have the right!"
Kadın gece sokakta eğlenirse / taciz hakkı var	If a woman has fun out at night he has the right to harass her
Serbest serbest dolaşa/maz k<u>adın</u>	A woman can't walk around freely
Doğru ya sokak senin m<u>alın</u>	The truth is: the street belongs to you!
So/kak senin mek<u>ânın</u>	You own the streets!

In "Dişi Köpek," the subject position constructed, both in the textual content of the song and in the rapping style used to deliver it, is not that of a hesitant *girl* but a mature, self-confident, defiant *woman*. The Turkish word for *girl* (*kız*), which permeated Ayben's verse in "Yüz Yüze," has specifically been replaced in "Dişi Köpek" by the word for *woman* (*kadın*). The frame of reference—and the intended audience—have also been expanded from the relatively insular world of Turkish hip-hop to embrace Turkish society as a whole. As she explained in the interview excerpt quoted earlier, the song is addressed to all, women and men, who are willing to listen to her, including the men whose sexist behavior she criticizes in the song. The position of authority Ayben claims, to speak for Turkish women, is also bolstered by the authoritative way she establishes her command over the stylistic resources of rap. Along with her move from *girl* to *woman*, indeed part and parcel of this transition itself, comes her move from the tentative old-school style of her debut recording, with its stereotyped rhyming and singsong intonation patterns, to the complex rhythmic and rhyming patterns she deploys in this song. In "Dişi Köpek" she has a verbal message to get across, the content of the song text, but—importantly—this message is embodied in a sonorous vehicle that highlights the sounding language itself, with her attention to the sounds themselves of the words and syllables and with her particular use of alliteration, consonance, assonance, and rhyme. The irregular line lengths, syncopations, and enjambments form a sort of sonorous jagged leading edge for the message contained within them. This vocal jagged edge powerfully embodies the materiality of Ayben's sounding voice as it cuts through patriarchal attempts to "undo women" (Clément 1988). Ayben also calls attention to the embodied, corporeal dimension of her rapping in her live performances, where she emphasizes the sounds and rhythms with the physical motions of her hand chopping at the air with the side of the palm and jabbing outward with her outstretched fingers.

Conclusions: A Less Predictable Form of Vocality

Dunn and Jones pose the question "under what cultural conditions, and by what artistic means, can women (re)claim the authority of the female voice?" and argue that this issue is fundamental for the study of female vocality (1994, 10). Ayben's herstory shows how one woman in a specific cultural setting—urban Turkey in the first decade of the new millenium—has worked to reclaim such authority. As she works to "find the social space in which to have a musical voice" (Cusick 1999, 497), Ayben must negotiate the requirements and expectations that come with her choice to be a female rapper in Turkey—the requirements and expectations of family, of her local community, and of the community of Turkish hip-hoppers, all of which are specific instantiations of the broader patriarchal gender norms given in Turkish society.[14] In this negotiation she has found and developed her voice, both in literal terms—her personal rapping style in terms of *flow*—and in metaphorical terms—her agency in reclaiming her experiences and making them available to others, male and female, through her music, asserting herself as a self and subject rather than an object and men's other (Abu-Lughod 1991, 140).

Significant here is not just the simple fact of her choice to be a performer, with all that entails in Turkish society, but also the specific genre—rap music—that she has chosen to work in. Ayben's choice to be a rapper, what Dunn and Jones would refer to as the "artistic means" for her reclaiming of a voice, is especially daring in the Turkish context, where there have been very few women rappers, and the public face of hip-hop youth culture is decidedly male-dominated. In contrast to the endless array of Turkish female pop singers, Ayben's specific choice to work in rap music and develop her ability as a

Figure 3.3. Turkish
rapper Ayben in
performance, August
2006. Photograph by
Thomas Solomon.

rapper represent, in the Turkish context, a "more assertive, less predictable [form] of vocality" (Dunn and Jones 1994, 4). Ayben's rapping—and her very existence as a female rapper—thus challenge conventional representations of femininity within Turkish society, providing a space for alternative conceptions of what a Turkish woman's voice might be.

Acknowledgments

Thanks first to Ayben for taking time from her busy schedule of recording and performing to do an interview with me. Thanks also to Serkant Köseler for his transcription of the Turkish interview recording; to Deniz Akın for additional editing of that transcription, for checking my translations to English of the interview and song texts, and for many helpful comments on and suggestions regarding the ideas I explore here; and to Çağla Kulakaç for sharing with me her experiences as a Turkish feminist and her opinions about Ayben's music based on those experiences.

Notes

1. The event described here is "Hip Hop Jam Istanbul 2004," which took place on Sunday, May 23, 2004, in the performance space called Maslak Venue. My description here is based on my own attendance at the event, supplemented by some details from the clip mentioned in note 2.

2. A clip of this performance by Ayben can be watched on YouTube at http://www.youtube.com/watch?v=ThGSVEfF6jM (accessed March 2012).

3. My interview with Ayben was conducted on November 4, 2006, and lasted about ninety minutes. The interview was conducted in Turkish. Translations in this article of excerpts from this interview are by me.

4. Ayben's father Danyal Özçalkan is interviewed briefly in the rap music segment of German-Turkish director Fatih Akın's documentary film *Crossing the Bridge—The Sound of Istanbul*. In the interview he talks about how he had listened in his youth to rock musicians such as Eric Clapton and Jimi Hendrix and did not understand rap music when he first heard it, but later came to appreciate it as a valid and vital musical expression.

5. Türk aile yapısında genelde kızlar evin gülüdür, evin değerlisidir. Ama bir yandan da şey ister aileler. Her zaman okul çok daha önceliklidir. Belki Anadolu'da kızlarını okutmayan aileler de var, ama İstanbul için konuşuyorum. Ailem şeydir, tutucu. Bir kızın gece sokağa çıkması yanlış düşünülebilir. Ya da o kültürden, o şeyde yetişmiş insanlar için bir kızın sahneye çıkması kötü bile karşılanabilir. Aslında o geleneklere bağlı bir aileden geliyorum. Bir yandan babamın da müzik dinliyor olması, gençliğinde hani bu 68 kuçağı dediğimiz kuşaktan geliyor olması, hani görmüş geçirmiş bir adam olması bizim için çok büyük bir avantaj oldu en başta. Tabi her şey göründüğü gibi değil de. Başından beri babamın desteklediği, desteklemediği zamanlar da olmuştur, ama bunları ben yaşamadım. Abimin başarısını gördükten sonra daha çok "Konu komşu ne der" şeyi oldu hep. Sonuçta annemiz babamız küçüklüklerinden beri aynı kültürdeler. Üsküdar'da yetiştik, onlar da Üsküdarlılar, vesaire. Yaşadığımız çevrede bir şey var . . . Türk aile gelenek ve görenekleri şeydir: saygı, sevgi tabi ki çok önemlidir. Onun dışında, garipsenebilir ya sahneye çıkmakla alakalı bir şey. Hani bunun yanlış bir şey olduğunu düşünen bir yanı var Türk insanının. Sahneye çıkan insanlara birazcık garip gözle baktıkları var . . . Türk aile gelenek ve göreneklerinde, akraba, aile bağları sağlam bir aileden geliyorum. Aile bağlarımız çok kuvvetli, birbirimize kenetlenmiş durumdayız. Onun dışında komşuluk ilişkilerimiz çok önemlidir. Ben yine mahallenin kızı Ayben'im. Onun yanı sıra ben hala evde yemek yapan, evde bulaşık yıkayan, çamaşır yıkayan, ev temizleyen, cam silen Ayben'im bir yandan da. Bu da bununla birlikte devam ediyor, beraber sürdürüyorum. Nereye kadar sürer bilemiyorum tabi ki ama. Nereye kadar bunları birbirine karıştırmadan sürdürürüm bilemiyorum ama.

6. I discuss this group and some of their songs in Solomon (2005a,b).

7. Çocukken bir heves ettim tabi graffiti yapayım. Ama benim çizim yeteneğim hiç yok. Dans etmek istedim, yeteneğim yok. Yapabileceğim bir şey değildi. Ben yapayım,

şey kalayım değildi. Her zaman gönlümde rap vardı. Ama Türkçe yapılabileceğini hiç ummazken abimden öğrendim. Onun Türkçe de yapılabileceğini ondan gördüm ve ben de denemeye karar verdim ve Nefret albümünde "Yüz Yüze" parçasında bana bir şans verdi. Artık oldu, artık yapabilirsin dedi ve ben de yaptım. Ondan önce de yazıyordum, ama işte bir türlü belki beğendirememiştim kendimi. Ve de o da ilk albümdü. "Hadi bakalım söyle" dediğinde çok heyecanlanmıştım. O stüdyo gününü hiç unutamıyorum yani. Oldu, bitti, yaptık, güzel de oldu.

8. The format for and many of the conventions of the two rhythmic transcriptions in this article are inspired by, but do not follow exactly, those used in the transcriptions in Adam Krims's book *Rap Music and the Poetics of Identity* (2000).

9. In contrast to the *lexical stress* inherent in individual words, *prosodic stress* is associated with larger units such as phrases or sentences.

10. Ben aslında sürekli yazdım. Rapten uzak kalmamaya çok özen gösterdim çünkü rap benim için o dönmde, ben o dönemde—annem hastaydı ve saire. Ben böyle çok fazla rap ortamından uzak kaldım, ama rapten uzak kalmamak için elimden geleni yaptım. Sürekli olarak yazdım ve işte yazdım. Hatta evde kendim şey yapardım böyle. CD'den çalıp, mikrofonu CD'nin yanına koyup ben de onunla birlikte okuyup o şekilde bilgisayara kaydettiğimin zamanları hatırlıyorum ve onları diskete kaydedip millete—abimin yanında: "Abi dinletir misin? işte bak ne güzel oldu, ne güzel yaptım" falan dediğim günleri hatırlıyorum. Şimdi o zamanlara baktığımda sanki o zaman daha mı şeydi—ey—nasıl diyeyim? Daha zordu yani—şimdi baktığım zaman bir şeyleri daha böyle teknik açıdan görebil—görmeye başladım. Bir şeyler gelişiyor demek ki yani ben bu işe—artık profesyonel olarak başladığım için bir de bunu iş, iş-meslek olarak da bir yandan yapıyorum ve, hani bu en büyük mutluluk benim için.

11. Benim çok fazla sıkıntı duyduğum bir konu. Sokakta cinsel taciz, erkeklerin laf atmaları vesaire gibi şeyler. Şöyle bir durum var, hani bir insan beğenebilir, beğenebilirsin. Ama bu çirkinleşmeye başlıyorsa, eğer sarkıntılık ve rahatsızlık verecek düzeye ulaşıyorsa gerçekten kötü. Beğendiğini söylemek ayrı. Ama sokaktayken rahatsızlık boyutunda bir el hareketleri oluyor, işte çok kötü sözler söylenebiliyor, kadınlara çok yapılıyor bu. Ve ben—en büyük şikâyetim bu. Sokakta yürürken rahat edememek, istediğini giyememek . . . Hani gece eğlenmeye çıkan bir kadına da kötü gözle bakılabilir, hani o erkekler tarafından, o laf atan—geri kafalı—aslında çok fazla ileri düzey zekâları olduğunu düşünen. Ama kadınlara sarkıntılık etmeyi de bir şey zannedip, ya da ne bileyim—gece kendi başına eğlenmeye çıkan kızlara o gözle bakabilecek zihniyette olan erkeklere, yani karşı bir nefret duyuyorum artık içimde . . . Sokakta laf atılmasına çok karşıyım, çok rahatsızlık duyuyorum ve bunu bir şekilde dile getirdim. Yani yaşadığım bir şeyi dile getirmek istedim. Böyle. Zaten—hani benim—sözlü savunma sanatı, rap benim için. Bir bakıma özgürlük, her istediğimi anlatabilmek için bir yol. Belki sokakta bana laf atmış olan bir insan benim şarkımı dinleyecek. "Vay be" diyecek ve, "Haklı söylüyor. Bu kız bir şeyler diyor evet haklı ya, gerçekten öyle olmaması gerekir" diyecek. Belki aklı başına gelecek, ya da "Bu da ne diyor" deyip kapatacak. O da belli olmaz, ama ben bunu söylemek istedim, gönlümden geçen buydu ve yaptım.

12. I have analyzed the text of the first verse of "Dişi Köpek" as containing 18 textual lines, on the basis of each line containing one complete independent clause in Turkish. Other analyses of the poetic structure of this verse may, however, be possible, depending on how one analyzes the clause structure of Turkish sentences.

13. The musical backing track for this song, called "beat" in hip-hop parlance, was

produced by Ayben's friend Elif, who had also rapped on the song "Yüz Yüze" from 2000. Elif had decided to leave rapping and work instead as a rap music producer. Now going under the artist name Roka, she is, as far as I know, the first and only woman in Turkey to make a professional career as a rap producer.

14. I am aware that throughout this chapter I have left *patriarchy* untheorized and have assumed rather than demonstrated the patriarchal underpinnings of rap music in the United States of America and in Turkey. In an unpublished longer version of this paper, I discuss Ayben's subject position as being overdetermined by the twin patriarchies of masculinist-oriented hip-hop, on the one hand, and the conservative segment of urban Turkish society she grew up in and continues to live in, on the other. In that much longer analysis I use Turkish social scientist Deniz Kandiyoti's concept of "bargaining with patriarchy" (1988) to explore in more detail Ayben's strategic negotiations with(in) these constraints, and the resulting contradictions within her music and in her visual image. Space restrictions prevent me from including that analysis here.

References

Abu-Lughod, Lila. 1991. "Writing against Culture." In *Recapturing Anthropology: Working in the Present*, ed. Richard G. Fox, 137–62. Santa Fe: School of American Research Press.

Atamert, Engül. 2001. *Tango and the Invention of Modern Turkey*. MA thesis in Ethnomusicology, Department of Advanced Studies in Music, Istanbul Technical University.

Bernstein, Jane A. 2004. "Introduction: On Women and Music." In *Women's Voices across Musical Worlds*, ed. Jane A. Bernstein, 3–12. Boston: Northeastern University Press.

Bryant, Rebecca. 2005. "The Soul Danced into the Body: Nation and Improvisation in Istanbul." *American Anthropologist* 32(2):222–38.

Clément, Catherine. 1988. *Opera, or the Undoing of Women*, trans. Betsy Wing. Minneapolis: University of Minnesota Press.

Cusick, Suzanne G. 1999. "Gender, Musicology and Feminism." In *Rethinking Music*, eds. Nicholas Cook and Mark Everist, 471–98. Oxford: Oxford University Press.

Doubleday, Veronica. 1999. "The Frame Drum in the Middle East: Women, Musical Instruments and Power." *Ethnomusicology* 43(1):101–34.

———. 2006 [1988]. *Three Women of Herat: A Memoir of Life, Love and Friendship in Afghanistan*. New York: Tauris Parke Paperbacks.

Dunn, Leslie C., and Nancy A. Jones. 1994. "Introduction." In *Embodied Voices: Representing Female Vocality in Western Culture*, eds. Leslie C. Dunn and Nancy A. Jones, 1–13. Cambridge, U.K.: Cambridge University Press.

Feld, Steven, and Aaron Fox. 2000. "Music." *Journal of Linguistic Anthropology* 9(1–2):159–62.

Feld, Steven, Aaron A. Fox, Thomas Porcello, and David Samuels. 2004. "Vocal Anthropology: From the Music of Language to the Language of Song." In *A Companion to Linguistic Anthropology*, ed. Alessandro Duranti, 321–45. Oxford, U.K.: Blackwell Publishing.

Greve, Martin. 2003. *Die Musik der imaginären Türkei: Musik und Musikleben im Kontext der Migration aus der Türkei in Deutschland*. Stuttgart: Verlag J. B. Metzler.

Jones, L. JaFran. 1987. "A Sociohistorical Perspective on Tunisian Women as Professional Musicians." In *Women and Music in Cross-Cultural Perspective*, ed. Ellen Koskoff, 69–83. New York: Greenwood Press.

Kandiyoti, Deniz. 1988. "Bargaining with Patriarchy." *Gender and Society* 2(3):274–90.
———. 1995. "Patterns of Patriarchy: Notes for an Analysis of Male Dominance in Turkish Society." In *Women in Modern Turkish Society: A Reader*, ed. Şirin Tekeli, 306–18. London: Zed Books Ltd.

Krims, Adam. 2000. *Rap Music and the Poetics of Identity*. Cambridge, U.K.: Cambridge University Press.

Naroditskaya, Inna. 2000. "Azerbaijanian Female Musicians: Women's Voices Defying and Defining the Culture." *Ethnomusicology* 44(2):234–56.

O'Connell, John Morgan. 2006. "The Mermaid of the *Meyhane*: The Legend of a Greek Singer in a Turkish Tavern." In *Music of the Sirens*, eds. Linda Phyllis Austern and Inna Naroditskaya, 273–93. Bloomington: Indiana University Press.

Olsen, Miriam Rovsing. 2002. "Contemporary Issues of Gender and Music." In *The Garland Encyclopedia of World Music, Volume 6: The Middle East*, eds. Virginia Danielson, Scott Marcus, and Dwight Reynolds, 299–307. London: Routledge.

Rose, Tricia. 1994. *Black Noise: Rap Music and Black Culture in Contemporary America*. Hanover: Wesleyan University Press.

Sakata, Hiromi Lorraine. 1987. "Hazara Women in Afghanistan: Innovators and Preservers of a Musical Tradition." In *Women and Music in Cross-Cultural Perspective*, ed. Ellen Koskoff, 85–95. New York: Greenwood Press.

Solomon, Thomas. 2005a. "'Living Underground Is Tough': Authenticity and Locality in the Hip-Hop Community in Istanbul, Turkey." *Popular Music* 24(1):1–20.

———. 2005b. "'Listening to Istanbul': Imagining Place in Turkish Rap Music." *Studia Musicologica Norvegica* 31:46–67.

van Nieuwkerk, Karin. 1995. *A Trade Like Any Other: Female Singers and Dancers in Egypt*. Austin: University of Texas Press.

Yurtbaşı, Metin. 1993. *A Dictionary of Turkish Proverbs*. Ankara: Turkish Daily News.

Discography

All items are Turkish CD pressings unless otherwise noted.

Ayben. *Sensin O*. Pozitif Müzik Yapım PMY 011 (2008).

Aylin Aslım ve Tayfası. *Gülyabani*. Pasaj 1717 (2005). [Includes "Gelinlik Sarhoşluğu (Bana Ne)," duet with Ayben.]

Ceza. *Rapstar*. Hammer Müzik/Hipnetic Records (2004). [Includes "Araba" and "Sinekler ve Beatler" featuring Ayben.]

Nefret. *Meclis-i âla İstanbul*. Hammer Müzik/Hipnetic Records HPNCD001 (2000). [Includes "Yüz Yüze" featuring Ayben and Elif.]

Nil. *Tek Taşımı Kendim Aldım*. Sony BMG/Epic 82876856542 (2006). [Includes "Peri," duet with Ayben.]

Websites

http://www.myspace.com/ayben34 (accessed March 2012).
http://www.youtube.com/watch?v=ThGSVEfF6jM (accessed March 2012).

4. Ixya Herrera

Gracefully Nurturing "Mexico" with Song in the U.S.A.

RUTH HELLIER

My throat releases as my mind's ear re-members a moment of embodied, sonic, sensory thrill. I can hear and feel a singing voice—my body responds kinesthetically with muscular and emotional shaping in my jaw, lungs, and breath. I recall that I am sitting in the packed auditorium of the Autry National Center, Los Angeles, California, on a warm and sultry Sunday afternoon in summer 2008. A young woman, Ixya Herrera, is onstage singing "El Pastor" ("The Shepherd"), a classic Mexican *huapango*.[1] With the distinctive vocal shift to falsetto and sustained high notes, accompanied by the syncopated strum-ming of the guitar and *jarana*, this piece is a favorite of audiences in the United States of America and Mexico. As I listen to Ixya there are reflexive resonances with my life: as a former professional singer my breathing and vocal appara-tus silently and almost imperceptibly respond; as a past resident of Mexico manifold memories reverberate. On stage, creating an air of enchantment and stillness, Ixya wears her "signature look"—a long evening gown, with a silk *rebozo* (shawl) draped over arms and shoulders, hair pulled back and adorned with a flower, complemented by large earrings and red lips (inspired by her muse, Linda Ronstadt). She is accompanied by a small ensemble of musicians comprising her father and two brothers, playing harp, guitar, and jarana.

Drawn from the metropolis of Los Angeles and its environs, the audience in the concert hall embraces all ages of people with a multiplicity of lifestyles and heritages, including many for whom a Mexican cultural identity is cen-tral. Here, notions of shifting boundaries, border-crossings, and compound identities create a rich tapestry, in great measure woven through singing voices. Here, "stories of all peoples of the American West [connect] the past with the present to inspire our shared future," as the mission statement for the venue expresses. Here, Ixya's vibrant voice and presence resonates with personal and collective lives.

. . .

I am mesmerized—the whole audience seems mesmerized—spellbound, enthralled, and thrilled. Ixya's voice balances on a tight rope—it feels as if we are all balancing on a tight rope that spans two worlds. Her voice is refined and raw, fragile and robust—there is no contradiction, no dichotomy. She sings a high falsetto note—1 . . . 2 . . . 3 . . . 4 . . . 5 seconds . . . the air is motionless, even as waves ripple through the space, seemingly drawing us with a shimmering sonic thread—delicate, fine, and very strong. She is intertwining silk strands, creating an embodied tension through highly emotive sound—6 . . . 7 . . . 8 . . . 9 . . . 10 seconds . . . she is willing us to come with her—the resonance is clean, brilliant, shining. Time transforms and stands still as each person seemingly holds their breath and breathes to the utmost depths of their beings, as that voice dissolves, converges, suspends, and liquefies borders between then and now . . . between here and there—11 . . . 12 . . . 13 . . . 14 . . . 15 . . . Ixya is playing, taking risks, and leading us to the edge, weaving a spell and charming us—she is crafting a direct connection, organic and unmasked, producing iridescent waves and flow through the warm summer air in the auditorium.

In an instant she resolves the tension with another flip of her voice, eliciting vocalized whoops of joy and percussive, applauding admiration from the audience. Ixya's voice is sweet sounding, beautiful, teasing, full of clarity, and strength. She delights in the control and power—control of her breath, the audience, the space—and the power to enchant. Her sense of playfulness and risk-taking through her vocality are striking.[2]

. . .

Seven

When I first heard her album Canciones de mi Padre [Songs of My Father] I was seven years old at the time. I still remember that day so well when my dad brought the cassette home and he put it on . . . oh . . . just hearing that voice . . .[3]

Ixya's voice trails away—she is lost in an enchanted, sonic world, transported and transfixed by a singing voice—her body responds kinesthetically with muscular and emotional shaping in her jaw, lungs, and breath. Ixya (pronounced *ee-shaw*) is recalling a weighty occasion of epiphany in her home in 1987, in Oxnard, a town in southern California, sixty miles north of Los Angeles. Her face lights up and her throat releases as her mind's ear re-members a profound moment of embodied, sensory thrill she experienced listening to a recording of a singer, which changed her life forever.

I had no idea who she was. I'd never heard of her but the first time I heard her voice it just blew me away. I was completely mesmerized. I was really young—but I knew, I knew that I wanted to be a singer. . . . Of course I didn't have a voice! I was out of tune—atrociously out of tune, but I confiscated that cassette and listened to it everyday and sang along and in my head I thought that I sounded just like her.

Ixya Herrera, a little girl of just seven years old, heard and was captivated by a woman's singing voice—a voice that stimulated her to sing and to pursue a career as a singer. As the youngest of five children, Ixya was raised in a home saturated with music. Her father, renowned harpist Fermín Herrera, and her two brothers, Xocoyotzin and Motecuhzomah, all performed professionally, while her mother, Carmen, and two sisters sang and danced at gatherings of family and friends.[4] In this environment many genres of music were in circulation, including classical, blues, rock, and various Mexican styles, from the rhythmically complex *huapango* to the driving and regular *canción ranchera* and the lyrical and romantic *bolero*. Musical visitors frequently called at their home, including eminent musicians such as Nati Cano, renowned director of the most famous mariachi ensemble in the United States of America, Mariachi Los Camperos.[5]

By the age of seven Ixya had listened to many singers, yet "that voice" created a new sensibility for her. Here is a weighty instance of "the impossible account of an individual thrill that I constantly experience in listening to singing," an idea propounded by Roland Barthes in his influential essay "The Grain of the Voice" (1977, 181). "That voice" belonged to Linda Ronstadt, U.S.A. megastar of rock and country music. Named "Queen of Rock" in the 1970s, she is one of the most successful women recording artists in U.S.A. history and is credited with opening many doors for women in rock and roll and other genres of the United States of America music business. After nearly twenty years as a star of rock and country, in 1987 Ronstadt recorded the album *Canciones de mi Padre*, a selection of Mexican songs that she had grown up listening to and singing in her family home in Tucson, Arizona, in the southwest United States of America. This release was Ronstadt's first public foray drawing on her Mexican cultural heritage.[6]

Ixya was already familiar with a varied repertoire of Mexican songs in the Spanish language when she listened to *Canciones de mi Padres*. Yet, on hearing Ronstadt sing, the instantaneous connection was not through genre or language: Ixya is very clear—what captivated her was "that voice."

She was beguiled by what might be called the "intensities and irritations" (Primavesi 2003, 66).[7]

It wasn't the style of music, but her voice that's influenced me. Had I heard her singing rock I would have been blown away—and her versatility . . . the clarity in her voice, the strength, the control—especially for the soft beautiful pianissimo notes. I think that she can sing those like no other. It's such a full voice . . . it has so much body to it, but it's such a sweet sounding voice, a very beautiful voice.

These narratives concerning the aesthetics of Ronstadt's vocality are vital in understanding Ixya's own crafting of herself as a singer. From childhood, through teens, to adulthood Ixya has developed her own unique voice, taking a profound pleasure in singing and desiring to enchant and move others in the way that she was mesmerized in 1987. Transforming and translating sonic elements and embodied sensibilities into words is a challenge. Deploying adjectives to talk about singing voices and performance can be problematical, for, as Barthes observed, the adjective is "the poorest of linguistic categories. . . . The adjective is inevitable: this music is *this*, this execution is *that*" (1977, 179). Yet Ixya's descriptions of Ronstadt's vocality provide a way to appreciate and comprehend her own values—versatility, clarity, strength, control, sweet sounding, so much body, and very beautiful. Her account resonates with Barthes's and Simon Frith's attempts to classify and capture attributes of singing voices, particularly in terms of the presence of the body in the voice, voice as body, and the volume of the singing voice—denoting capacity and space rather than decibel level (Frith 1995, 1, and 1996, 191; Barthes 1977, 182). As one who takes delight in Ixya's singing, I can bear witness to her realizations and accomplishments, and would indeed make use of these very descriptions to evoke Ixya's own voice.

• • •

Twelve

When I was twelve my dad was invited by the director of Mariachi Los Camperos, Nati Cano, to tour with Los Camperos and Linda Ronstadt, because by that time she had released her second Mexican album and they needed a harpist. Nati became friends with my dad—he would go to the house and so had heard me sing, and asked me to come along to one of the rehearsals.

Ixya recalls the momentous occasion of transformation that took place at the Tucson Mariachi Conference, Arizona, in April 1992. Staged annually since 1982, this large-scale fund-raising performance event is highly significant, engaging mariachi ensembles—the most iconic of all Mexican musical group-ings—and Ballet Folklórico troupes, which present codified and theatrical-ized regional Mexican dances (see Hellier-Tinoco 2011). The potency of the occasion draws on the inherent Mexicanness displayed on terrain where the political border between Mexico and the United States of America has shifted, and where notions of borderlands, barriers, and crossing territorial boundaries is part of the very fabric of the place. Over the years the event has attracted major stars, including performances by Linda Ronstadt, one of Tuscon's most distinguished homegrown artists. In 1992, Ronstadt was tour-ing with the material of her second album, *Mas Canciones*,[8] which included the well-known huapango, "Tata Dios" ("Father God").[9]

It was during a sound check that Nati asked me to sing "Tata Dios." So her [Linda's] personal assistant runs and calls Linda, who was somewhere in the back of the theater, and tells her "you have to come out here—there's a little girl singing 'Tata Dios,'" and she heard me, and she loved it, and she asked me if I wanted to sing with her . . . so what do you say to that? "Sure!" So . . . my first performance ever was with Linda Ronstadt when I was twelve, which was just amazing for me because she's the reason I became interested in singing in the first place. I sang with Linda sixteen times after that and she became a good friend and a mentor.

Just five years had passed between Ixya's epiphanic experience as a little girl of seven being mesmerized by Ronstadt's voice, to the moment when she dueted with her idol in person, in front of a crowd of thousands on stage in a huge auditorium in Tucson. Of course, she had sung with Linda Rondstadt many times before, but always in the privacy of her bedroom and living room, imagining herself on stage alongside her. Now it was happening for real. The song "Tata Dios," composed by Valeriano Trejo and made famous by great Mexican singers such as Pedro Infante and Miguel Aceves Mejía—"the King of Falsetto"—required great vocal clarity, power, and control, particularly for the falsetto and held notes, all of which Ixya had rehearsed meticulously. Her five years of self-motivated, dedicated practice had already produced rewards.

Marking Ixya's transition into the professional world, and following her debut at the Tucson Mariachi Conference, she performed with Ronstadt in the "Fiesta Mexicana" tour and was subsequently invited to sing as a soloist, both in the United States of America and in Mexico. She crossed territorial borders to sing and traversed genre borders, developing a varied Mexican repertoire. At age fourteen she sang for Televisa, one of the largest and most powerful television channels in Mexico. Future engagements looked extremely promising. However, national events took a dramatic turn as the disastrous devaluation of the peso in 1994 plunged the nation into economic crisis, impacting on the possibilities for Ixya to work for Televisa. During the same period, in another noteworthy performance, she was invited to sing, as one of just two soloists, at the Mariachi Conference in Las Cruces, New Mexico, United States of America. The other soloist was the long-renowned Mexican star and "la reina de la música ranchera" (Queen of Ranchera music), Lola Beltrán. For this event it was Beltrán who crossed the border from Mexico to sing in the United States of America, performing on the same stage as Ixya.

• • •

Sixteen

By the time I was sixteen I released my first CD, which I called Primavera *[Spring] . . . underneath we put* Xopancuicatl, *which also means primavera in Náhuatl.*[10] *We chose the name Primavera because everything grows in the spring of course . . . everything blossoms again.*

I grew up listening to my dad's old records . . . he has a lot. He had this old album that he bought when he was nineteen years old, with this trio called Los Hermanos Luna—two brothers and one sister . . . this old album with the bacon sizzling in the back, with the sister singing and the brothers playing guitars . . . all huapangos, with just guitar and voice.

Significantly, the recording of *Primavera* took place in a studio in Los Angeles, engaging an arranger from Mexico City, and renowned musicians from Mexico and Cuba, performing on marimba, flute, huasteco violin, guitar, and salterio.[11] Crossing territorial borders was an important element of the venture. Together, Ixya and her father chose a selection of Mexican songs, ranging from the well-known to the less-familiar. Since inception Ixya's undertaking has not concerned replicating the past and singing "old" songs because they are old per se, but rather because she herself loves to sing them and listen to them and therefore has a desire for others to share her enthusiasm and sense of thrill. Giving new life and nurturing are central to Ixya's career and passion as a singer.

When I heard Canciones de mi Padre *I didn't know they were old songs. This is really interesting to take these old songs and give them life. Some of them [that we chose] had not been recorded since the 1950s. There was this piece that I loved, "El Prófugo" ["The Fugitive"]—about this man who was in jail, he escaped prison to see his dying mother—you know how some of these Mexican songs can be very intense . . . this lovely song hasn't received any attention . . . so it's like we were giving it life again.*

I try to transport people with the songs. . . . There's definitely an attempt to take people back even if they're not that old. I get feedback saying "thank you . . . you took us to a different world." It definitely helps to keep the music alive. So many people thank me for singing these songs, especially older people—they say "You're so young, and you're keeping these songs alive, thank you."

As an enabler and facilitator, Ixya also teaches and gives lecture-demonstrations in schools and colleges in Los Angeles County, specifically engaging children and young people. By talking about different styles of Mexican music, and also voice technique, she inspires these students to take an interest in stories of the past and to appreciate the singing voice as an instrument.

• • •

Enchantment

Oh, I've got a great story. A couple of years ago I was invited to perform at the Schwob School of Music, Columbus, Georgia. This town borders Alabama, so it is very, very southern and a small town, but with a beautiful school of music. The theater had no microphones and it was all wood—a gorgeous place. There were a couple of Mexicans in the audience—everyone else was white and Southerners. For the performance it was just myself and Elias Torres, the guitarist—we said "ok, here goes nothing." But the people loved it. Afterwards, this little old lady came up to me and said, "I was watching you sing and the whole time I was looking at you going up and down the stage and I wanted to be you." Mission accomplished—I was able to take her to another place.

Throughout the almost twenty years of her career Ixya has sung for diverse audiences in concert halls large and small in the United States of America and Mexico, including the Lincoln Center for the Performing Arts in New York City (figure 4.1), the John Anson Ford Amphitheater in Hollywood, and the Teatro de la Ciudad de la Paz in Baja California. Sensitive and attentive to the needs of her audiences, she introduces and explains each song, enabling her public to feel comfortable with their experience, even as she leads them into new terrain. Most songs are in Spanish (with one or two in Náhuatl); however, for her concerts in the United States of America Ixya engages both English and Spanish for salutations and explanations. Speaking to the audience her voice takes on a tender and soft timbre as she caresses the air with an aesthetic of grace and control, which soothes and facilitates trust. Very aware of the contrast between her vocality when speaking and singing she deliberately engages this as a facet of her energy, bringing into focus questions of the "femininity" of the singing and speaking voice, and playing with what Judith Peraino might call the "expectations of an alignment between voice and gender" (2007, 63).

It definitely impresses some people. . . . Some people say "how does that voice come out from that tiny body" . . . my speaking voice is much softer than my singing voice. I think it helps. It just makes them wonder about me. I think that's pretty cool.

Drawing on a varied repertoire of Mexican genres Ixya selects her song list carefully, mixing well-known familiar classics with little-heard songs. She engages a complex network of choices concerning vocal aesthetics (sung and spoken), genre, language, gesture, movement, and clothes/costume. Her use of falsetto and long, sustained notes are two forms of reiterated vocality that enable moments of thrill and recognition. As a physical presence on stage, Ixya imbues the space with her own sense of grace and poise. Traits of her "look" are stereotypical of old and half-imagined Mexico, yet Ixya is also utterly of the twenty-first–century milieu of the great conurbation that is Los Angeles. Her performances function "as vital acts of transfer, transmitting social knowledge, memory, and sense of identity" through reiterated behavior—a notion expressed by Diana Taylor, scholar of performance studies in the Americas (2003, 1). A convergence of present-past-future-elsewhere

Figure 4.1. Ixya Herrera in concert at Lincoln Center, New York, 2002. Photographer unknown. © Ixya Herrera.

permeates Ixya's performances, with her desire to enchant and transform. There are parallels with Texan singer Lydia Mendoza's role in "transcending physical and temporal boundaries, serving as a consolidating agent across generations and across regions" (Broylez-González 2002, 194). Ixya has developed the ability to communicate intimately with her audiences—audiences with a desire for negotiation of collective visions and individual lives. She generates an awareness of closeness and rapport, guiding her listeners into places and spaces profoundly familiar, half-remembered, and unknown, and creating atmospheres of "in-ness" as she enables her public to feel at home in her presence.

$$\bullet \quad \bullet \quad \bullet$$

Father

It's a collaboration. That's something my father and I have worked at. I started taking voice lessons at twelve and he sat in on every class and took notes. To this day, he's the one who guides me. He says "I don't think you should prolong that note," or "this note should be softer," so it's been the two of us.

Fittingly for a singing career that was set in motion by a father giving his youngest daughter Ronstadt's album entitled *Songs of My Father*, the relationship between Ixya and her father is a very special one. With her father as accompanist, producer, language-coach, and agent, Ixya's career could be expressed as songs *with* my father. As Ixya entered the professional world at twelve years old, she took Ronstadt's recommendation to receive lessons. With the advantage of living near Los Angeles she took lessons with major singing teachers, always with her father in attendance. To this day her father continues to accompany her musically on harp for many of her performances. Commenting that he is a very caring dad, Ixya explains how she values her father, appreciating that he is very objective, always having her best interest in mind.

Ixya's musical career has been embedded in family life. Even when she was a child, once her parents realized that this was not simply a childish fad, they began to support her unremittingly. Mother, father, brothers, and sisters have all undertaken roles to assist and facilitate her choices, acting as agent, engineer, and advisor in shaping her vocality, stage presence, and repertoire. Her brothers play *requinto jarocho*, guitar, *jarana*, and they sing backing vocals, often performing as an accompanying ensemble for her concerts.[12]

We rehearse in the living room, so being the only girl, the only woman with all these men, sometimes it can be difficult. . . . But there is an understanding that they're there to support me. Otherwise we would be a conjunto [ensemble].

Although it is useful to be connected with a well-known musical family—her father and brothers have their own conjunto performing son jarocho music—Ixya has to make it clear that she is not part of their conjunto. Reflecting on her sense of performance status and selfhood, she stresses that her father and brothers accompany her solo singing rather than forming an ensemble with her, indicating her desire for individual agency. She is a soloist, creating her own pathway. Dealing with close family requires careful negotiating as she moves between the private and the public, and between home and profession. Rehearsals often take place in the living room, a private space imbued with home life, so the transformation of this personal setting into an environment that will transpose to public stages is a complex and ongoing process, and one that concerns notions of self-crafting.

• • •

"I am"

I just say that I'm Mexican. Yes, I'm Mexican American, but why add the American part? And yes I'm also Chicana—it's the same as being Mexican, right . . .

I grew up with the term "Chicano" because my family has always used it and because family members have been historically involved in the "movimiento." My grandfather worked with César Chávez in Oxnard. My uncle and father— also, my mother and aunt—were involved in the Brown Berets.

I learned Mexican music in the USA. My model and idol, Linda Ronstadt was also a Chicana.[13]

As Ixya and I sit having lunch at the Arts and Letters Cafe in Santa Barbara, California, in April 2008, my question concerns self-identification: "Ixya, do you think of yourself as Mexican American?" Although the issue does not involve vocality per se, self-identification and representation relating to ethnicity have multiple and complex implications for her performance choices. As a young woman singer in the United States of America, and as a Mexican/Chicana, she places herself in front of a public, and is inherently performing a political act that is complex, multiple, and dichotomous. Choice matters. Ixya's self-identification exhibits ambivalence and confidence in a context where labels and classifications of ethnicity and heritage have weighty consequences. In narrating Ixya's decisions and self-crafting as a singer and woman, knowing and comprehending something of the political and ethnic context is crucial. An awareness of the possible choices that have been rejected reveals the potency and agency of the decisions that she has taken.

Self-identifying as Mexican and Chicana invokes an ideological and political trajectory. Drawing on Chicana scholars Norma Cantú and Olga Nájera-Ramírez, the term "Chicana" refers to "women of Mexican descent who reside in the United States" (2002, 2). In the 1960s, *el Movimiento Chicano* (the Chicano movement) "mobilized thousands of Americans of Mexican descent into militant struggles for civil rights, cultural equity, and self determination" (Ybarra-Frausto 2003, xv).[14] Although embracing all Mexican Americans in the United States of America, it particularly centered on the southwestern states, including California. The whole Chicano movement formed at a significant moment in the long and complex histories of contested, acquired, and seized territories, cultural practices, languages, and peoples. In the nineteenth and twentieth centuries these narratives in the United States of America involved border changes (of territories that were formerly part of New Spain and Mexico) and border crossings (often with the full complicity of the U.S.A. government). Political and cultural discourse and tropes of the Chicano movement and Chicanismo concern assimilation, hegemony, resistance, and rights, often invoking a binary of Anglo and Latino.

Some women have identified concerns that the Chicano agenda was men-led and men-centered, for the movement "derived its impetus from antiracist politics and from a recuperation of cultural traditions based on an ethos of group solidarity and cultural distinctiveness . . . which often reproduced gender hierarchies and heterosexual identities" (Espinoza 2003, 99). Consequently, a Chicana feminist movement became, and continues to be, active in political and academic environments, with central elements of Chicana feminism involving not only resisting agendas of assimilation but also claiming and crafting identities that are multiple, complex, contradictory, and ambivalent. "The Chicana feminist concept of the borderlands, a formative space where cultures and identities converge" became a focal metaphor for shaping lives in the United States of America (Cantú and Nájera-Ramírez 2002, back cover).

Ixya lives with the legacy of the Chicano movement: in her personal family life; in her vocality and stage presence; and in the local, regional, and national politics of Oxnard, California, and the United States of America. Oxnard, the city in which Ixya was born and raised, has a large Mexican American population. Carmen, Ixya's mother, was born in Oxnard, spent her early childhood in Mexico, but returned to Oxnard at age twelve; Fermín, Ixya's father, was born in Mexico, raised in Oxnard, studied Náhuatl in Mexico City, and returned to California to take up a post as professor of Náhuatl. Both her parents were advocates for civil rights, as part of the Brown Berets, an activist movement within the larger Chicano movement, campaigning for educational equality and struggling against police brutality. Although Ixya has only distant family living in Mexico, her Mexican identity is central.

Being and/or identifying as Mexican, Chicana/o, or Mexican American in the United States of America often calls for a heightened awareness of cultural heritage, and, as is normal in myriad global contexts, music and performance therefore play important roles both in shaping the identities of the participants and as representational practices. In Ixya's generation young singers and musicians often opt to disrupt, transgress, and push at the boundaries through choice of genre and vocality—using punk, rap, and other elements of hip-hop culture and drawing on the Mexican genres of *conjunto* and *technobanda* as forms of upbeat and driving sounds. Even in the first wave of the Chicano movement, and following a politics of hybridity, bands combined rock 'n' roll and the Mexican Trío tradition as a form of resistance. Musical aesthetics often encompass elements that are brash, aggressive, irreverent, and purportedly sexy.[15] Explicit gendered transgression and border crossings have been marked by other women singers and musicians who have chosen to perform in male-dominated genres in the United States of America.[16] Young Chicana/o singers and musicians engage with explicit models of dress, in line with other youth fashion, such as tattoos, piercings, short skirts, and tight pants to display forms of resistance.

borderlandsborderlandsborderlands

What is significant about Ixya as a young Mexican woman singer in the United States of America is that she does not have any stories and acts of *overt* rebellion and resistance—that Ixya takes a different path is noteworthy because they are *her* choices and *her* acts of self-crafting. Her acknowledgement of her heritage and Mexican cultural identity is present as she enacts and envoices agency and subtle activism on concert stages and in recordings. Ixya's vocal and stage aesthetics involve enchantment, grace, nurture, and all the qualities that she admired in Linda Ronstadt's performance: power, versatility, strength, control, and beauty. By her own admission, her only form of obvious proselytizing is in relation to one particular song, "La Borrachita" ("The Drunken Woman"), a song of social protest.

Yet Ixya clearly inhabits borderlands: it is easy to interpret many elements of her performance as a singer through notions of convergence, negotiation, contradiction, and multiplicity in genre, vocality, language, and dress. Some attributes are clear markers of her Chicana heritage. With her chosen repertoire of Mexican songs of multiple genres she overtly inhabits the past and Mexico. Singing in Spanish in the United States of America is a weighty mark of her Mexicanness. She also sings in Náhuatl, an important signifying element of the Chicana/o movement, and profoundly symbolic of indigenous prehispanic Mexico, with a real and mythical past.[17]

Notions of the stereotypical are wholly appropriate, for as Ixya crafts her own sense of self on stage she is fully awake to the possibilities. Her resistance to some stereotypes and her compliance with others demonstrate her agency. Although her singing and speaking voice are of primary importance, her awareness of movement and dress on stage are central to her performance as a singer.

> *You're performing . . . nobody wants to see the girl next door. It's a transformation. . . . I don't try to be sexy but I do want to come across as classy and yet graceful—hidden in there is the whole sensual side, I want to entice my audience and take them to a different place. Being a woman, I take advantage of the fact that we have the ability to be more graceful than a male . . . through my performances, through my vocal performances and how I move about on stage, I try to be enchanting. Of course all of this is rehearsed. I practice how to gracefully move my hand. You have your performers like Beyoncé and Madonna who can get away with being very sexual and sexy and all that. . . . I don't sing that type of music, so my sexiness has to be cleverly hidden. But it's not even about being sexual, it's more about being graceful.*

Ixya is clear about her views of what sexy entails, and therefore what she aspires to and what she rejects. In describing her rejection of an overt sexuality performed through costume and movement she gives an example of a highly successful young singer from Los Angeles who has made a name for herself in the Mexican male-dominated genres of *banda*, *corrido*, and *norteña* music, and who engages poses and costumes that overtly display her cleavage. This embodiment seems to fit with global Latina[18] stereotypes and also with one Chicana feminist view of Latina beauty and bodies—both of which Ixya resists. Global stereotypes often connect explicit sexuality with certain body parts (hips, breasts, thighs) and with baring skin. Somewhat paradoxically, these essentializations have coherence with one particular Chicana feminist position inscribed in academic writing. This notion configures a "pan-Latina body," which involves "the beauty of enhancing and accentuating one's particular ethnic and physical signifiers—butts, breasts, thighs—. . . as identificatory markers" (Figueroa 2003, 269),[19] and draws up a bold dualism, in terms of assimilationist and negotiated versions of beauty, relying on essentialization through a binary of "white" and "Latina." Ixya's version of beauty and her "signature look" do not involve these essentialist Latina stereotypes (figure 4.2).

Ixya's signature look of long gown (not a traditional Mexican gown) and her rebozo create quite another signification. For Ixya the gown is a way of

Figure 4.2. Ixya
Herrera, 2009.
© Ixya Herrera.

masking sexuality, even as it is viscerally sensual, accentuating the very essence of her gracefulness and enchantment. In another performance context
such gowns have been read as inherently "sexy" (Citron 2004, 49),[20] yet Ixya
chooses her gowns as a deliberate resistance to such implications. Another
option for Ixya might be the *charro* outfit—the stereotypical costume of men's
Mexicanness, associated in the music world with mariachi ensembles—consisting of tight high-waisted jackets and pants. Women ranchera singers and
mariachi musicians replace the pants with a long straight skirt (Pérez 2002),
and occasionally overtly appropriate men's clothing, as exemplified by Los
Angeles's ranchera singer Rita Vidaurri who wears pants (Vargas 2010).[21]
However, as Ixya sings a wide range of genres, she is not drawn in this direction. She prefers to "play around" with her rebozo. She says that it has become
her thing that she has worked with throughout the years, practicing "how
to work the rebozo on stage. It's a beautiful shawl made of beautiful material."[22] The rebozo is an icon of traditional Mexican womanhood—a form
of womanhood that is regarded as potentially problematic by some Chicana
feminists, for, as Pérez has noted, "in contrast to the charro suit, the codes of

traditional dress for Chicanas in many ways promote gender roles of sexual partner, childbearer, and nurturer. Anzaldúa 1987 points out that *"la gorra, el rebozo, y la mantilla* (hat, shawl, and veil) convey the message that women must be protected" (2002, 148).[23]

Yet, when Ixya sings wearing her gown and rebozo, her performances can be read as playful, powerful, full of nuances, subtleties, and contradictions, as her garments converge and cohere in sartorial form with her vocal aesthetics, such as the flip into falsetto and long, sustained notes, creating resonances other than protection and sexuality.

As for nurturer, Ixya assertively strives to be a nurturer. She nurtures her audiences and her listeners, caring for them and enabling them. Perhaps some might critique Ixya's model, wishing her less stereotypical as nurturer, heterosexual, and graceful, and yet her sense of creativity and playfulness are deeply significant.[24] In her discussions concerning the "'acting out' of the dilemmas of femininity," the literary and critical theorist Mary Russo proposes the idea of the "flaunting of the feminine," whereby "to put on femininity with a vengeance suggests the power of taking it off" (1997, 331), which, as musicologist Sheila Whiteley has noted, offers "the possibility of using stereotypical aspects of femininity as a political tool" (2000, 216). Narrating her choices in terms of womanness and femininity, Ixya's awareness of her self-crafting in this area is palpable, suggesting an aesthetic of the hyperfeminine, and also association with the multiplicity of postfeminism. As Ixya crosses the age-border into her thirties and reflects upon her almost twenty years as a professional singer, she says that she's always been very feminine and girly but is open to all options. Moving into her future she will continue to make bold choices concerning expressions of her own femininity through voice and body.

• • •

Future Unknown

On hearing Ixya's voice at a recent rehearsal in Los Angeles, renowned Chicana performance artist and cellist Maria Elena Gaitán exclaimed: "Wow! You sing with your ovaries!" This expression of vocality is significantly not adjectival but embodied, and is a testament to Ixya's vocal power, control, and inherent womanness. Gaitán was reacting to hearing the sustained notes and strength of voice as Ixya was rehearsing a performance of "La Llorona" ("The Crying Woman"), a quintessential Mexican song. Ixya had been invited to sing with Gaitán and two other distinguished Chicano musicians, Willie Herrón and Xiuy Velo, all of whom have used musical expression, experimentation, and improvisation as a form of political interaction over the last thirty years.[25] For this experimental performance of "La Llorona," Ixya vocalized around and within the recognizable musical structures of the well-known song, and sartorially chose to dress without her gown or rebozo.

Ixya's future is open to possibilities and challenges. With a CD release and concerts on the horizon, an enthusiastic fan base networking through the website *ixyafans*, and a close and supportive family, she has many opportunities. Recently in her private life, Ixya has undergone some extremely painful and traumatic times. Concurrently, the political context in the United States of America is uncertain with divisive issues around border-building with Mexico; documented and undocumented migration; and discriminatory environments. Despite and because of the uncertainty, Ixya chooses to gracefully nurture and proclaim her Mexicanness through song in the United States of America with old and half-forgotten songs, enchantingly enabling her audiences to experience an individual and collective thrill through her singing.

Xochicuicatl Flower-Song/Poetry
Quin oc tlamati noyollo My heart is content
Pampa niquitta in xochitl Because I see a flower
Pampa niccaqui in cuicatl Because I hear a song
Quin oc tlamati noyollo, quemah My heart is content—yes[26]

Acknowledgments

I thank Ixya for her generosity of spirit in taking time to talk with me, and I look forward to much fruitful collaboration with her in California, wishing Ixya every success with all her singing projects over the coming years. I also thank Juan Zaragoza for recommending an initial contact with Ixya.

Notes

1. *Huapango* refers to a genre of music from the northeastern region of Mexico (known as La Huasteca) and includes a large repertoire of fixed, composed songs and also *son huasteco*, which tends to be improvised and less predictable.

2. "*I love the falsettis—for Mexicans if you're going to sing 'El Pastor' you better have really good breath control, because they're expecting that long falsetti—that's your time to show off, and so when I recorded it I did about ten seconds on each falsetti, but when you're doing it live you've got to prove to your audience that you're worthy of singing it. They're really expecting you to prolong those falsettos, so that's what I love about it—I love the challenge. It doesn't require a big voice, there are no big chest notes in the song, but it requires a lot of control in the voice, and your breath control to allow those falsettos to come out beautifully, purely, the vibrato just has to be very consistent, it cannot waver, . . . you just gotta let it flow as long as you can.*"

Singing in falsetto, a process that Ixya describes as "a simple flip of the voice," is usually associated with men's voices, disseminated through comments such as those claiming that "a falsetto is, after all, a man's voice (there's no such thing as a female falsetto)" (Frith 1995, 4). Women can and do produce falsetto, a shift that alters the timbre of the voice. Falsetto raises issues of "natural" and "unnatural" or false vocal characteristics, particularly because falsetto by men's voices is perceived to be more overt due to the pitch expectations associated with men's and women's physiology, which affects the sheer literal range that is possible. When women use falsetto there is often an assumption that this is an appropriation of a man's domain and technique, with an implication of emulating masculinities. Musicologist Judith Peraino has posed the question of whether a singing voice must bear the indelible mark of a binary gender system, or whether the singing voice could offer an escape from that structure (2007, 63). Ixya's use of falsetto plays with the high pitches expected of a woman's voice, but it also draws attention to possibilities in terms of quality, tone, and timbre as she shifts between notes sung in falsetto and those sung in the usual modal voice.

3. All verbatim material is drawn from interviews and other personal communication with Ixya. We communicated in English, except for a few clarifications concerning Spanish terms.

4. El Conjunto Hueyapan de la Familia Herrera (The Hueyapan Ensemble of the Herrera Family) was founded by Fermín Herrera in 1973.

5. See Hellier 2003 and 2006.

6. Ronstadt titled her album after a booklet by her aunt Luisa Espinel, herself a singer, published in 1946 by the University of Arizona. Her album, released in 1987, is the biggest selling non-English language album in U.S.A. record history. Ronstadt's paternal grandfather was German, and her maternal grandfather was Mexican. Ronstadt has many fans who applaud her for drawing on her familial ties and roots. However, she has also been critiqued because she is not a Spanish-speaker. What is undeniable is that through her Mexican albums she has had a tremendous and lasting impact in terms of disseminating a Mexican repertoire, sung in Spanish, to listeners in the United States of America and in many global contexts, including Europe and Australasia. In personal terms, I first heard the album *Canciones de mi Padre* in 1993 in England, having been given a cassette copy. I still have the cassette in my treasured collection.

7. "I suggest a kind of performance analysis that tries to focus not so much on elaboration of systematic structures or concepts (as in semiotic or linguistic approaches) but rather on attention to intensities and irritations" (Primavesi 2003, 66).

8. The album's title as published is cosmetically incorrect. According to Spanish orthographical rules, the word *más* ("more") must have an accent over the vowel to disambiguate it from *mas* ("but").

9. Ronstadt's album *Mas Canciones* was released in 1991, and included "Tata Dios," with vocals by Ronstadt and her two brothers (neither professional musicians) attempting to capture the setting and atmosphere as they sang in their living room when growing up.

10. At the time of the sixteenth-century Spanish incursion in Mexico, Náhuatl was the predominant language in central Mexico. Today, it is spoken by over one and a half million people. As part of the ongoing Chicana/o movement in the United States of America it linguistically represents a form of resistance to oppression and marginalization.

11. Arranger: Daniel Garcia Blanco.

12. *Requinto jarocho* and *jarana* are plucked and strummed string instruments.

13. *"I grew up with Mexican music but have never felt that it was the music of Mexico. It is the music of Mexican background people. Sort of like how in the U.S. we speak English but we do not say that we speak the language of England. Likewise, we Mexicans/Chicanas speak Spanish but we do not say that we speak the language of Spain. I sing Mexican music, not the music of Mexico. I learned my music here in California. Yes, there is an interaction with fellow musicians from Mexico but the relationship has always been one of peers."*

14. The "a" and "o" endings of Chicana/o indicate gender distinctions.

15. There are links here with what is often called third-wave feminism of the United States of America and the United Kingdom of the late twentieth and early twenty-first centuries, in which punk music was used for its overtly rebellious, irreverent, brash, and bold characteristics.

16. For example, Selena who performed Tex-Mex music (see Figueroa 2003) and musicians playing in and with a mariachi ensemble (see Jáquez 2002; Pérez 2002; Vargas 2010).

17. Richard T. Rodríguez posits that perhaps Chicano (male) rappers and their audiences "feel the need to hold on to the Aztec past that would at once help them retain a sense of historical being while countering the powerless positions they and their listeners are frequently placed in" (2003, 118).

18. A highly debated, controversial, and generic term, "Latina/o" is used in the United States of America as an ethnic category, variously encompassing all those with heritage in the Spanish-speaking Americas and also the Caribbean and Brazil.

19. In discussing Selena, (the Tex-Mex singer who died at age twenty-three in 1995), Figueroa suggests that Selena "embodies a boldness that distances her from an assimilationist drive toward monolithic beauty (thin white body) and brings her closer to a pan-Latina body" involving "the beauty of enhancing and accentuating one's particular ethnic and physical signifiers—butts, breasts, thighs—. . . as identificatory markers" (2003, 269).

20. Citron discusses the clothes worn by young women classical musicians in concert performances, using her own interpretations related to gowns. She reads a so-called low-cut or strapless gown as inherently "sexy" and equates this dress code with "popstars and movie actresses," seemingly considering this to be appropriate for the pop star and movie actress world, but not appropriate for a classical music world, and invoking the terms "sex" and "sexuality" with these gowns.

21. "Chicana singer Rita Vidaurri is one of very few women to ever perform publicly in Mexico wearing charro pants. . . . Traditionally, what has literally and figuratively stitched masculinity and mexicanidad [Mexicanness] together has been the charro costume, in particular the pants and hat" (Vargas 2010).

22. In a recent photographic exhibition, "Wearing Our Stories, Costume and Cultural Identity in the Latino Community," Ixya chose to be depicted wearing her signature rebozo (Museum of Ventura County, 2009).

23. Gloria Anzaldúa was a renowned Chicana cultural theorist, poet, feminist, and author of *Borderlands/La Frontera* (1987).

24. Some might critique my own authorial position, because I am not a "native scholar" (Cantú and Nájera-Ramírez 2002, 1), but a British woman ("Anglo" in U.S.A. terms) regarded as "white" in a generic white-Latina binary. Yet my connections with Ixya, with

borderlands, and with Mexico are many, including my former career as a professional singer; the many years living in Mexico and my previous marriage to a Mexican man; my transcontinental life moving between Mexico, the United States of America, and the United Kingdom; and my own pleasure listening to *Canciones de mi Padre* in 1993 in the United Kingdom on a home-copied cassette handed to me by the Catholic priest of the high school where I was Head of Music. I am a borderlands dweller and border-crosser with multiple herstories. (See Hellier-Tinoco 2010 and forthcoming.)

25. "An Evening of Chicano Performance: The Adventures of Connie Chancla," April 7, 2011, with Los Vex Pistols (aka, Los Illegals). Chicana/o Studies Performance and Theatrics Lecture Series, California State University. They utilize musical and oratorical skills to examine cross-cultural, race, gender, and class issues affecting Chicanas/os in the United States of America.

26. This is Ixya's choice as the song she feels closest to. It is a traditional Nahua song, translated by Fermín Herrera. With regard to meaning: "in xochitl" (the flower) and "in cuicatl" (the song) together make a diphrasal metaphor meaning "poetry."

References

Anzaldúa, Gloria.1987. *Borderlands/La Frontera: The New Mestiza*. San Francisco: Aunt Lute.

Barthes, Roland. 1977. *Image, Music, Text*. London: Fontana Press.

Broyles-González, Yolanda. 2002. "Ranchera Music(s) and the Legendary Lydia Mendoza." In *Chicana Traditions: Continuity and Change*, eds. Norma E. Cantú and Olga Nájera-Ramírez, 183–206. Urbana: University of Illinois Press.

Cantú, Norma E., and Olga Nájera-Ramírez. 2002. "Introduction." In *Chicana Traditions: Continuity and Change*, eds. Norma E. Cantú and Olga Nájera-Ramírez, 1–11. Urbana: University of Illinois Press.

Citron, Marcia J. 2004. "Feminist Waves and Classical Music: Pedagogy, Performance, Research." *Women and Music* 8:47–60.

Espinoza, Dionne. 2003. "'Tanto Tiempo Disfrutamos . . . ' Revisiting the Gender and Sexual Politics of Chicana/o Youth Culture in East Los Angeles in the 1960s." In *Velvet Barrios: Popular Culture and Chicana/o Sexualities*, ed. Alicia Gaspar de Alba, 89–106. Basingstoke: Palgrave Macmillan.

Figueroa, María. 2003. "Resisting 'Beauty' and Real Women Have Curves." In *Velvet Barrios: Popular Culture and Chicana/o Sexualities*, ed. Alicia Gaspar de Alba, 265–82. Basingstoke: Palgrave Macmillan.

Frith, Simon. 1995. "The Body Electric." *Critical Quarterly* 37(2):1–10.

———. 1996. *Performing Rites: On the Value of Popular Music*. Oxford: Oxford University Press.

Hellier, Ruth. 2003. "Reviews: Special Feature: New Books and Compact Discs in Mexican Music." *British Journal of Ethnomusicology* 12(2):107–15.

———. 2006. "Review of ¡Llegaron Los Camperos!—Concert Favorites of Nati Cano's Mariachi Los Camperos and Aztec Dances—Xavier Quijas Yxayotl." *World of Music* 48(1):159–61.

Hellier-Tinoco, Ruth. 2010. "Dead Bodies/Live Bodies: Death, Memory and Resurrection in Contemporary Mexican Performance." In *Performance, Embodiment and Cultural*

Memory, eds. Colin Counsell and Roberta Mock, 114–39. Newcastle: Cambridge Scholars Publishing.

———. 2011. *Embodying Mexico: Tourism, Nationalism and Performance*. New York: Oxford University Press.

———. Forthcoming. *Creativity/Memory/History: Contemporary Theatre and Performance in Mexico*. Bristol: Intellect Press.

Jáquez, Cándida F. 2002. "Meeting La Cantante through Verse, Song, and Performance." In *Chicana Traditions: Continuity and Change*, eds. Norma E. Cantú and Olga Nájera-Ramírez, 167–82. Urbana: University of Illinois Press.

Peraino, Judith. 2007. "Listening to Gender: A Response to Judith Halberstam." *Women and Music* 11:59–63.

Pérez, Leonor Xóchitl. 2002. "Transgressing the Taboo: A Chicana's Voice in the Mariachi World." In *Chicana Traditions: Continuity and Change*, eds. Norma E. Cantú and Olga Nájera-Ramírez, 143–63. Urbana: University of Illinois Press.

Primavesi, Patrick. 2003. "A Theatre of Multiple Voices." *Performance Research* 8(1):61–73.

Rodríguez, Richard T. 2003. "The Verse of the Godfather: Signifying Family and Nationalism in Chicano Rap and Hip-Hop Culture." In *Velvet Barrios: Popular Culture and Chicana/o Sexualities*, ed. Alicia Gaspar de Alba, 107–22. Basingstoke: Palgrave Macmillan.

Russo, Mary. 1997. "Female Grotesques: Carnival and Theory." In *Writing on the Body: Female Embodiment and Feminist Theory*, eds. Katie Conboy, Nadia Medina, and Sarah Stanbury, 318–36. New York: Columbia University Press.

Taylor, Diana. 2003. *The Archive and the Repertoire: Performing Cultural Memory in the Americas*. Durham: Duke University Press.

Vargas, Deborah. 2010. "Rita's Pants: The *Charro Traje* and Trans-Sensuality." *Women and Performance* 20(1):3–14.

Whiteley, Sheila. 2000. *Women and Popular Music: Sexuality, Identity, and Subjectivity*. London: Routledge.

Ybarra-Frausto, Tomás. 2003. "Notes from Losaida: A Forward." In *Velvet Barrios: Popular Culture and Chicana/o Sexualities*, ed. Alicia Gaspar de Alba, xv–xviii. Basingstoke: Palgrave Macmillan.

Discography

Ixya Herrera. *Cantares Mexicanas*. 2004. Xochicuicatl Productions.
Ixya Herrera. *Primavera*. 1996. Xochicuicatl Productions.
Linda Ronstadt. *Canciones de mi Padre*. 1987. Elektra/WEA.
Linda Ronstadt. *Mas Canciones*. 1991. Elektra.

Interviews with Ixya Herrera

May 19, 2008 (Santa Barbara); May 22, 2009 (Oxnard); April 22, 2011 (Oxnard).

5. Kyriakou Pelagia

The Housewife/Grandmother-Star of Cyprus

NICOLETTA DEMETRIOU

"As punctual as an Englishwoman," she shouted, before I even got out of the car. *"Right on time."* I said hello, and walked with her across the small yard that led to the kitchen door. It was late morning and the sun was already burning. The colorful flowers in her garden had just been watered to guard them against the looming heat of noon. She was wearing an old work dress and black open-toe slippers. I noticed that her feet and toenails were dirty with the fertile red soil of the village. *"I was in the field,"* she said, as if she had read my thoughts. *"I went with my son's mother-in-law. We all go together and help."* We entered the house through the kitchen door. Her husband was sitting at the kitchen table, smoking serenely. I greeted him, and she immediately called me to follow her into the living room. She pulled a couple of chairs and put them the way she had the previous day, one right opposite the other. There was a sense of urgency. Noon was just round the corner, and the food cooking in the kitchen had to finish in time for lunch. I felt that my interview was something of an inconvenience, meddling in my interviewee's daily routine. Anxious not to lose any of our precious time, I awkwardly took my notebook out of my handbag, and began asking the questions I had so carefully planned. It was in vain. I was clearly not the one deciding how the interview would be conducted. This dynamic grandmother in front of me, who walked out of the room every few minutes to check on her food, interrupting our chat abruptly, was unlike anyone else I had ever interviewed.

"A Housewife, Not a Singer"

The early 1990s witnessed an unmatched transformation in Cyprus's radio-scape.[1] In 1990, when permission was given for the establishment of private radio stations, hundreds of new voices suddenly resounded through the boxes that for nearly four decades had only broadcast the CyBC.[2] The monopoly and sternness of the state-funded CyBC gave way to a number of light-hearted radio stations and phone-in programs. This dramatic change from a monotonous and predictable radio schedule to an unprecedented and previously unimaginable variety had an immense impact on Cypriot audiences and, following on from that, on Cypriot popular culture. Radio shows were no longer solely formulated by strict timetables and a handful of presenters and producers, but by audiences themselves. Virtually anyone, irrespective of social or educational background, could phone in to dedicate a song to a loved one, comment on current affairs, recite a poem, or sing a song.

Just as so many others at the time, Kyriakou Pelagia,[3] a housewife from Paralimni then in her midfifties, saw this as an opportunity to express herself and showcase her village's poetic tradition on air. Paralimni is the center of a group of villages in eastern Cyprus collectively known as *Kokkinohoria* (literally Red [soil] villages). In addition to sharing the red soil that gives the region its name, the area of Kokkinohoria prides itself on having the largest and most talented community of poet-singers of improvised fifteen-syllable rhyming couplets, *tsiattista*.[4] An integral part of everyday life in Paralimni in the past (much less so now), being able to improvise couplets on the spot was seen as proof of one's talent and skill. Pelagia's father, Damianos Kouzalis, was one such poet-singer, adept at improvising rhyming couplets. Ever since Pelagia was a child, Damianos had challenged her with his witty tsiattista, to which she had to provide a swift, rhyming, and equally clever response.

Growing up in a village where opportunities for women to sing in public were very limited, and where being a woman singer was "misunderstood," Pelagia's responses to her father and singing at family events were all she had.[5] For, even though women were not discouraged from improvising and singing at home or in family events, the public expression of *tsiattisma* (i.e., the art of making *tsiattista*) in festivals and fairs (e.g., saints' name days) was exclusively reserved for men. And that was a cause of great sorrow for Damianos. He had learned his art from his father, who had learned it from his own father. But, unlike them, Damianos could not pass his knowledge on to any of his descendants, because he and his wife, Maria Koutsolouka, had only daughters—five of them. Kyriakou, his second daughter, shared his wit for improvising and passion for singing. But she was a girl, and—in his mind—no self-respecting girl or woman in the 1940s and 1950s would sing in public. And so Damianos spent his days thinking that his family's art and talent would die with him, once exclaiming with frustration: "Too bad, Kyriakou, that you were born a woman, or you could beat ten men in *tsiattisma*." To this, his daughter, confident of her skills, replied: "*I inherited [my talent in] poetry, my property, from you; and even though you're my father I beat you [at it] seven times!"* (Papapetrou 2006; Pelagia 2006).[6]

That same confidence was still present in Kyriakou Pelagia some four decades later. In the early 1990s, with the new radio stations inviting audiences to take part by reciting or singing, it was time for her to reach out further. She began to phone in to entertainment shows and to talk to presenters and radio listeners almost always in rhyming verse. Pelagia was, of course, not the only middle-aged lady who phoned in to recite her verses or sing on air (cf. Syrimis 1998, 217–18), but it did not take long for her to stand out from the rest. Her nasal voice and the way she delivered her witty couplets became her trademark. Radio audiences soon got to recognize the voice of Pelagia from Paralimni, whose straightforwardness and dynamism were evident long before her newfound fans got to know her face (figure 5.1).

Seeing Pelagia's popularity on her impromptu radio appearances, Michalis Hadjimichael and Ilias Kouloumis, the founders of the musical ensemble Mesogeios (Mediterranean), approached her and asked her to record a song with them for the group's first CD. Mesogeios, a group playing traditional music[7] from Cyprus and the Greek islands, was only just beginning

Figure 5.1. "I have three loves: poetry, music, and flowers." Kyriakou Pelagia in her garden in Paralimni, October 2008. Photograph by Nicoletta Demetriou.

to take shape. Hadjimichael and Kouloumis, both part-time amateur musicians with an audience limited to their village and the surrounding area, needed to get someone on board who could drive their popularity outside the confines of the village. Pelagia, a connoisseur of the local song repertory with a skilled voice and—due to her radio performances—a constantly rising number of fans, was the perfect candidate. When Hadjimichael and Kouloumis first asked Pelagia to join them she dismissed them, finding their proposal "*ridiculous*":

Initially I thought it was really ridiculous. To take a housewife from her kitchen, her fields, her orchard [pervolia], to take her and teach her how to make recordings [of her songs], I thought it was a ridiculous thing. I used to tell them "goodbye [piainnete sto kalo], I don't want such things. I'm a housewife, not a singer" (Papapetrou 2006).

Unbeknown to her at the time, the very fact that she was a housewife was what would catapult her popularity in the years that followed this incident. Hadjimichael and Kouloumis's insistence to get Pelagia to record her songs finally paid off. She recorded not one, but seven out of the twelve tracks of Mesogeios's first CD, which was clearly marketed with her as the principal singer. The CD, released in 1995, was called *Ta Paralimnitika* (*[Songs] from Paralimni*). According to Hadjimichael (2005), despite its title, the songs featured on the CD are not found exclusively in Paralimni, but throughout Kokkinohoria. But the title was chosen as a tribute to Pelagia (the CD's main star) and her origins, and also to honor the Municipality of Paralimni that sponsored the recording.[8]

The popularity of the CD was almost instant. Pelagia sang love songs, wedding songs, and a religious song, and her fellow musicians completed the recording with more love songs and some new compositions mainly on patriotic themes. The traditional music ensemble of violin, *laouto* (a long-necked plucked lute tuned in double courses arranged in fourths), and percussion (in this case *darbukka*) was complemented by the clarinet, accordion, *def*, guitar, and bass.[9] Pelagia was the only traditional singer on the CD, in the sense that she had no formal training in music and had learned the repertory aurally in the village. She also had never sung with a musical ensemble consisting of so many instruments before, and she found having to synchronize her singing with the strict rhythm imposed by the percussion instruments, as well as the time constraints imposed by the recording studio, very difficult to get used to (Hadjimichael 2005). Of all the songs on the CD, "Eipa sou" ("I told you"), a lively love song, had huge success; it was played on the radio repeatedly, captivating audiences all around Cyprus and turning Kyriakou Pelagia into a household name. It was not long before Pelagia came to be characterized as "the voice of the land of Cyprus"[10] and to be given the title "*mastorissa*" (mistress/expert) by her colleagues. Her success was followed by live concerts with Mesogeios and invitations to appear on TV and radio shows.

But why did Pelagia agree to sing in the first place? After all, she had found Hadjimichael and Kouloumis's proposal "ridiculous." "*I have three loves,*" she says, "*poetry, music, and flowers.*" If love for singing gave her the first push, the popularity of *Ta Paralimnitika* and the projection and recognition that it brought with it was what kept her going. That was why in 1997, when Mesogeios tried to repeat their success by releasing the sequel of *Ta Paralimnitika*, *Ta Paralimnitika 2*,[11] Pelagia had no objections to recording more songs. She sang twelve out of the CD's fifteen tracks, a mixture of religious, narrative, and love songs. Supported by the audience's acceptance (as well as improved recording technology), the group felt freer to experiment with richer, more inventive instrumentations. Gradually, Pelagia's repertory opened up to include songs that were previously unknown to her, and which she learned by listening to Hadjimichael's private recordings. By 2003, when Mesogeios released their third, most recent CD, *Oloaspron Pezouni* (*White Dove*), their experimentations produced a wholly different sound compared to that of the 1995 CD.

In addition to the violin-laouto-percussion ensemble, the 2003 CD features the *saz*, *ud*, *cura*, and, in a number of tracks, a prominent *kanun* accompaniment. The combination of these instruments with the inventive *taksim* in several of the songs gives the recording a clear Middle Eastern/Eastern Mediterranean color. *Oloaspron Pezouni* was an attempt to move further away from the conventional instrumentation (violin, laouto, percussion) and performance style of Cypriot music, aiming to appeal not only to traditional music devotees, but also to world music fans. Mesogeios's reinvented sound is sharply contrasted by Pelagia's very traditional-sounding voice. This union of old (Pelagia's voice) and new (Mesogeios's instrumentations)—the sound of a traditional voice of an older lady singing to the accompaniment of a very contemporary and lively ensemble—has proven very successful. With the modern instruments and, significantly, the underlying beat, Pelagia's songs have become pieces that can be played at parties and nightclubs. And this latter fact undeniably propelled her into an entirely new sphere, making her the first Cypriot music singer whose songs are played in nightclubs.

The trend was introduced with "Eipa sou," which was—without Mesogeios's permission—remixed by an as yet unidentified person, given a very prominent beat, and used for dancing at parties. Seeing that the song had become even more popular as a result, Mesogeios took no legal action against the perpetrators (Pelagia 2006; Hadjimichael, pers. comm. 2008). In fact, one could argue that their subsequent recording endeavors to an extent tried to follow the trend, albeit not openly, by enriching their instrumentation and by adding a more prominent beat. By 2008, when I conducted my fieldwork for this chapter, Kyriakou Pelagia's fame as the woman protagonist of the Cypriot music scene, and as a star of Cypriot popular culture, was firmly consolidated.[12]

Her principal collaborator, Michalis Hadjimichael, sees a number of different reasons behind Pelagia's popularity. First and foremost, it was the emergence of private radio stations that were ready to support and promote an "audience-catcher" such as Kyriakou Pelagia. The singer herself admits (in couplet form) that radio stations were a vehicle for her success:

> I hold Cyprus's tradition on my shoulder[s],
> but radio stations too open the way for me.

Novelty was also an important factor, says Hadjimichael: she was the first female traditional singer in Cyprus to release commercial recordings. Her songs were original too, in the sense that very few, if any, people outside of Paralimni and the surrounding villages knew them. But Hadjimichael and his group were, according to him, far from inactive when it came to promoting their CD to the newly created radio market. Pelagia's persona also played a dramatic role in her popularity, Hadjimichael claims: she reminds many people of their grandmother (or a model of a generic village grandmother) and her tsiattista—that quintessentially Cypriot form of poetry in popular imagination—remind them of "old-times Cyprus" with its tradition-bearing "grandfathers" (Hadjimichael, pers. comm. 2008).

Echoing Hadjimichael's words, during our meetings Pelagia insisted on reminding me that she was first and foremost a housewife and a grandmother—both of them exclusively female roles—and treated the fact that she was a singer (and a very successful one for that matter) as something of secondary significance. She told me how she had been repeatedly asked to sing at private functions and pose for magazine covers. Her reply was always the same and equally firm: "*I'm a housewife, not a singer.*" And as if to strengthen her point, and to highlight that she is not only a housewife but also a proud mother and grandmother, at the end of almost every meeting she would show me pictures of her three children with their families, and glow while talking to me about her grandchildren.

While dismissing the stardom in which Cypriot media place her as "*pellares*" ("[an act of] craziness"), at the same time she takes pride in talking about her fans' love and admiration: "*A woman from Germany came to Paralimni to see me and brought me a gift. . . . You won't believe how many people called me on my name day to wish me well. . . . Someone called me 'the nightingale of Paralimni.'. . . People show me their appreciation, their love."* But after basking in her success for a little while, she feels that she needs to redress the balance.

I'm the same as I have [always] been, nothing changes in my life. . . . I told them [people] I'll never consider myself a singer. I'm a housewife. Does recording three or four CDs make you a singer? A singer is one who comes and goes to the studio day and night, and rehearses, does this and that. I'm not a singer. What [songs] I have known since I was little, [that's what] I sing now.[13]

She is a typical Cypriot *"housewife,"* she says, a woman *"who likes to take care of her house . . . and her husband."* It is because of being a housewife and not a star that she refuses to leave her house and husband and give concerts with Mesogeios abroad, and it is for the same reason that, until very recently, she refused any invitations to sing anywhere in Cyprus that was deemed to be "far" from Paralimni.[14]

One could well assume that this domestic persona is the result of a well-planned marketing strategy. But meeting Pelagia in person is enough to dismiss that assumption. The first time I interviewed her at her house, in May 2006, I was completely unprepared for what I was going to encounter. What immediately became apparent upon meeting her was how much at ease she was with cameras and microphones. She knew exactly where to sit, where to look, and was not intimidated in the least. (In fact, if anyone was intimidated in that first interview, it was certainly I.) All this was perhaps to be expected given her previous experience on the radio and television, but I had, at the time, not yet grasped her ease with the whole setting. What caught me completely off guard, however, was the overpowering dynamism that she exuded, the directness of her speech, as well as her implicit determination to control both the content of the interview and its length. After about half an hour of talking (and barely having gone through a third of my questions), she exclaimed: *"We've said enough! Are we going to be talking till tomorrow?"* Even though I was considerably better prepared when I met her again in the autumn of 2008 (deciding to spend several days in Paralimni, and to interview her for only a few minutes every day), after our first thirty minutes of talking she once again told me that we had said enough for the day. From what was going on, I gathered that cutting the interview short had nothing to do with her being a "star" and behaving like one. She was cooking and wanted to finish her house chores before lunch and, crucially, before Giorgos, her husband, returned home. (The previous day she had interrupted the interview as soon as her husband got home in order to make him a coffee.) Chitchat of any kind—ethnographic interview included—was clearly not to her liking.

By reacting in this way, Pelagia once again put her role as a wife before that of a singer—or, in this case, a research subject—and aptly demonstrated where her priorities lay. But her explicit concern about her husband and his well-being showed much more than simply that. *"If I had to argue with my husband [for being a singer], I wouldn't [do it],"* she says, always being quick to acknowledge his support and hence his role in her success. She knows very well that without his complete and utter backing none of her achievements would ever be possible.

When social conventions relaxed and made it possible for Pelagia and other women to start singing more publicly in the village (in the early 1980s),[15] negative comments abounded.[16] Many—especially older—members of the audience saw public singing as a typically male activity where women had no place. It is a story well known in Paralimni (though nowadays told only privately) that other women who began performing at the same time as Pelagia later withdrew because of their husbands' reaction to village gossip. Women singing in public was evidently something not everyone in the village approved of. Pelagia's insistence on emphasizing her role as a housewife could, then, be read as a preemptive defense against comments directed at women singers. By labeling herself as a "housewife," and by making sure that she takes care of her husband, Pelagia not only keeps the balance of her household right, but she also publicly announces that her "social duty lies in conformity to her ideal domestic role" (Auerbach 1989, 30), thus avoiding any danger of being accused of abandoning her social role in the village.

However, the notion of housewife itself is not a passive one. As Salamone and Stanton have argued for the case of Amouliani in Greece, "women's power and prestige is *formalized*" in "*nikokyrio*, 'household,'" which "historically has dictated the 'balance of power' between men and women in rural Greece" (1986, 97–98; emphases in original). Tellingly, the word for *housewife* in Greek, *nikokyra*, literally means *houselady* or *housemistress*. So being a nikokyra—a woman in control of her house and family—can be very empowering, and declaring it only makes the woman's position stronger: "A woman's happiness, sense of self worth, and effectiveness will depend as much on her acceptance of the ideal of nikokyra as on its public realization" (ibid., 99).

Seen under this light, and despite Pelagia's protests, being both "housewife" and "star" (in this case, a woman singer with a public persona) is not necessarily mutually exclusive. Certainly some of Pelagia's choices confirm this: in the 2006–7 TV season, for instance, she sang the title song of a comedy series (*Deixe Mou Ton Filo Sou*, i.e., Show Me Your Friend) alongside a hip-hop artist. Her couplets, sung in Cypriot dialect to a traditional tune, served as the refrain of an otherwise hip-hop song sung in modern Greek. Not only did Pelagia sing the couplets, but she also appeared on the clip together with the young hip-hop singer.

Why did she do it? I asked, puzzled by her unlikely pairing with the young artist and her insistence on telling me that she is only a housewife. Was it money? It seemed improbable. The amount of money that she received for composing the lyrics and appearing on the clip was negligible. Recognition—being recognized wherever she goes, being loved by young people (the likely audience of the hip-hop singer) and loving them back—was what prompted her decision. And the empowerment this recognition brought with it, the contrast between the impossibility of singing in public with which she began her life and the possibility (or, better, the reality) of her very public career as a woman singer at present, keeps motivating her day after day.

Pelagia's successful appearance on *Deixe Mou Ton Filo Sou* showed that it is precisely this unlikely—but not incompatible—combination of star and housewife, old and new, traditional and modern in her persona that makes her so popular in Cyprus. By successfully uniting these seemingly antithetical images and by showing—however unintentionally—that one does not have to preclude the other, Pelagia managed to turn the tide: instead of the negative comments of the past about women singing in public, she is now something of a national treasure in Cyprus, and certainly a source of pride for her village.

Nevertheless, several other women of Pelagia's generation still see the perceived boundary between star and housewife as insurmountable. Prior to the extensive urbanization that followed Cyprus's independence from British colonial rule in 1960 and the ensuing modernizing societal trends, performing music professionally—either singing or playing an instrument—was seen as improper and disrespectful for women. The only known professional female performers were those singing and dancing in theatres, cafés, and cabarets. As with other countries in the Mediterranean (see Magrini 2003), the stereotypical picture of female performers in Cyprus was invariably linked with drinking, smoking, drugs, and prostitution. Hence for most women of Pelagia's age, singing in public—professionally or otherwise, outside the family and village environment—was, and in several cases remains, problematic.

But despite the general disapproval toward women musicians in Cyprus in the first half of the twentieth century and the public's customary perception of them as decadent, oral narratives reveal that some women did become known for performing music in public without being seen as immoral. What was important for them, however, was for characteristics seen as typically female to be left aside—either because of disability (an example given to me was that of a blind woman fiddler) or because of behavior that differed from that of the typical female Cypriot. Many of the women performing in public were, in my informants' words, *antrogenaitzes*, literally "manly women," therefore certainly differing from the female stereotype. In the case of Pelagia, the very confidence and dynamism that make her popular are also two of the traits that make her different from most other women of her generation who sing, but did or do not dare to come forward. What sets her apart is her extremely vocal and visible dynamism, a trait that in traditional Cypriot society (and specifically for women of Pelagia's generation and social background) is not stereotypically feminine. The way she speaks portrays no hidden modesty or fear or—to use a word loaded with Mediterranean associations (see Peristiany 1965)—"shame."

This very direct way of behaving is also reflected in her singing voice. Even though vocal aesthetics and delivery are, as yet, a nondiscussed subject in Cyprus, by carefully listening to Pelagia's voice and comparing it to recordings of older, traditional folk poets and singers (such as those on the recordings of the Peloponnesian Folklore Foundation 1999 [1988]), one can begin to understand how greatly responsible they are for her success. Influenced by Greek *laïka* (popular) singers, in recent years a number of Cypriot traditional singers sing with a deliberate slight delay—their voice falling right after the beat, rather than on the beat, something that is perceived as expressive of love, sorrow, or passion. In contrast, Pelagia's articulation is crisp and crystal clear, and her voice always falls exactly on the beat. Even though Cypriot audiences would not, if asked, readily identify diction (in this case the way she enunciates words) as one of the pivotal elements of Pelagia's aesthetic, it does, somewhat instinctively, strengthen their view of the "traditional" in her voice. However, contrary to other singers in the Eastern Mediterranean, such as Zeki Müren in Turkey and Umm Kulthum in Egypt (discussed in Stokes 2003 and Danielson 1997, respectively), in Pelagia's case, diction does not connect her to a higher social class nor does it give her "high prestige" (Stokes 2003, 315). Rather, her clear, direct way of speaking and singing, the care—if not the pride—she takes in enunciating clearly the lyrics of her songs, connects her to a time in the Cypriot past when the dialect was used in all settings of everyday life without it being connected to notions of peasantry or illiteracy.[17] In turn, this connects her to village life and tradition, perhaps also to a Cypriot "age of innocence."

Nasality, a shared aesthetic value in several musical cultures of the Mediterranean, also has a share in Pelagia's popularity. Discussing the nasal quality in Umm Kulthum's voice, Virginia Danielson maintained that many Egyptians saw it as "an important marker of authentic singing" (1997, 138). Later, however, with the impact of Westernization, nasality came to be seen as "rustic, countrified, or unsophisticated" (ibid.). It is precisely this "rustic" and "countrified" aspect of a nasal voice that is important in the case of Pelagia. Though not seen as an essential trait in Cypriot singing, the distinctive nasal quality in her voice, and, once again, the way this affects the way she enunciates the words of her songs, also adds to the "village" aesthetic of her persona, and completes the puzzle of what many Cypriots perceive as the "ethnic maternal voice" (Antelyes 1994, 217).[18]

"The Pelagia Phenomenon"

When in September 2004 Kyriakou Pelagia sang as a guest star in Anna Vissi's concert at the GSP Stadium in Nicosia, the visual contrast could not have been greater. Vissi—a Cypriot-born pop singer, one of the best-selling singers in the Greek-speaking world—wore a white miniskirt, a black see-through top, white boots, and had her long, dyed blond hair down. Pelagia appeared on stage wearing a long and loose beige dress that covered most of her body, with her cropped gray hair and no trace of makeup, and with flat black shoes that, from a distance, looked suspiciously similar to slippers. The encounter began with the recitation/improvisation of a few couplets by Pelagia to Vissi's excitement, who addressed her openly in Cypriot dialect and tried to imitate her couplet-making, as if in a quest to reaffirm her Cypriot roots. When Vissi prompted Pelagia to start singing, she playfully complained that the grandmother's songs were even more popular than hers: "Your *souxe* [hits] are greater than mine, I think."[19]

Pelagia began singing her best-selling "Eipa sou," first on her own, then joined by Vissi, with the audience frantically cheering and clapping. Next to the intensely sensual and erotic Vissi, dancing suggestively to the sound of the song, stood the inconspicuous grandmother, without moving, almost stiff, in an image of impossible incongruities. The visual antithesis was extended into their vocal performance as well, Pelagia singing by attacking the notes directly, without embellishments, and Vissi singing with turns and delays that accentuated her voice's deliberate sensuality. With every sound and move Vissi seemed to draw attention to her sensuality and eroticism—two vital components of both her image and voice. In contrast, Pelagia showed no apparent desire to play a role other than being herself: a village housewife and grandmother.

Why has this elderly woman become so popular, and why now? The 2004 Pelagia and Vissi concert crudely juxtaposed a seductive pop singer—a symbol of the sensual and the erotic—and a modestly dressed elderly lady with no wish to even hint at the sensual,[20] and who, in strictly traditional contexts, might be seen even as deviating from her prescribed gender role. Despite their marked differences, however, both singers were equally accepted by their mainly young audience. Has Pelagia—the housewife, grandmother, villager, farmer—become so popular *because* of the contrast she presents to the overabundance of half-naked, good-looking singers? Does her overwhelming acceptance mark a turn toward a more conservative neo-Cyprus, or does it signify a long-awaited (by traditional musicians) turn of the younger generation to traditional music? And what does it tell us of the associations people in Cyprus make regarding traditional singers?

If I consider three commercially successful Cypriot traditional singers of the last fifty years,[21] I come to the following conclusions: they were all men; they have all had conservative appearances/public images; they have all had conventional lives within the prescribed societal norms (i.e., they have all had full-time jobs other than singing, and they have all been married with children); they have all shown some connection with religion (some more strongly than others); and finally, they have all appeared to be pillars of the Cypriot music tradition, trying to save it from decay. With the exception of gender, Pelagia shares all these traits with her fellow singers. (However, as I discuss later, a crucial difference also lies in *how* she tries to save Cypriot music.) I am therefore inclined to ask: Does a Cypriot traditional singer have to remain within Cypriot society's prescribed norms in order to be accepted by the public?[22] In other words, is the term "Cypriot traditional singer" synonymous with conservatism? If so, where does this connection come from?

The first major traditional singer in Cyprus, Theodoulos Kallinikos, was not simply conservative in his attire and looks; he was the chief cantor (*protopsaltis*) of the archbishopric of Cyprus for almost seven decades, from 1935 until his death in 2004. In the minds of older people in Cyprus (those who experienced the CyBC's exclusivity and could not have escaped his performances), Kallinikos *is* Cypriot song. The cantor was the first to produce commercial recordings of Cypriot songs and dominated Cypriot radio in the 1960s and beyond (see Demetriou 2008, 75–128). Has the association of Theodoulos Kallinikos in people's minds with Church/conservatism/tradition (the triptych known in Greek as *patris-thriskeia-oikogeneia*, i.e., homeland-religion-family) been so powerful that every traditional singer who wants to be successful in Cyprus *needs* to comply with this recipe? Most male traditional singers in Cyprus today certainly admit that, to some extent, they have been influenced by Kallinikos, with all that this implies.

But also the whole notion of tradition in the Greek-speaking world has been connected to conservatism, to the past, to the old and peasant. Significantly, however, it has also been connected to the creation of the "national"—

in arts, poetry, and, above all, folk songs (see Herzfeld 1982; Beaton 2004 [1980], 10–11).[23] At the turn of the twentieth century, folk songs were seen as "monuments of the word" (also known as *zonta mnimeia*, i.e., living monuments), connecting the modern Greek world with the ancient via Byzantium (Herzfeld 1982). In the early 1950s, Kallinikos's book of folk song transcriptions was seen as providing a "service" that was both "musical and *national*" (Michaelides in Kallinikos 1951, no page; my emphasis). More recently, Michalis Hadjimichael described Mesogeios's work as "carrying to today . . . the ancestors' four gospels" (Hadjimichael 1997, 3).[24] Rarely have folk songs in Cyprus been just what they are: songs.

Similarly to other singers in Cyprus who perform the old songs, Pelagia exudes a sense of traditionalism or conservatism—in terms of the way she presents herself visually (conservative clothes, gray hair, no makeup, etc.) and also socially (married woman, good housewife, mother and grandmother, etc.). In a sphere that is still predominantly male, it is this conservatism—along with her very visible and audible dynamism—that put her on a par with her male colleagues. Contrary to most of her colleagues on the Cypriot music scene, however, Pelagia does not get involved in theoretical discussions—e.g., on the radio, TV, or in written outputs—about Cypriot tradition and its "preservation" (a perennial favorite among her fellow singers). Although this followed as a natural effect of her character and behavior, rather than being a purposely adopted strategy, it guaranteed her even more success—especially among the youth. Singers' theoretical discussions on saving tradition often have the opposite effect of what they strive for, presenting them as elitist: their theoretical predisposition does not allow them to become involved in genres (or collaborate with groups of people) that are seen as responsible for traditional music's decay. Rather than lecturing young people about tradition, Pelagia *does* tradition; what she wants to say, she says through her verses and songs:

> I give my opinion to both poor and rich: they who honor their roots honor themselves too.
>
> The thieves and the outlaws put up the wires;[25] if tradition goes too, Cyprus will die out completely.

By consistently avoiding preaching at her young audience, Pelagia not only secured her triumph as a national grandmother, but also, by implication, inadvertently marked a small victory for Cypriot music. Without ever turning down her role as housewife/grandmother or her conservative look, she sings with pop and hip-hop singers. She appears as guest star on TV series (always as herself), and on TV and radio shows with a modern outlook. She does not try to be modern, she is always herself (which is itself a role, one could suggest). Yet at the same time she does not negate pop culture, she becomes part of it, without getting lost in it. So much has pop culture accepted her as a result, that Cypriot Eurovision fans debate whether she should represent Cyprus in a forthcoming contest, being the only one "who can project" the country and attract votes.[26]

In keeping with her grandmotherly role, the singer always makes sure to tell her interviewers—as always in couplet form—how much she loves the youth, and how much they love her in return. "*Youth are right, I don't blame them, for we also did what [young people] were doing back then.*" That many young people seem to be more interested in "foreign songs" is not something that she minds, provided, of course, that they keep loving their roots too:

> *Whatever a person learns is surely to their honor; but they should certainly know what their origins are.*
> *They ask us "Where are you from?" We state "Cyprus."*[27] *So youths should get to know Cypriot [songs/dialect] too.*

But young people are not her only fans; Pelagia's success also turned her into a role model for older women, and elderly people in general. In fact, so great has the effect of her popularity been on collective imagination that she unwittingly created what Michalis Tterlikkas, another well-known Cypriot traditional singer, called "the Pelagia phenomenon." The fact that Pelagia combined her domestic roles with a very public career as a singer showed other women of her generation that it is possible to do both. Significantly, for women who grew up with the notion of "singer-equals-decadence," she also demonstrated that being a singer can be a respectable thing. Ever since Pelagia became popular, Tterlikkas says, several elderly ladies (and a handful of men) have been hoping to be discovered and promoted, and become "the new Pelagia" (pers. comm. 2008):

> When I meet elderly ladies and ask them to sing for me, they invariably ask me, anxiously: "Will you play my songs on the radio? Will you make a CD of me? Will I become like Pelagia?"

The appeal of being recognized in the streets, of being known and admired—in short the temptation of glory—is hard to resist.

In many ways Pelagia's case is paradoxical: she is one of the very few stars of the Cypriot music scene, in a country where women performers of traditional music are a rarity and where traditional music stars, irrespective of gender, are even rarer. This housewife/grandmother-star has been able to transcend borders within Cypriot society, and appeal to young and old, traditional and modern, folk and pop music fans alike. In examining her popularity, one should, then, not consider that she became famous *in spite* of her age, but *because* of it: her status as a village housewife and grandmother who—due to her popularity—has become everyone's grandmother has provided her with a nonsexual status that goes well with what is expected from traditional singers' conservative public personae. Pelagia's popularity reflects how effectively she embodies that persona, and, for that reason, how successfully she represents "new Cyprus": one where conservatism is combined with modernity and what is typically described as *horkatiko* (peasant), one that is laughed at for being precisely that, but which, at the same time, is—secretly perhaps—loved and admired.

Notes

1. In July 1974, following a coup backed by the military government of Athens aiming to overthrow the Cypriot president, Turkey (one of Cyprus's guarantor powers, along with Greece and Britain, according to the country's constitution) invaded the northern part of the island. As a result, thousands of Greek Cypriots living in the north of Cyprus were forced to move to the south and, similarly, thousands of Turkish Cypriots living in the south fled to the north. Cyprus has been de facto partitioned ever since. The southern part of the island is governed by the Republic of Cyprus—founded in 1960 following independence from Britain, and a member of the EU since 2004—and the northern part is governed by the Turkish Republic of Northern Cyprus, proclaimed in 1983 and recognized only by Turkey. In the context of this chapter, "Cyprus" refers to the southern part of the island, and similarly "Cypriot" refers to "Greek Cypriot." I do this not to negate the existence of Turks or other ethnic groups on the island, but simply to avoid repetition.

2. The Cyprus Broadcasting Service was founded by the British authorities during colonial times (radio 1953; TV 1957). It was renamed Cyprus Broadcasting Corporation (CyBC) after independence from Britain in 1960.

3. "Kyriakou" is her first name, diminutive of "Kyriaki." "Pelagia" is her surname, which she acquired after her marriage to Giorgos Pelagias in 1958. She was born Kyriaki Kouzali on July 8, 1936, in Paralimni, a village on Cyprus's east coast. With one exception, in this chapter I chose to call her "Pelagia" (rather than "Kyriakou"), as this is how she is customarily being referred to in Cyprus.

4. *Tsiattista* (singular *tsiattisto*) is a form of improvised verse in Cypriot Greek dialect that can be either recited or sung to recitative-like tunes. Tsiattista consist of two fifteen-syllable verses, each of which is made up of two half-lines of eight and seven syllables. (Hence a complete tsiattisto would be in the form of 8+7 / 8+7.) Even though in their strict sense tsiattista involve two or more performers exchanging verses of antagonistic content in dialogue, nowadays in Cyprus the word is commonly used to identify any kind of rhyming couplet, irrespective of content.

5. All quotations by Pelagia are taken from my interviews with her, unless otherwise noted.

6. All translations in this chapter are mine, unless otherwise stated.

7. This is a translation of *paradosiaki mousiki*, the term that performers of this music in Cyprus typically use to describe it. Another, equally accepted, term is *kypriaki mousiki* (Cypriot music), or *kypriaki paradosiaki mousiki* (Cypriot traditional music). Up until the 1970s, Cypriot music scholars employed the terms *dimodis* or *dimotiki* (folk), or even *laïki* (popular) to describe this same music (see Michaelides 1944; Kallinikos 1951; Ioannidis 1968). The term *dimotiki* is still occasionally used; however *paradosiaki* is the preferred term used on, for example, contemporary Cypriot music CDs. The term *laïki* is now used only to describe a specific genre of Greek popular music. Because there is no documentary evidence to indicate what precipitated the change from *dimotiki* to *paradosiaki*, the reasons can only be supposed. According to a Greek perspective, the support of dimotiki mousiki by the military junta of Athens (1967–74), and hence the connection of the term with that regime, was reason enough for it to become grossly unpopular (Kallimopoulou 2009, 17–23). Even though this might have had repercussions in Cyprus as well, based on my fieldwork experience in Cyprus I would suggest that the term *paradosiaki* (traditional) has acquired more prominence because of an intense preoccupation with tradition in general (i.e., not only musical tradition) and "lost homelands" following 1974 (see Syrimis 1998, 212). In the same vein, paradosiaki mousiki has been eligible for sponsorship from several funding bodies (see note 8) in the last couple of decades, hence performers consciously or otherwise tend to use the same term when marketing their music.

8. Despite sponsorship by the Municipality of Paralimni, *Ta Paralimnitika* remained a private enterprise made for commercial purposes. Sponsorship of traditional music CDs by various bodies is extremely common in Cyprus, and many government and church bodies, or other public organizations, have budgets for what is usually termed their "cultural mission." In return sponsors get advertisement of their logos on CD covers. The Municipality of Paralimni relies on tourism as a main source of income, and sponsoring the CD means extra publicity for the area.

9. The traditional percussion instrument used is *tampoutsia*, a kind of frame drum. The recording also featured the piano but only in a song performed by a choir, not in the ones sung by Pelagia.

10. These words are attributed to the Greek singer Giorgos Dalaras, and have been reproduced in the booklets of Mesogeios's last two CDs (Hadjimichael 1997, 11; 2003, 6).

11. Even though successful, *Ta Paralimnitika 2* did not reach the first CD's popularity. By October 2008 *Ta Paralimnitika* had sold 9,000 copies, whereas *Ta Paralimnitika 2* had sold only 6,500 (Hadjimichael, pers. comm. 2008). To put this in context, selling 3,000 CDs in Cyprus equals a bestseller, or a *chrysos diskos* ("golden disc").

12. The Cypriot traditional music scene is made up of ensembles of semiprofessional musicians, who perform primarily during the summer months at open-air concerts organized by local communities and frequently sponsored by the state. As a genre that is still largely connected to Cyprus's rural past (alluded to in the lyrics of many songs, and invoked by the use of outdated words of the Cypriot Greek dialect), it typically does not attract younger audiences. That is why Pelagia's case—i.e., the fact that she has so many young fans—is both interesting and unique.

13. This, of course, is not entirely true. As I have written earlier, since she began recording, Pelagia has learned several new songs from Hadjimichael.

14. This usually involved villages in the Paphos region, a maximum of a two-and-a-half hours' drive from Paralimni.

15. What made this possible was the change in Paralimni's (and more broadly Cyprus's) social structures. Following the events of 1974, a large number of internally displaced people from the north of Cyprus moved to Paralimni, thus changing the demographics, structure, and dynamics of the village. As a result of the same events, some of Famagusta's roles—the second-largest city in Cyprus prior to 1974, and the administrative, commercial, and tourist center of northeastern Cyprus—were gradually transferred to Paralimni, which evolved from a small agricultural village to a tourist-thriving town.

16. I found out about the negative comments circulating in Paralimni regarding women singers in the 1980s by talking to members of the audience of those early concerts. When I asked her, Pelagia claimed that she had never heard any negative comments about women singers in the village (Pelagia 2008). This implies either that criticism was not publicly voiced or that she was indifferent to it precisely because she enjoyed her husband's support.

17. For a brief discussion on Cypriots' internal conflict pertaining to the use of Cypriot Greek dialect (and its perception as "peasant") and that of standard Greek, see Argyrou 2005 [1996], 136. Bryant (2004) examines the dynamics between the local dialects (Greek and Turkish) and the official languages of education in Cyprus, and their connection to nationalism.

18. I borrow this term from a different context, Peter Antelyes's discussion of "Red Hot Mamas" (1994:212–29).

19. http://www.youtube.com/watch?v=48kKauXou4k (accessed March 2012).

20. In the course of the concert, Pelagia revealed that her dress was a gift from Vissi. In buying her the gift, did Vissi want to make sure that the contrast between them would be present by deciding what Pelagia was going to wear, or did she simply reproduce what she already saw as Pelagia's public image?

21. I am referring to Theodoulos Kallinikos (1904–2004), Christos Sikkis (b. 1946?), and Michalis Tterlikkas (b. 1955). My comparison is limited to those singers who released commercial recordings with some success, and who have therefore had a public persona.

22. This is certainly not the case with pop singers. Vissi, for example, is divorced and has appeared in public with a number of different partners over the years.

23. In this paragraph I am using the term *folk songs* instead of *traditional songs* because this is how the songs are referred to in the works cited.

24. Michalis Hadjimichael is among those singers in Cyprus for which preservation of Cypriot music and how best to achieve it is an extremely important issue. Even though Hadjimichael often uses the booklets of Mesogeios's CDs as outlets for his views, Pelagia has nothing to do with either the booklets' writing or the selection of the music material itself.

25. This is a reference to the barbed wire that runs along the demarcation line of 1974, which has since separated Cyprus into two parts.

26. See http://www.eurovisionclub.com/articles.asp?id=234&comments_pg=4&comments_psize=20& return_to_pg=4&return_to_psize=&arxeio=1 (accessed March 2012). More recently a Facebook page was created in support of Pelagia going to Euro-

vision. See http://www.facebook.com/ group.php?v=wall&gid= 95179713936 (accessed March 2012).

27. In the original Cypriot verse the word she uses—for rhyming purposes—is "Cypriots" instead of "Cyprus."

References

Antelyes, Peter. 1994. "Red Hot Mamas: Bessie Smith, Sophie Tucker, and the Ethnic Maternal Voice in American Popular Song." In *Embodied Voices: Representing Female Vocality in Western Culture*, eds. Leslie C. Dunn and Nancy A. Jones, 212–29. Cambridge: Cambridge University Press.

Argyrou, Vassos. 2005 [1996]. *Tradition and Modernity in the Mediterranean: The Wedding as Symbolic Struggle.* Cambridge: Cambridge University Press.

Auerbach, Susan. 1989. "From Singing to Lamenting: Women's Musical Role in a Greek Village." In *Women and Music in Cross-Cultural Perspective*, ed. Ellen Koskoff, 25–43. Urbana: University of Illinois Press.

Beaton, Roderick. 2004 [1980]. *Folk Poetry of Modern Greece.* Cambridge: Cambridge University Press.

Bryant, Rebecca. 2004. *Imagining the Modern: The Cultures of Nationalism in Cyprus.* London: I. B. Tauris.

Danielson, Virginia. 1997. *The Voice of Egypt: Umm Kulthum, Arabic Song, and Egyptian Society in the Twentieth Century.* Chicago: University of Chicago Press.

Demetriou, Nicoletta. 2008. "The *Fones* Discourse: Ideology and Practice in Greek Cypriot Folk Music." Unpublished PhD thesis. SOAS, University of London.

Hadjimichael, Michalis. 1997. *Ta Paralimnitika 2. Dimotika Tragoudia tis Kyprou* (*[Songs] from Paralimni 2. Folk Songs from Cyprus*). Booklet accompanying the recording. Paralimni: Municipality of Paralimni.

———. 2003. *Oloaspron Pezouni. Dimotika Tragoudia tis Kyprou* (*White Dove. Folk Songs from Cyprus*). Booklet accompanying the recording. Paralimni: Municipality of Paralimni.

Herzfeld, Michael. 1982. *Ours Once More: Folklore, Ideology, and the Making of Modern Greece.* New York: Pella.

Ioannides, C. D. 1968. "A Short Collection of Cyprus Folksongs." *Kypriakai Spoudai* ΛΒ' (32):265–300.

Kallimopoulou, Eleni. 2009. *Paradosiaká: Music, Meaning and Identity in Modern Greece.* Farnham: Ashgate.

Kallinikos, Theodoulos. 1951. *Kypriaki Laïki Mousa* (*Cypriot Popular Muse*). Nicosia: Neos Kosmos, Thomas G. Kyriakidis.

Magrini, Tullia, ed. 2003. *Music and Gender: Perspectives from the Mediterranean.* Chicago: University of Chicago Press.

Michaelides, Solon. 1944. "Kypriaki Laïki Mousiki" ("Cypriot Popular Music"). Reprint from *Kypriaka Grammata* Θ' (9):3–14 (originally 115–26).

Papapetrou, Paschalis. 2006. *Kyriakou Pelagia.* Short documentary for CyBC TV.

Peristiany, John. 1965. *Honour and Shame: The Values of Mediterranean Society.* London: Weidenfeld and Nicolson.

Salamone, S. D., and J. B. Stanton. 1986. "Introducing the *Nikokyra*: Ideality and Reality in Social Process." In *Gender and Power in Rural Greece*, ed. Jill Dubisch, 97–120. Princeton: Princeton University Press.

Stokes, Martin. 2003. "The Tearful Public Sphere: Turkey's 'Son of Art,' Zeki Müren." In *Music and Gender: Perspectives from the Mediterranean*, ed. Tullia Magrini, 307–28. Chicago: University of Chicago Press.

Syrimis, George. 1998. "Ideology, Orality, and Textuality: The Tradition of the *Poietáridhes* of Cyprus." In *Cyprus and Its People: Nation, Identity, and Experience in an Unimaginable Community, 1955–1997*, ed. Vangelis Calotychos, 205–22. Boulder, Colorado: Westview Press.

Interviews

Hadjimichael, Michalis. 2005. Private interview with Nicoletta Demetriou. Nicosia, November 2, 2005; Frenaros, December 18, 2005.

Pelagia, Kyriakou. 2006. Private interview with Nicoletta Demetriou. Paralimni, May 11, 2006.

———. 2008. Private interview with Nicoletta Demetriou. Paralimni, October 7 and 8, 2008.

Discography

Pelagia, Kyriakou, and Mesogeios. 1995. *Ta Paralimnitika. Tragoudia tis Paradosis ([Songs] from Paralimni. Traditional Songs)*. Paralimni: Municipality of Paralimni.

———. 1997. *Ta Paralimnitika 2. Dimotika Tragoudia tis Kyprou ([Songs] from Paralimni 2. Folk Songs from Cyprus)*. Paralimni: Municipality of Paralimni.

———. 2003. *Oloaspron Pezouni. Dimotika Tragoudia tis Kyprou (White Dove. Folk Songs from Cyprus)*. Paralimni: Municipality of Paralimni.

Peloponnesian Folklore Foundation. 1999 [1988]. *Kypros—Dimotiki Mousiki. Cyprus—Popular Music* (bilingual edition). Nafplion: Peloponnesian Folklore Foundation.

6. Lexine Solomon

Songs of Connection and Celebration by a Torres Strait Islander

KATELYN BARNEY

Katelyn's Journal Entry, June 12, 2008

I've just got back home after a night at the Dreaming Festival of Indigenous Performance at Woodford, Queensland, Australia. I saw Lexine perform and it was amazing. She was singing in a huge tent and, even though it was cold outside, the tent was warm from hundreds of people singing and dancing. The crowd was an eclectic mix of young and old, Indigenous and non-Indigenous. Some were sitting on the ground or on plastic chairs. Some were dancing. Clearly, all were happy and the room was a buzz of excitement. As I arrived, Lexine was on the stage with her band and was teaching the audience the words to her song, "This Is Woman."

Her band was following her closely and she worked well with them. Her two regular band members on keyboard and guitar were playing and her cousin was playing the drums. Lexine was singing with confidence and her smooth voice effortlessly filled the room. She was wearing a bright colorful scarf that reached almost to the ground and swayed with her when she sang. I walked in, a little tentatively, trying to find somewhere to sit. From the stage Lexine saw me and winked as she sang, "This is woman, and she lives, this is woman, and she loves, this is woman, and she believes." I instantly relaxed, joined the crowd, and let the music wash over me. After "This Is Woman" Lexine sang a cover of "Over the Rainbow" and after that, she taught us all how to sing a Torres Strait Islander song, "Baba Waiyar." Even though she must have been *hot under the lights, Lexine looked relaxed and as more and more people came in, her energy lifted and her captivating and smooth voice effortlessly filled the tent. It was an experience that I will carry with me for a long time.*

• • •

Raised in Australia's North Queensland, Lexine Solomon is a Torres Strait Islander who has performed nationally and internationally as a singer for over twenty years. The Torres Strait Islands are a group of islands situated between Cape York, Australia, and Papua New Guinea. Yet, like many Torres Strait Islanders, Lexine was born and lives on mainland Australia. Her music encompasses a diverse range of styles and languages and an overarching theme is her identity as a Torres Strait Islander woman. I have known Lexine for seven years and have worked collaboratively with her on a research project to draw attention to the work of Torres Strait Islander women singers. In this chapter, she is the research subject and I will draw on interviews, conversations, and experiences to explore how she uses her singing voice to connect with the Torres Strait Islands. I also examine how she uses her songs to express her family history and celebrate Torres Strait Islander women. Like Beverley Diamond and Pirkko Moisala I believe that "moving our usually untold experiences from the privacy of our memories to the printed page" is "an important step" (2000, 17; Ellis 1998; Humphreys 2005). Overall, this chapter is about how Lexine connects with her family, community, and culture and celebrates her identity through song.

A Singing Workshop in the Classroom: Introducing Lexine

Lexine stood in the front of the lecture room and tapped her laptop to begin her PowerPoint presentation. She turned to face the class and looked out at the sea of thirty faces. Green, blue, and brown eyes of non-Indigenous students looked back at her. She had sung at many performances but seemed a little nervous in the university setting.

She began:

I acknowledge the traditional owners of the land on which we meet today. Thank you Katelyn for inviting me to your class.

We smiled at each other. I was very keen for Lexine to attend this class, which was part of a course that I was coordinating on Indigenous Australian[1] women at The University of Queensland.

I'll start off by telling you a little bit about myself, if that's okay. Then we can do some singing.

I noticed that a few students shifted uncomfortably while others smiled in anticipation.

As a child I used to make up songs all the time. But then getting paid to sing—I have been performing for over twenty years now—since I was eighteen in 1981! One time when I was fifteen or sixteen I was asked to sing for a double wedding in my church and people kept saying how much they enjoyed it. Then in Bible College I was backup singer with a band then became the lead singer and did solos in the church—singing in the church choir—I guess I just loved to be part of the joy that people enjoyed whenever I sang—it's been an amazing journey.

Lexine clicked to another slide that showed her two album covers (figure 6.1).

These are my two albums that I've released independently. This Is Woman I released in 2002 and Strike a Pose in 2006. There are original songs and covers of songs from other artists on both of them. I'm really inspired by the people around me and it is community focused. I received some funding from the Australia Council to record the first album and saved up my own finances. I wrote eleven of the tracks, there are three on there that I co-wrote with Aboriginal performer Warren H. Williams, then there's a song that belongs to Torres Strait

Figure 6.1. *This Is Woman* album cover, Lexine Solomon, 2002. © Lexine Solomon.

Islander Miseron Levi called "Baba Waiyar," and "Amazing Grace," which has become a signature song for me. The second album was part of a research project I undertook where I interviewed women family and friends to produce a DVD collection of interviews with Indigenous Australian women who have had an impact on my life to encourage and empower other Torres Strait Islander and Aboriginal women to reflect on their own life experiences.

I interrupted, "Lex, can you tell the students about why you release your songs independently rather than through a record company?"

Well, I've found that for myself as a songwriter/singer I just have more control. It just means I can decide where the music goes. As a female, and Indigenous, it's really important that I'm creating my own music—only I know what I'm looking for—I become executive producer of my work. I recorded that album of mine This Is Woman *in a small home studio but I got to achieve the sounds I was looking for.*

She took a sip from her water bottle and then clicked to the next slide that showed a photo of her working at the Central Australian Aboriginal Media Association.[2]

I was the first Torres Strait Islander woman employed as music manager/producer at the Central Australian Aboriginal Media Association (CAAMA) in Alice Springs, Northern Territory from 2002 to 2005 which was a great experience, I got to work with some great artists. I've performed in New Zealand, the United States of America and across Australia. I manage myself and organized the tours myself. In 2007, I was featured in the documentary "Canberra's Best Kept Secret" where the director won Best Senior Director of the competition. You can check it out on YouTube can't you Katelyn?

"Yes I think so," I answered.

The next slide was a picture of Lexine and me (figure 6.2).

Ah, my life with Doctor Katelyn Barney.

She giggled and I wondered what she was going to say.

I first met her in 2004 when she came to interview me for her doctorate, then in 2006 I asked Katelyn if she'd like to work with me on a project. We secured some funding and over the last three years we've been working on a research project together interviewing my fellow Torres Strait Islander women singers.[3] It's been quite a journey and it's become a strong friendship, hasn't it Katelyn?

"Yes, it has. I've given the students a couple of our articles too," I said.[4]

Figure 6.2. Lexine and Katelyn at the Dreaming Festival, Australia's International Indigenous Festival in Woodford, Queensland, Australia, 2008. Photograph by Patricia Barney.

Alright let's do some singing. I wrote the title song on the album This Is Woman *for an International Women's Day Dinner in 2000. I wanted to write songs about women and who they are to us—and why they make us who we are. I'll sing it through and then you can try it too.*

She started the backing track and her uneasiness about being a lecturer immediately disappeared as she confidently sang:

> What is woman made of?
> A question of all time
> A woman found with virtue
> This is not a rhyme
> She has purpose
> She gives love
> She has all she needs
>
> This is woman, and she loves
> This is woman, and she lives
> This is woman, and she believes

What is woman made of?
Sugar and spice
She holds the link to carry life
She has purpose, she gives love
She has all she needs

This is woman, and she loves
This is woman, and she lives
This is woman, and she believes

Woman is made of charity
I have faith to find there's hope for me
I have purpose, I am loved
I have all I need[5]

Okay your turn now, repeat after me.
The students slowly began to learn the verses.
"Any questions?" Lexine asked after they had finished.
A student at the front with short, curly, red hair raised her hand. "What does the reference to sugar and spice mean?" she asked.

Well, I always thought of that nursery rhyme "Sugar and Spice and All Things Nice." I grew up without a mother but I've still turned out alright and the sisters that I raised were great too. We had faith, hope and we learnt how to have charity. That's what that last verse is about.

Singing to Connect with the Torres Strait Islands

I was raised by a Torres Strait Islander father on the mainland of Australia. Since I was not raised in the Islands I only have a kindergarten understanding of language but my understanding of culture and custom, and some of the traditions make up who I am because of my father. There are lots of cultural ties back to the Islands that I have, and without "living" parents, my connection is only as strong as I make it. I first went up to the Torres Strait Islands in 1992. I went up not sure where I was going. . . . I went to St Pauls on Moa Island and I just soaked it in. I just took it in. This is where my father was, he walked on this beach, he saw these coconut trees. It was worth it.

• • •

Jeremy Beckett writes that "to be an Islander you must have an island, but for the mainland-born this 'island' has to be discovered all over again, and imagined" (2004, 13). Approximately 33,100 people identify as Torres Strait Islander, and 20,200 people identify as both Torres Strait Islander and Aboriginal (Australian Bureau of Statistics 2006). The majority of Islanders now live on mainland Australia, yet approximately 6,800 people still reside in the Torres Strait. For Lexine there is a tension between being born on mainland Australia yet wanting to sustain an Islander identity.

It's not always easy to be a mainland based Islander and be accepted. As a mainland Torres Strait Islander, discomfort has several layers. I was raised by a Torres Strait Islander father whose values were embedded in how I was raised as the eldest daughter of seven children.

Lexine's comment points to the ways mainland-based Islanders can feel a sense of illegitimacy and unbelonging because they have not grown up in the Islands and because they are physically distanced from the Islands. As Chris Lawe Davies and Karl Neuenfeldt note, "herein lies the essential paradox of the diasporic imagination: although the geographic space known as the Torres Strait is a group of islands between Australia and Papua New Guinea, the majority of its population are mainland based, not island-based, Australians" (2004, 138). Lexine discusses the importance of identifying as a Torres Strait Islander woman.

To me it's my tie to why I am [laughs]! I belong [laughs]! You know, there's that whole link back to my father—there are people who know me because of him—they relate to me even after he's been gone twenty-plus years now. It's a link to people who are still living, the old people and their families.

Her songs provide a medium for Lexine to connect with the Torres Strait. An example of this is her song "I Belong":

> Generations may come and go
> Still the memories linger on
> But the stories tell me who I am
> There is truth in the words they spoke
> It's not a tale and it's not a joke
> These words tell me why I am
> I am the land, I am the trees
> I am the sand, and the seas
> My people they walked this land and I belong.[6]

The notes to her CD state that "I Belong" is about "heritage and a yearning to identify with people and culture and how generations carry memories and stories handed down through me." In October 2001, "I Belong" was the theme song for the inaugural National Gospel Happening in Canberra.

I've taken that around the world actually, and a lot of races have said that it's like it was written for them. I took it to New Zealand, to New York and Chicago and sang it for different races of people. . . . I took it to the Islands, and they were like, "this is about us!" you know, so that's been pretty amazing, yeah.

Singing gives me an opportunity to tell a story of how I fit and connect to the Islands.

Lexine's connection to the Torres Strait region is also expressed through singing a Torres Strait Islander *kores* (chorus) called "Baba Waiyar." *Kores* are one major strand of Islander sacred music and are post-1960s evangelical songs sung in Torres Strait Islander languages Meriam Mer, Kala Lagaw Ya, Kriol, along with English and other languages such as Tok Pisin from Papua New Guinea. *Kores* are usually simple in structure with a single brief stanza that is repeated a number of times. Karl Neuenfeldt points out that "new melodies are composed or old ones recycled, including the melodies and sometimes the words of well-known and copyrighted contemporary popular songs" (2008, 170). Lawrence suggests that because *kores* are easier to remember and learn, they are performed more frequently than the older language hymns, which were introduced from Pacific Islander missionaries who introduced or in some cases banned particular styles of music (2004, 47). Certainly Christianity became the main religious and social force throughout the Torres Strait. Following the arrival in 1871 of the London Missionary Society (LMS), the introduction of Christianity to the Torres Strait Islands is referred to by Islanders as the "Coming of the Light" and is celebrated annually (ibid.). Lawrence notes that

> Christianity has not completely replaced the old religious beliefs, for Christian ideals and some of the older spiritual beliefs and cultural practices continue to coexist, especially in the eastern islands. . . . In attempting to wean the Torres Strait Islanders away from pre-Christian music and dance, as practised during cult ceremonies, the LMS missionaries forbad[e] the use of the skim drum (warup) to accompany hymns. (ibid., 46, 55)[7]

"Baba Waiyar" is a well-known kores in the Torres Strait and it is sung in an eastern Torres Strait Island language with vocal harmonies that are common in Torres Strait Islander music, and with Island-style guitar and drum.

"Baba Waiyar" was written by an uncle up in the Islands [the late Miseron Levi] and I was in Canberra when I was recording that album, and I had met up with one of my aunties, and she actually came and played guitar for me, and she taught it to me the Island way but I still sing it the way that I learned it, so that was pretty special, and she asked if I could put it on the album.

Although "Baba Waiyar" is the only identifiably Torres Strait Islander song that Lexine has recorded, she leaves open the possibility and the creative freedom to draw on her Torres Strait Islander heritage in her songs.

I included "Baba Waiyar" on my album This Is Woman *with the Island style of guitar and the drum because it's still a part of my heritage. And I still should be able to have access to it even though I live in the today world.*

"Baba Waiyar" and her own song "I Belong" allow Lexine to express her "Islanderness" and illustrate that an Islander identity can be constructed and maintained through song.

Singing to Connect with Family

I do not profess to have lived a life any harder than the next person. I was seventeen when my mother passed. It was a Saturday morning, a normal day of chores and then without any warning, my mother hemorrhaged. We were all shaken. The breast cancer won. My father stopped coming home from his job on the railway and, as the eldest of seven, eventually I was left alone to raise my siblings. Many times my brothers and sisters have longed to hear stories about themselves to remember things from their childhood, but without parents there is no one to tell us. So one day I got this idea that I could record an album of songs to tell my siblings our story, remember our parents through songs and stories I carried through these years to tell them about "us," that might answer their questions about life. I'm really protective of the recording because it is a journey and a story.

• • •

Lexine emphasizes that one key reason for recording her songs is the preservation of her family's stories for future generations. She states that her album *This Is Woman* was originally written just for her family rather than for a wider audience.

It was never an album to be released . . . it was specifically written for my family so that they could find answers in their lives. . . . It was important that they got to remember, because I think by then, as you know, my parents had died, my mother had been gone twenty years, so it was very important for my family, it was important that I could deliver it to them.

She notes that some of her family members were initially uneasy about her singing about and recording information about their family:

I have been very candid and revealed some home truths—my big brother had some problems with me doing this—but I let them have input into the recording and revealing who we are—because of the women in our "past"—who are really in our lives ah! You know things like a dysfunctional family, like lots of people I suppose, but I decided that I could tackle some of the issues about what mothers expect of others . . . there's lots of history we don't have—it's gone with our parents.

Yet at the same time, it has become an important source of information for her siblings and a way of finding out more about their family history.

I've had my brothers and sisters ring me "oh Lex . . . " they remember something from their childhood and I've said "listen to that song and read what I wrote in the CD notes."

The album opens with a song called "Cut to the Chase" which is about Lexine asking her mother to give her strength to raise her brothers and sisters on her own:

> I know I've done you wrong.
> You died when I was 17.
> Did I turn my back on you?
> To do my own thing.
> But how do I say the words?
> Help me cut to the chase, to speak the words
> I failed you once again.
> My heart is longing to hear you say
> Everything's okay
> Help me cut to the chase.
> How can you love me now you're gone?
> Help me cut to the chase
> So we can carry on.[8]

She explains the meaning of the lyrics in the following way:

Oh well I guess "cut to the chase" is a very "white" saying, meaning "get to the point." All the information about this song that I ever wanted to say is on the album cover, but what I've found is that while I am aging and maturing some of my concepts have aged and matured too. I remember in the early morning after my mother died feeling in my heart, Lord the sun has come up and my mother is dead. Does anyone know how I feel? How we feel? We are just children—please how can we endure this? My siblings didn't understand. That was the end of life as we knew it. "Orphans" was what people called us, and still do.

Singing her songs, and particularly recording her songs, allows Lexine to express her family history and preserve her families' stories for future generations. She uses her songs to document and tell history to her siblings and celebrate important family members, particularly her mother.

Singing to Celebrate Torres Strait Islander Women

Anna Shnukal writes that Torres Strait Islanders are "a minority within a minority and the women a minority again—triply invisible" (1999, 180) and certainly there is very little literature that focuses on the experiences of Torres Strait Islander women in general (e.g., Osborne, 1997; Barnes, 1998). Similarly, Elizabeth Osborne (1997, 2) notes that Torres Strait Islander women's knowledge has been historically "devalued and suppressed," while Torres Strait Islander journalist Rhianna Patrick (2004) notes that the inclusion of an Islander woman's perspective is "something that isn't seen very often at all." Lexine aims to bring the focus on Torres Strait Islander women by singing about their importance in the community.

I wanted to write songs to celebrate women in my family and who they are to us—and why they make us who we are.

"This Is Woman," the title song on her album of the same name, refers to a generic "woman" who "lives, loves, and has purpose," which could connect to any woman, but Lexine notes that it is specifically meant to connect with the Torres Strait Islander women in her own family.

Torres Strait Islander women's roles and their songs are often undervalued. Women are so important to see a family make it through, to be complete. Torres Strait Islander men are still a minority but women are a minority within a minority.

Her comments resonate with McRose Elu's assertion that Torres Strait Islander "women are the keepers of the household, the nurturers and managers of the family. We have a very important position . . . as homemakers, gardeners, food-gatherers, child-bearers and comforters and we play a major role in maintaining social harmony" (2004, 140). Woven throughout the discourse about and by Torres Strait Islander women is a theme of marginalization and the struggles for recognition and identity that Torres Strait Islander women experience. My collaborative research project with Lexine attempts to bring the voices and experiences of Torres Strait Islander women performers to the foreground and to highlight the ways Torres Strait Islander women sing, perform, speak, play, and self-define more diverse and dynamic identities as Indigenous Australian women. Lexine also attempts to celebrate women in her family through song. As Lexine highlights, the song "This Is Woman" also refers to herself.

This is what I can become, the chorus talks about I'm a woman of purpose, I give life, I am loved and I've tried to remain true to that.

Singing for Self: The Sustenance of Song

Lexine and I are sitting in a roadside service station having lunch on the way to Canberra, Australia's capital. We've presented together at a music conference in Newcastle in New South Wales on our research collaborations together interviewing other Torres Strait Islander women singers. We had talked openly about the difficulties, dilemmas, and ethics as well as the benefits of cross-cultural collaborative research. Lexine had sung a Torres Strait Islander welcome at the beginning of the presentation but her voice is now sore and husky.

Lexine clears her voice as we sit together eating a snack before continuing the drive.

It's so frustrating, my voice, losing my voice. I can feel it.

She puts her hand up to her throat.

I don't know if I'm going to be able to sing at the next conference.

"Don't worry if you can't; it doesn't matter," I say, trying to soothe her anxiety. "It must be so frustrating."

You have no idea, I just want it to be better. I've got all these gigs coming up. And not only that, singing at these events and conferences helps me show people who I am. Singing about it is a stronger way of expressing identity for me than just speaking about it.

I take a sip of my coffee and think to myself, singing is so important to Lexine. "Was singing always important to your identity?"

In my twenties even though I was singing, I had no idea I was "a singer." Then when I started to lead songs in a church I knew it was serious. Singing is just sustenance, it just brings you through, you don't believe how it can carry you. I remember I had to sing to the producer and I got through two lines and I just burst into tears . . . when the tears come it breaks it, like water falling on hard ground, and all of a sudden it is fallow ground, it's all just broken up and something can grow out of it. I just felt a great relief that day.

• • •

Lexine Solomon sings for many reasons. The overarching motive is for both connection and celebration: connection with the Torres Strait Islands as an Islander woman born and raised on the mainland; connection with family, and particularly siblings whom she raised as a result of her mother passing away; and celebration of Torres Strait Islander women who have been historically marginalized. She also sings for herself.

No matter what happens to me, despite whatever adversity I face and rejection I experience, I still have song.

She chooses to release her albums independently with the assistance of Commonwealth or state government funding. While this could be read as marginalization of a Torres Strait Islander woman by the music industry, she asserts that she consciously chooses not to release her songs through major record companies in order to retain artistic control over her sound. She manages her own music career and sells her albums herself directly to audiences at her performances. Torres Strait Islanders living all across Australia, including those in the Islands themselves, buy her CDs, as well as non-Indigenous people who see her perform and run workshops at festivals such as the Dreaming Festival of Indigenous Performance. She is well known within the Indigenous community in Australia, performing at community events such as annual National Aboriginal and Torres Strait Islander Day of Celebration (NAIDOC) events.

Our relationship over the years has grown into a strong friendship as we have undertaken research, traveled, presented, and written together and I continue to be amazed by her singing voice and her life experiences as a Torres Strait Islander woman. Her guest lectures and workshops in courses I've taught at The University of Queensland to (mostly non-Indigenous) students gives them an opportunity to hear about the voiced experiences and contemporary songs of a Torres Strait Islander woman and enter into a dialogue about a wide range of issues facing Torres Strait Islander women on the mainland. Lexine is part of the diasporic population of approximately two-thirds of all Islanders "separated by time, place and situation from their origins" (Lawe Davies and Neuenfeldt, 2004, 137). Yet like other mainland-born Torres Strait Islanders, it remains essential to Lexine to maintain connections with the Torres Strait Islands. She uses her songs to celebrate and make ties with the Torres Strait and affirm for other mainland Torres Strait Islanders that constructing an Islander identity is possible and can be lived out through song. As Helen Reeves Lawrence notes, "wherever Islanders live—whether on the home islands or in mainland cities—they express their culture and identity through music" (1998, 4). Singing remains a key platform for Lexine to maintain and sustain her identity and celebrate proudly and loudly that "this is woman, and she loves, lives and believes" in herself and in the importance of her fellow Torres Strait Islander women.

Acknowledgments

Thank you to Lexine for your continuing friendship, research collaborations, and lots of laughs.

Notes

1. In the Australian context, it is accepted practice that the first letter of Indigenous is capitalized. Not doing this is regarded by many Aboriginal and Torres Strait Islander people as being "racist, offensive and belittling, a way of negating our identity and nationality and can be similar to misspelling a person's name (gail or dianne) or another country name (chinese, european) by not capitalising" (Huggins 1994, 14; see also Heiss 2002).

2. See Ottosson (2007) for more information on CAAMA.

3. From 2007–10 Lexine and I worked together on the Australian Institute of Aboriginal and Torres Strait Islander Studies funded project "Performing on the Margins: Torres Strait Islander Women Performers." For further information in the project see Barney and Solomon, 2009a,b, 2010.

4. See Barney and Solomon, 2009a,b.

5. Copyright Lexine Solomon. Permission given to reproduce lyrics.

6. Copyright Lexine Solomon. Permission given to reproduce lyrics.

7. See Lawrence 2004 for more information about the influence of Christianity in the Torres Strait.

8. Copyright Lexine Solomon. Permission given to reproduce lyrics.

References

Australian Bureau of Statistics. 2006. *Census*. Canberra: Australian Government Printing Service.

Barnes, Ketrina. 1998. "Torres Strait Islander Women." *Australian Journal of Indigenous Education* 26(1):25–30.

Barney, Katelyn, and Lexine Solomon. 2009a. "Looking into the Trochus Shell: Autoethnographic Reflections on a Cross-Cultural Collaborative Music Research Project." In *Musical Autoethnographies: Making Autoethnography Sing/Making Music Personal*, eds. Brydie-Leigh Bartleet and Carolyn Ellis, 208–24. Bowen Hills, Qld.: Australian Academic Press.

———. 2009b. "'The Memories Linger On, but the Stories Tell Me Who I Am': A Conversation between an Indigenous Australian Performer and a Non-Indigenous Australian Music Researcher." In *Musical Islands: Exploring Connections between Music, Place and Research*, eds. Elizabeth Mackinlay, Brydie-Leigh Bartleet, and Katelyn Barney, 70–93. Newcastle: Cambridge Scholars Publishing.

———. 2010. *Performing on the Margins: Conversations with Torres Strait Islander Women about Music*. St. Lucia, Qld.: Aboriginal and Torres Strait Islander Studies Unit.

Beckett, Jeremy. 2004. "Writing about Islanders: Recent Research and Future Directions."

In *Woven Histories, Dancing Lives: Torres Strait Islander Identity, Culture and History*, ed. Richard Davis, 2–14. Canberra: Australian Aboriginal Studies.

Diamond, Beverley, and Pirrko Moisala. 2000. "Music and Gender: Negotiating Shifting Worlds." In *Music and Gender*, eds. Pirrko Moisala and Beverley Diamond, 1–19. Urbana: University of Illinois Press.

Ellis, Carolyn. 1998. "What Counts as Scholarship in Communication? Autoethnographic Responses." *American Communication Journal* 1(2):1–5.

Elu, McRose. 2004. "Cooking, Walking, and Talking Cosmology: An Islander Woman's Perspective of Religion." In *Woven Histories Dancing Lives: Torres Strait Islander Identity, Culture and History*, ed. Richard Davis, 140–50. Canberra: Australian Aboriginal Studies.

Heiss, Anita. 2002. "Writing about Indigenous Australia—Some Issues to Consider and Protocols to Follow: A Discussion Paper." *Southerly* 62(2)(Summer):197–206.

Huggins, Jackie. 1994. "Respect vs Political Correctness." *Australian Author* 26 (3):12–14.

Huggins, Rita, and Jackie Huggins. 1994. *Aunty Rita*. Canberra: Aboriginal Studies Press.

Humphreys, Michael. 2005. "Getting Personal: Reflexivity and Autoethnographic Vignettes." *Qualitative Inquiry* 11(6):840–60.

Lawe Davies, Chris, and Karl Neuenfeldt. 2004. "Mainland Torres Strait Islander Songwriters and the 'Magical Islands' of the Torres Strait: Song as Identity Narrative." In *Island Musics*, ed. Kevin Dawes, 137–51. London: Berg Publishers.

Lawrence, Helen Reeves. 1998. "'Bethlehem' in Torres Strait: Music, Dance and Christianity in Erub (Darnley Island)." *Australian Aboriginal Studies* 2:51–63.

———. 2004. "'The Great Traffic in Tunes': Agents of Religious and Musical Change in Eastern Torres Strait." In *Woven Histories Dancing Lives: Torres Strait Islander Identity, Culture and History*, ed. Richard Davis, 46–73. Canberra: Australian Aboriginal Studies.

Neuenfeldt, Karl. 2008. "Ailan Style: An Overview of the Contemporary Music of Torres Strait Islanders." In *Sounds of Then, Sounds of Now: Popular Music in Australia*, eds. Shane Homan and Tony Mitchell, 167–80. Tasmania: ACYS Publishing.

Osborne, Elizabeth. 1997. *Torres Strait Islander Women and the Pacific War*. Canberra: Aboriginal Studies Press.

Ottosson, Ase. 2007. "'We're Just Bush Mob': Producing Aboriginal Music and Maleness in a Central Australian Recording Studio." *World of Music* 1:83–104.

Patrick, Rhianna. 2004. "Review of *Woven Histories Dancing Lives: Torres Strait Islander Identity, Culture and History*." http://www.abc.net.au/message/blackarts/review/s1152746.htm (accessed March 2004).

Shnukal, Anna. 1999. "Review of *Torres Strait Islander Women and the Pacific War*." *Journal of Australian Studies* (March):180.

Discography

Solomon, Lexine. 2002 *This Is Woman*. Lexine Solomon, LS1000.

———. 2006. *Strike a Pose*. Lexine Solomon, LS2000.

7. Marysia's Voice

Defining Home through Song in Poland and Canada

LOUISE WRAZEN

"Who am I?" "What kind of person am I?" Marysia is prompted to ask herself when explaining the contemplative process that contributes to her creativity as a singer. She reflects that she needs to stand—to stop—and think about her current life before being able to effectively capture it in her songs. Rather than implying any misgiving about her own identity, however, such provocative self-questioning reveals a self-conscious and deliberate consideration of her current life in Canada as opposed to her past in Poland. In fact, Marysia is confident in who she is, on the one hand drawing on her strong roots to proclaim that she remains Górale[1] (or Highlander; from the Podhale region of southern Poland) with her entire being, and on the other remaining secure in an assured womanhood founded on years of active motherhood and happy marriage. In this chapter I explore the ways in which Marysia's fundamental question has informed her vocality across migration and its contingent memories to locate her unequivocally in today's world. In using the word *vocality* here, I include what Dunn and Jones have identified as "the performative dimension of vocal expression, that is . . . the dynamic, contingent quality of both vocalization and audition" (1994, 2). In doing so, I consider primarily the "literal, audible voice" (ibid., 1) as the site of potential agency, even while taking as my point of departure a silence that has been associated with broader concepts of the voice denied, as derived from its use as a metaphor in feminist discourse (Bernstein 2004, 4).

This introduction to Marysia addresses the silence of the story often left untold, and reflects on the extent to which the individual woman's voice may have been lost within a discourse surrounding globally mediated sounds. Within these stories unwritten or unheard, the musical experiences of women whose self-identity revolves explicitly around their maternity and homes remain particularly well masked (see also O'Reilly 2007). This chapter, therefore, is a response to silence: the first is that of those local stories of women (and mothers) untold; the second is that which characterizes an anonymity that can result from dislocation to a new home; and the third is that of the absence of the singing voice from the resonant contours of a landscape left behind. The story of Maria (Marysia) Mąka here overtakes these three silences: as a talented yet only locally known singer, Marysia's singing voice has remained remarkably active ever since moving from Podhale, Poland, to the Toronto area of Canada, where it has helped her to define a home for herself, her husband, and her twelve children. Under demanding circumstances where it would be all too easy to become overwhelmed into musical silence, or to remain defined primarily through her role as a mother, Marysia's resounding singing voice and musical energy have assured her a much broader personal identity.

As an individual reflection in a larger volume devoted to women singing in global contexts, this chapter continues to explore the musical voice in its resolute local distinctiveness. Although mindful of Dunn and Jones's theoretical differentiation between vocality and voice, my concern here is less to develop a "conception of vocality as a cultural construct" (1994, 2)—compelling though it is in relation to Górale singing—than to explore the emergence and agency of Marysia's singing voice through the particularity of her experiences. While linguists may define the concept of voice as "the linguistic construction of social personae, [that] addresses the question 'Who is speaking?'" (Keane 2000, 271), this paper considers the musical construction of the social persona and revolves around the question "Who is singing?" This arises quite naturally from Marysia's opening question "Who am I?" since the potentially emergent and subjective state of being (or becoming), implicit in Marysia's question when confronting herself in the current moment, contributes to any ongoing (re)formulations of herself as a singer—forming an ongoing dialectic.

As an exploration of one individual's musical responses to some of the vicissitudes and challenges of daily life, this discussion responds to an agenda built on the value of exploring the diversity of women's lived experience (Wolf 1992, 118; see also Doubleday 1988; Mack 2004; Wrazen 2007). The challenges of adequately representing the individual remain problematic, as explicitly illustrated in the writing of Diamond (2000), Koskoff (1993), and Rice (1994, 9–12). Drawing on my time spent with Marysia over several years, I have constructed a narrative that rarely uses direct quotes, even though Marysia's words have guided my writing as it explores a number of themes here.[2] These themes are articulated by specific song texts, significant to Marysia in some way, organized in a manner that belies continuous narrative sequence. In this way, they are intended to correspond to the nature of singing by Górale in Podhale, which is characterized by short songs that may be initiated (in principle) by anyone present. An initial incipit-like opening by a soloist is taken up by anyone else who wants to join in the singing on a lower part. As the three short phrases of one song are finished, another song can emerge from elsewhere in the crowd of a room or landscape. The result constructs a sonorous quilt of self-contained musical/textual vignettes of no predictable order or certain conclusion, entirely dependent on the performative inspiration of those present. The four segments of the subsequent sequence, which consider themes of encounter, creativity, displacement, and home, are not presented, therefore, as though the lines of a consistently woven narrative, but rather as largely self-contained verses in an (ongoing) lyric episode intended to explore individual subjectivities and musical experiences. These are also not unlike the fragments of conversation from which they are sometimes drawn, culled from times often interrupted by the needs of a small child or household matter requiring immediate attention.

1) Encounters and Withdrawals

Hej poco ześ tu przysła,	Hey why did you come here
siwo mgła siwo mgła;	grey fog grey fog;
Hej tyź mi do wirsycka,	Hey you've hidden the road
chodnicek zaległa.	to the small hill from me.[3]

This text was the first sung to me by Marysia and her ensemble during a rehearsal after I met her in 1985. She may well have been wondering why I had "come there" at the time, in this way accessing potentially personal feelings in the opening before moving to the poetic images of a familiar landscape in the closing. At the time, Marysia (born in 1963) was twenty-two, with two children and pregnant with her third (figure 7.1). Despite trying to farm an inhospitable piece of land in the village of Stare Bystre in the northern area of Podhale (the southernmost region of Poland on the fringes of the Tatra Mountains) and building a new home, Marysia and her husband Jasiek coordinated and taught the local song and dance troupe for the area. During this era of the communist-led government in Poland, the formation of ensembles was encouraged in the region, and the pay provided to Jasiek (as leader) offered a valuable supplement to an otherwise meager income. The daughter of a well-known village fiddler, Marysia grew up with music around her and continued to make it an active part of her life, singing for special occasions at church as well as performing and teaching in the ensemble. She lived on the family plot with her family—her father having moved to Canada with her two younger siblings to join Marysia's mother several years earlier. Despite living in an isolated enclave of homes on the crest of a hill accessible only by crossing a potentially treacherous river on a precariously narrow, long log, Marysia regularly journeyed to the local community center to sing and practice with the local youth (often with her children). Having heard about her singing from her father, I first recorded her while at one of these rehearsals.

Where poetics may personalize the relationship between the known and the unknown in this text in a way that made me pause to retrospectively reflect on its possible significance, it was the physicality of Marysia's voice that ultimately rendered this song intimate and personal. Sung in a hearty and resonant chest timbre uninhibited by any restrictions of place, Marysia's

Figure 7.1. Marysia and two of her children, Peter and Anna, in Podhale, Poland, 1989. Photograph by Louise Wrazen.

voice located her unequivocally as being of this region, where singing voices could be resplendent among the acoustics of the outdoor expanses of hills and valleys. The singing voice is here produced with the intent to engage with its surrounding landscape—the physicality of the sound embedding itself in the contours of the land to offer the chance to extend and echo beyond the immediately audible. Where this sonically expansive gesture is able to generate an intimacy between singer and landscape, it can also draw the attentive listener into a visceral response to the physicality and grain of this voice (Barthes 1988). Standing close to her as she sang, Marysia's voice reached me as it might have entered an expansive landscape and, when combined with her deeply personal engagement with the singing, created a sense of intimate connection that has stayed with me ever since.

Marysia's family had grown to five children by the time I returned to Podhale in 1989. Quickly outgrowing their tiny two-room home, she and her husband were trying to finish building a new house. Frequently cooking for a group of about ten workers in addition to caring for her own family when I was there, Marysia continued to enjoy singing and teaching others to sing. On several notable occasions, a group of five or more young girls came to sing with her. Despite tight quarters, frequent interruptions, and ongoing examples of multitasking stretched to new limits, Marysia patiently and expertly guided them through their repertoire. Opening her home to these girls (as well as to me), even in the midst of a domestic life challenging in its demands on her, Marysia shared her small kitchen as well as generous voice with us all. It was also here that she and her husband sang for me, so that I might record her singing for her father. Ongoing economic hardships combined with the changing politics of Poland in subsequent years led Marysia to move to Canada in 1992, following her husband, who had left in 1990. Their home in Stare Bystre remains unfinished, though in Canada, where they now live just outside of Toronto, their family has grown to twelve children.

2) Public Intimacies and the Creative Process

Regle moje regle,	Small hills my hills,
ukochane regle;	Beloved hills;
Kie jo se zaśpiywom,	When I sing,
to se mi łozlegnie.	my voice will extend/echo.

When in her twenties, Marysia spoke of both tunes and texts as though developing a personal relationship with them. Though tunes and texts are interchangeable in Podhale, Marysia explained how she would learn a new tune by singing it with a single text until she became fully accustomed to it.

Similarly, she contemplated the words intensely when singing. For example, when singing of *regle* (small hills), as in the above text that she sang to me, she would let the words ring out through her voice in a manner befitting their evocative quality. In so doing she would strive to create some of the acoustic resonance that a voice might achieve when actually singing amid such hills. Poetics, therefore, here assist the performer in vocally inscribing the acoustic implications of the landscape mentioned in the text onto the performance itself—wherever it might be performed. In contrast, Marysia admitted that she might sing other texts more provocatively. Through the public use of her voice in performance, the singer, therefore, is effectively inviting others to participate in this, her more personal, vision of the world. Insofar as the concept of intimacy can be understood most broadly as a very special sort of knowing[4] among persons, that (as a corollary) requires a very special sort of sharing, the voice here serves as an invitation to intimacy, enjoining the listener into the possibility of a special relationship with the singer. Its strong viscerality and association with poetics allow it to serve this role particularly well (Barthes 1988, 2008 [1985]).

This deliberate manipulation of her voice and feelingful association with the poetics of song have remained with Marysia. Now in her forties, she has continued to nurture this vocal and poetic sensitivity to the extent that she has become increasingly active in composing. Most frequently, Marysia composes new texts to known tunes, and often does this for special occasions. She laughs when she admits that when a special occasion arises, people now frequently expect her to have composed something new to sing for the event. As she explains it, she composes within a contemplative process in which she is aware of asking herself three main questions. First, she asks "Where am I?" In doing so, she is aware of deliberately positioning herself within a present, rather than a past, reality. Although she roots herself musically within the structures of music-making from Podhale (including tunes, polyphonic singing style, vocal timbre), she strives to orient her texts to the current world that her children know in Canada—as opposed to that which she and others may remember from Poland. Second, she asks "What would I like to change?" Insofar as she even asks such a question, she views her role as having great potential influence. Music links people, she advised me. As one able to touch others with this music, she therefore occupies a position of strength insofar as she is able to participate in instigating changes. Where life may be difficult or challenging, she wonders what she can do to help. Not only does she speak of framing a broader relevance for her own children, but of helping others who may be at a loss (for reasons of unemployment or alcohol, for example). Significantly, her optimism for the possibilities inherent in this position overrides any feelings of insecurity that she might otherwise have as a relatively new participant in a foreign country.

Third, Marysia asks herself how the world feels—that is, how do people feel. In framing this question, she seeks to understand the current mood in the world around her, and the human experience within it. In trying to feel the pulse of human emotion around her, with the possibility of helping to change it if necessary (question 2), she approaches composing not unlike motherhood: if a baby is hungry, she feeds it; if a child has a fever, she seeks to guide it to health. Therefore, Marysia's role as the empathetic nurturer, arising so naturally out of her long experience of motherhood, here also compellingly guides her approach to composition.

3) Private Certainty and Diasporic Memory

Hej bedym jo se śpiywoł,	Hey in the Górale style I will sing,
hej po góralsku chodzeł;	hey in the Górale style walk;
Hej choć jek sie nie w Tatrak,	Hey even though not in the Tatras,
hej ba w Kanadzie rodził.	but in Canada born.
Hej bo se w mojej piersi,	Hey because in my breast,
hej serce łojców bije;	hey the heart of my parents beats;
Hej i tam se nucicka,	Hey and there the melody/tune,
hej starodowno zyje.	hey [that's] old-fashioned lives.

Marysia actively perpetuates her regional Górale roots both inside and outside her home. The strong local identity associated with the Tatra Mountains and Podhale (with its distinctive dialect, material, and expressive culture), has long animated Górale both in Poland and abroad, as well as contributing to a broader nationalist discourse (Cooley 2005; Wrazen 2008). Górale have no difficulty in understanding who they are, Marysia suggests. Maintaining Górale traditions is not optional for her, but the result of an inner need or compulsion rather than a conscious choice. Such sentiments are inflected not only with Marysia's strong sense of regionalism and responsibility, but also with a clarity of purpose that is driven by a confident and personal self-awareness. This locally derived identity is foundational for Marysia and provides her with a self-assurance that is sustaining even amid some of the uncertainties and contradictions that she experiences in raising her children in their Canadian surroundings.

Together with her husband, Marysia nurtures a family life built on traditional values now carried into new settings. A strong belief system revolving around the structures of the Roman Catholic Church is fundamental. Sundays, holidays, and special feast days, including those particularly noted in

Poland if not in Canada, continue to guide their family's life; these are often marked in their parish by Górale music that includes Marysia's singing—frequently of her own compositions. Nature and rural ways also continue to guide their lives. Despite now living within the boundaries of a quickly expanding greater Toronto area marked by urban development, Marysia and Jasiek have settled into a home on a road that remains relatively secluded. As a self-employed builder, Jasiek has worked to expand this home to meet the growing demands of their family. They also own property outside the city where they plant a large garden and frequently go to provide some freedom for their children to run around, and to offer Marysia some respite.

Ongoing and active engagement with a larger community of Górale has included providing opportunities for their children to experience the traditional music and dance of Podhale here. Over the years, Marysia and Jasiek have initiated a number of different local ensembles, with Marysia teaching singing and her husband teaching dancing. She has explained that her confidence in her own Górale identity leads her to want to spread this among others. The text that opens this section, composed by Marysia for the occasion of a Canadian visit by Cardinal Stanisław Dziwisz in 2008, proudly locates the young people singing and performing as now effectively bridging two realities that contribute to their emerging identities. As distinct from most Polish ensembles, Marysia focuses exclusively on the Podhale region with her members. This is not about changing costumes, she explains rather dismissively when comparing what she wants to do with other performing ensembles of young people, who present medleys from a variety of regions of Poland. When organizing any ensemble or performance, she believes in the need to begin with the music (that is, the string ensemble of fiddles and *basy* (three-string cello-like instrument) that is characteristic of Podhale), not with the dancers. In this way, she deliberately wants her ensemble to be different, even though she admits that it may be more modest in other ways.

In particular, Marysia wants it to be authentic. Her aim of including stories and spoken texts that represent a larger segment of life in performances would assist in creating a sense of authentic culture in the children, she suggests. This authenticity, therefore, is not defined by Marysia in reference to codified performance practices that might serve as criteria for evaluation—such as found, for example, at some of the festivals in which ensembles may participate (Cooley 1999; Wrazen 2005). Rather it derives from the immediacy of deeply felt personal experience. She strives, therefore, to assist in recreating this total experience for the children both inside and outside the performance arena. Marysia is eloquent when she describes that she wants the children themselves to feel what is deep within them; the authenticity of this Górale experience does not reside in the act of performing or playing, she maintains, but in the very state of being. In this way she brings the certainty of her own understanding of herself, and her past, to influence the growth and future of the children around her, whether her own or those of fellow Górale who may be less committed to this process.

4) Creating a Voice Away from Home

Choć Kanada inna,	Even though Canada is different,
kraj casem nie ludzki;	the country sometimes not inhabitable;
Ale tutok z nami,	but here with us,
przysły nase bucki.	came our trees.
Morskie Oko wieksze,	The great lake (Lake Ontario)[5] is larger,
drzewa szlachetniejsze;	the trees are more noble;
Ziym urodzaniejsza,	the land is more fertile,
Jagody ładniejsze.	the berries are nicer.

The relevance and vibrancy of culture as lived tradition as opposed to imposed construct animates Marysia's creative energies. Her conception of culture (*kultura*) links it as integral to the experience of life. In Podhale, she recalls that people worked and sang as though everything went naturally together. Now, she fears that culture is imposed by the media to encourage a style of clothes, makeup, or behavior. In her effort to protect her children from what she regards as this artificial construct, she seeks to broaden the range of options available to them, as well as others, through her musical activities, in this way assisting each person to recognize who they are—just as she is certain of who she is. With her strong underlying musicality and uninhibited vocality firmly rooted in her Górale origins, Marysia continues to explore her voice with this in mind, now deliberately reorienting it to the contours of the Canadian life experiences of those around her. To this end, she deliberately considers her subject position—both as a performer before an audience, and as a Górale singing in Canada.

As the performing context of a natural landscape is now supplanted by that of an attentive audience, performance dynamics also obviously change. Marysia has developed a particular sensitivity to performing for others in Canada. When preparing a program for performance, she imagines herself in the position of an audience member and asks herself how she would feel watching what is being performed. Raised on ensemble performances structured in a predictable sequence of solo/dance/singing (her summary) that continue to flourish both in homeland and in diaspora, Marysia tries to think of different options for her performances, often around a central narrative that includes poetry. She believes that she has a natural sensitivity to what an audience might want to see—in particular one that has already seen numerous performances structured around the usual sequence of songs and dances. She also wants to establish a connection with the audience that is based on the present. These concerns find their way into the composition of specific texts as well as in longer episodes that she conceives for performance. In rewriting the story of the Nativity, for example, she sought to explore some of the human emotions that could be associated with a story so well known and yet often told in a formulaic manner. Using known tunes, she composed a narrative based on some poetic recitations and a variety of Górale tunes. With several of her own family members participating in the performances, her version aimed to stress the intimacy of motherhood and infant life in a manner that might reach both audience members and her own children. And so, for example, she sang the following (drawing concisely on her own maternal experiences):

Synku mój malućki,	Son, my little one,
pociesynie moje;	joy of mine;
widzem zapłakane,	I see tear-filled,
ślicne łocka twoje.	your lovely little eyes.

More recently, Marysia has been exploring the possibility of rewriting the story of Janosik (born Juraj Jánošík 1688–1713), transposing the legendary Robin Hood–type brigand from the Tatras to North America, where he would address moral issues related to how to live a good life (addressing drugs and violence, for example), rather than fight against physical and economic oppression as he is said to have done in the eighteenth century. Much of this seems to be written, at least in her mind, though it is not certain when she will find the time and commitment from others necessary to see this ambitious project through to its performance.

Life in Canada provides a distinctive framework for Marysia—one that she chooses not to ignore in her creative life. She states explicitly, for example, that she does not like to sing about what is not there. To this end, she questions what relevance some of the older song texts can have to those who have never been to Podhale, wondering how anyone can sing about sheep if they have never seen any. Further to her belief that culture is integral to lived experience and that it should help one to live better, Marysia wants to ensure that song texts have relevance to those now singing them here. Her own compositions reveal that she fully understands how these traditional songs capture the everyday in their texts while also poetically addressing the more broadly universal and compelling. But where these have been defined by trees and mountains, sheep and shepherds in Podhale, the reality in Canada requires a different poetic vocabulary, which she is eagerly exploring. This commitment to reorient poetics through images more germane to the experiences of Górale now living outside Podhale suggests a progressive attitude that is not necessarily shared by others. She recalls that when explaining to a friend how important it is to compose texts that would be of relevance to those participating in Canada, he responded with some skepticism, wondering aloud what he might write about—going to a bank machine? In contrast, she questions why those here should always be singing about shepherds when there are more common frames of reference beyond the mundane, like birds singing and love.

The poetic content of Marysia's songs, therefore, aims to locate her singing voice compellingly in today's world. Just as the timbral resonance of her voice may draw others into the intimate acoustic presence of her singing, her texts seek to refer listeners to their current experiences. Where others may become preoccupied with the vast differences between modern life in a global age and the pastoral lifestyle of a time past, and relish in nostalgia or folkloric authenticities, Marysia understands the value of embracing the present. She has no patience for nostalgia, claiming that it is equivalent to an illness that prevents people from fully appreciating the current possibilities around them. Marysia has full confidence in her life here despite its hardships. This is reflected in the song that she wrote in honor of Pope John Paul II's visit to Canada in 2002. Two verses from this longer strophic song open this section: although the first opens with a sobering realization, it continues more optimistically by searching for the familiar and recognizing the ongoing presence of trees so beloved (even if not mountains) in this new land; and it concludes with a strong affirmation of the numerous merits (presented even as advantages) of this new home. Raising a growing family without a solid knowledge of English under uncertain financial circumstances in a foreign country has not diminished the steadfast resilience and energy that I recognized in Marysia in Podhale. Remembering her cramped kitchen in the small isolated house on the far side of the river in Stare Bystre and marking her determination even then, I'm not surprised by her current optimism or tenacity. Life is better here according to Marysia—even the blueberries are bigger! This is the new home that she now claims, and that she also strives to reflect in her singing (figure 7.2).

A naturally outgoing manner also assists Marysia in finding new places for her voice. Despite restrictions placed on her by her children, she enjoys those parties and occasions where musical conviviality is socially embedded.

Figure 7.2. Marysia singing with her husband, Jasiek (on her left), and Bolek Mąka (on her right), with Józef Siuty accompanying in the background, in Brampton, Ontario, Canada, 2008. Photograph by Louise Wrazen.

At a recent St. Andrew's Day party Marysia's voice animated the evening, first in some unaccompanied polyphonic singing around supper and then as accompanied by the string band that played for some general dancing after the meal. On another occasion, Marysia organized her family and friends to perform at a larger celebration of multiculturalism, where they provided an informal welcome to arriving guests with their music and dance. She coordinated the performances and sang exuberantly with the band while others listened or danced. Such occasions not only illustrate how Marysia engages others meaningfully through her singing and confirm the performative vitality of her vocality, but they also assert her vocal presence in a larger public space. Although she has sought to embrace a broader conception of poetic relevance through a distinctive compositional voice, her singing also has provided Marysia with a valuable entry into a broader social and musical world. Easily defined by her robust maternity, Marysia's self-assured public vocality extends her beyond the potentially confining isolation of motherhood to assert a more broadly defined womanhood.

Closing Reflections

This chapter arose as a direct response to the challenge posed by Ellen Kos-koff to "put real people and the truth of their musical lives back into the picture" (2005, 98) that has contextualized this entire volume (as already articulated in the editor's introduction). The value of relating music to real lives is similarly promoted by Suzanne Cusick when she notes that feminist musicologies "provide a theoretical legitimacy for reconnecting 'the music itself' with the fabric of human life. Thus, feminist musicologies provide an opening for us to rethink music as something that matters—and matters very much—to "'real' life" (2001 [1999], 498).

In turning to the local, the specific, and the individually meaningful, I have focused on the musical life of a woman who forms no part of a broader global, national, or even regional musical presence (in contrast to some of the other chapters in this volume). Marysia's life revolves very much around her home, family, and narrow local community. As consistent with this volume, for Marysia the intimacy of a rich home life intersects con-spicuously with an active community-based public presence in her singing voice—through which her womanhood as circumscribed by her roles of daughter, wife, teacher, artist, and mother converge. While Marysia has admitted that it is very difficult being a mother because of the need to give so much of herself—you have to *"give of your heart"*—this very generosity and potential intimacy similarly guide her vocality. Combining its strong natural timbral resonance with an ongoing poetic and musical sensitivity, Marysia explicitly and consistently engages her voice to reach others. Her generous vocality creates, elaborates, and sustains a variety of relation-ships (between past and present; performer and musical-poetic text; and herself and others) in ways that offer memorable lessons in compassion and optimism even while it also asserts her own acoustic presence onto a new landscape. While transnational structures of corporate power may influ-ence the musical marketplace to swell arenas and concert halls with adoring fans, it is often a more intimate single voice that remains most compelling in individual memory. As Barthes has suggested, the voice is the privileged site of difference: "there is no neutral voice" (2008, 80). This chapter asserts the ongoing significance of the musical, gendered voice in constructing spaces of comfort, opportunities for agency, and markers of resilience in times of hardship and change. Within the larger global construct of musical exchanges and influences, it remains particularly important, therefore, for us to continue to address the fundamental question of who is singing.

Notes

1. I adopt the plural "Górale" as both noun and adjective, singular and plural, masculine and feminine, in an effort to avoid the complexities of declensions and also as a way to promote gender-neutral designations.

2. Much of my time with Marysia has been in informal conversation. My research with her began in Podhale in the summer of 1985, continuing in 1989, with more intensive research in Canada beginning in 2007. Opportunities to observe Marysia perform included a church holiday (*odpust*) on September 9, 2007; Górale party (*Andrzejki*) on November 29, 2008; Górale Christmas party (*Opłatek*) on January 7, 2009; multicultural citywide festival (Carabram) on July 11, 2009. During this period I also visited Marysia in her home and had numerous phone conversations with her. I thank her for her kindness and generosity.

3. Translations of song texts are my own and tend toward a literal translation, thereby hardly doing justice to the poetic quality of these evocative texts (though an even more literal rendering of the final two lines of this text would read: "Hey, you've for me to the small hill the road hidden").

4. Although Lynn Jamieson (1998, 1) defines intimacy as "a very specific sort of knowing, loving and 'being close to' another person," John Scott and Gordon Marshall ("intimacy," *A Dictionary of Sociology*, John Scott and Gordon Marshall. Oxford University Press, 2009, *Oxford Reference Online* (accessed March 2012)) replace her word "specific" with "special" when citing her work—a change that is important for the purposes of this discussion.

5. Although Marysia explicitly mentions Morskie Oko (a famous lake in the Tatras), she explains that she is actually creating a reference to Lake Ontario.

References

Barthes, Roland. 1988. "The Grain of the Voice." In *Image, Music Text*. Essays selected and translated by Stephen Heath, 179–89. New York: The Noonday Press.

———. 2008 [1985]. "Music, Voice, Language." In *Music, Words and Voice: A Reader*, ed. Martin Clayton, 79–84. Manchester: Manchester University Press.

Bernstein, Jane A. 2004. *Women's Voices across Musical Worlds*. Boston: Northeastern University Press.

Cooley, Timothy J. 1999. "Folk Festival as Modern Ritual in the Polish Tatra Mountains." *World of Music* 41(3):31–55.

———. 2005. *Making Music in the Polish Tatras: Tourists, Ethnographers, and Mountain Musicians*. Bloomington: Indiana University Press.

Cusick, Suzanne. 2001 [1999]. "Gender, Musicology, and Feminism," In *Rethinking Music*, eds. Nicholas Cook and Mark Everist, 471–98. New York: Oxford.

Diamond, Beverley. 2000. "The Interpretation of Gender Issues in Musical Life Stories of Prince Edward Islanders." In *Music and Gender*, eds. Pirkko Moisala and Beverley Diamond, 99–139. Urbana: University of Illinois Press.

Doubleday, Veronica. 1988. *Three Women of Herat*. London: Jonathan Cape.

Dunn, Leslie C., and Nancy A. Jones. 1994. "Introduction." In *Embodied Voices: Representing Female Vocality in Western Culture*, eds. Leslie C. Dunn and Nancy A. Jones, 1–13. Cambridge: Cambridge University Press.

Jamieson, Lynn. 1998. *Intimacy: Personal Relationships in Modern Societies*. Cambridge: Polity Press.

Keane, Webb. 2000. "Voice." *Journal of Linguistic Anthropology* 9(1–2):271–73.

Koskoff, Ellen. 1993. "Miriam Sings Her Song: The Self and the Other in Anthropological Discourse." In *Musicology and Difference: Gender and Sexuality in Music Scholarship*, ed. Ruth A. Solie, 149–63. Berkeley: University of California Press.

———. 2005. "(Left *Out in*) *Left* (the *Field*): The Effects of Post-postmodern Scholarship on Feminist and Gender Studies in Musicology and Ethnomusicology, 1990–2000." *Women and Music* 9:90–98.

Mack, Beverley B. 2004. *Muslim Women Sing: Hausa Popular Song*. Bloomington: Indiana University Press.

O'Reilly, Andrea, ed. 2007. *Maternal Theory: Essential Readings*. Toronto: Demeter Press.

Rice, Timothy. 1994. *May It Fill Your Soul: Experiencing Bulgarian Music*. Chicago: University of Chicago Press.

Wolf, Margery. 1992. *A Thrice-Told Tale: Feminism, Postmodernism and Ethnographic Responsibility*. Stanford: Stanford University Press.

Wrazen, Louise. 2005. "Diasporic Experiences: Mediating Time, Memory and Identity in Górale Performance." *Canadian Journal for Traditional Music* 32:43–51.

———. 2007. "A Singer and Her Voice: Creating a Place of Her Own in the Polish Tatras." Unpublished paper presented at the ICTM conference, Vienna.

———. 2008. "Beyond the Polish Tatras: Performing Pride, Identity, Difference?" In *The Human World and Musical Diversity*. Proceedings from the Fourth Meeting of the ICTM Study Group "Music and Minorities" in Varna, Bulgaria, 2006, eds. R. Statelova, A. Rodel, L. Peycheva, I. Vlaeva, and V. Dimov, 231–37. Sofia: Institute of Art Studies.

8. Sathima Bea Benjamin

Musical Echoes and the Poetics of a South African–American Musical Self

CAROL MULLER

Ellington said when he brought me here, "You have the greatest gift
of all, the gift of imagination because if you can imagine things,
the sky is the limit in jazz and in life itself. . . . When you sing for
instance you are not just using your voice, you are using your
whole reaction to life, and jazz allows you to do that."
—Sathima Bea Benjamin March 16, 1990

In 2002, several years after receiving the words and melody of "Musical
Echoes" in a dream, South African born jazz singer, Sathima Bea Benjamin
traveled from New York City to Cape Town to record the song and produce
a CD of the same name. Her trio included American Steven Scott on piano,
South Africans Lulu Gontsana on drums, and Basil Moses on bass. My point
of entry to her life and music is the cover of the *Musical Echoes* recording, a
color photograph of Sathima at home, alone at the edge of the Atlantic Ocean
in Cape Town as the sun begins to rise. Sathima's name and the disc title
are italicized silver lines in the clouds. Her trio has no visual counterpart:
their names are inscribed on the right side of the image. Sathima stands to
the left of the frame, facing right, staring outward to the expansiveness of
the ocean, an ocean that eventually connects her to the Americas, her other
home. Her hands are clasped at her breast, layers of white chiffon envelop
her small frame, and an opaque shawl hugs her upper torso. She is barefoot
on freshly washed white sand.

A profound feeling of solitude, of deep reflection at the dawn of a new
day pervades the image. The tide is low: long, languid waves gently ebb and
flow. The echoes of the ocean caress the ears, the wisps of an early morning

breeze touch lightly without disturbing the peace. She knows where she is, but there are not the usual topographical or tourist markers in the image—the close-up view of the level top of Cape Town's Table Mountain, with Devil's Peak on the right, the cableway lining the mountain slope; or the view from Blaauwberg Strand—the Table Bay View or the sight of the Twelve Apostles mountain range. In Sathima's photograph there is a "this could be along any coastline in the world" feel to the scene. Ambiguity. Here the local and personally significant merge with the universally familiar. So too does Sathima's voice elide into the globally constituted, though still American-centered, world of jazz.

Standing at the edge of the ocean reminds us of Sathima's approach to jazz and to life itself: she is the romantic, the woman who privileges the natural, and the unprocessed but subtle, in her sound. We have no inkling of the intrusion of the noises of modernity, the bustle of the city, or the emotional stresses that come with everyday life. Rather the solitariness of the moment gives the singer the space to let her heart and mind roam freely: to imagine, remember, to dream, envision, and to return to the sounds of her childhood—family visits to the beach, the movies, to the sounds of radio and record, live and mediated, copies and originals, on stage and in the streets. As she revisits the echoes of sound she has carried inside for so long, the real and the remembered merge: it is this singularity, captured in the photographic moment, a coming full circle, uniting past and present, home and elsewhere, which ultimately heals.

To situate Sathima's music, biography, and ways of thinking about jazz into a more general discourse on women in jazz I begin with Margery Wolf's *Thrice-Told Tale* (1992), which provides a model for placing the South African–born singer in a larger lineage of jazzwomen using three textual forms. In the first part, I use the biographical to examine the formation of Sathima's "jazz self" in five distinct phases of her life. In contrast to the generalizing impulse of the opening discussion, the second part stresses the particular and idiosyncratic. We hear from Sathima "in her own words" to gain insight into how she has shaped the discourse of jazz to her own purposes, thereby placing herself firmly into its community of performers and composers. I conclude by reflecting on how Sathima has imagined herself as a woman in jazz by drawing on Nadia Serematakis's ideas about the poetics of the everyday and a self-reflexive femininity. I position her femininity in contrast to the forms of masculinity that Hazel Carby (1998), writing about Miles Davis, argues jazz instills for many male musicians.

Sathima's Life Story

The biographical is a useful analytical tool for thinking about many women in jazz for two reasons. First, the life story provides a comprehensive picture of the formative years, specific moments of transformation, and their long-term development as artists. This picture of the *longue duree* is necessary for those women for whom jazz is just one of many activities that occupy their time, and because developing a distinctive voice in jazz takes years, even for those who pursue their careers fulltime. For example, in contrast to her longtime husband and musical partner Abdullah Ibrahim, aka Dollar Brand, who has dedicated his waking hours to the pursuit of jazz, with the birth of their second child, Sathima's days were filled with the mundane—caring for the family, supporting Abdullah, paying bills, sorting out the taxes. Sathima's musical career has had to be squeezed into the routine demands of everyday life, extending out of what she was already doing for Abdullah. It is really only in the last decade or so that Sathima has begun to carve out her own place in jazz, while Abdullah has been regularly recording from the 1960s. In this frame the life story of many jazz women (particularly the older generation of living musicians) requires that our analysis is focused on the poetics of everyday life, on finding a balance intellectually between the forgetfulness and demands produced by the mundane, and the joyful remembering that creating, performing, and recording jazz instills in its makers, listeners, and scholars.

Sathima was born a woman of "mixed race" in segregated South Africa, where she lived through the transition to apartheid (1948) and its demise (1990 on) (figure 8.1). Surviving as a jazz musician required her to leave South Africa in 1962 and endure years of incessant travel in search of work, in unfamiliar countries and amid communities that simply didn't recognize her as a jazz singer coming from Africa. On the one hand her formative and migratory years profoundly shaped her sense of self as a woman, her output as a singer, and the strategies she has harnessed to articulate a place for herself in jazz.[1] On the other hand, decades of continuous movement and then prioritizing her place as mother of two children, have, nevertheless, impeded her capacity to position herself as a jazz musician in a single city or country, to build a loyal audience base, or even to secure a contract with a major label for her life's work such as Verve Records, as American singers Betty Carter, Shirley Horn, and Abbey Lincoln were able to do. Furthermore, Sathima projects herself as a particular kind of woman—she is a mother in New York City, simultaneously thrust into addressing the political issues that

apartheid imposed upon people of color like herself; she desires to be a supportive wife to Abdullah, though few jazz musicians survive as couples for
extended periods of time; and by her own admission, she is traditional, even
old-fashioned in her beliefs. Strong and passionate, her values are intense
and uncompromisingly articulated in her life and music.

I have divided her life story into five major moments: formative years,
falling in love, diasporic reflection, becoming a woman in jazz, and going
home. In many ways the pieces of Sathima's life have been shaped by South
Africa's political history from the 1930s through to the present. Even when
she went abroad, daily life for those in exile was shaped by the ups and
downs, and the pressures and struggles of the international antiapartheid
movement. In this sense, her life story differs from those of many other
women jazz musicians.

Figure 8.1.
Bea Benjamin in
Johannesburg,
South Africa, ca.
1958–59. From
Sathima Bea
Benjamin private
collection.

Phase One: Formative Years

Sathima's earliest memory of her own music-making was that it was inserted into the crevices or secret spaces of everyday life. The first source of such activity was her grandmother's radio and the popular songs that streamed out of the box daily while she did chores in the kitchen: cooking, cleaning, and ironing clothes. These songs were intended to work as background music, but Sathima remembers being deeply moved by the words and melodies and wanting to sing them herself. She secretly created a repertory that she sang in competitions held during intermission at the movies. Listening to and gathering songs was a forbidden pleasure—Sathima's grandmother did not know the girl was singing these songs in public from about age eleven, and it had to be kept secret—but this music transformed the daily schedule of cooking, ironing, and cleaning from the mundane into the memorable and musical.

At the time Sathima's repertory included songs like "Somewhere over the Rainbow" performed by white women from England and America. "You began by copying, by sounding just the same as Joni James or Ella Fitzgerald," Sathima recalled, "but eventually you had to move away from that. Eventually you had to sound like yourself. No two singers are the same." Sathima ultimately stopped singing those songs when she became more aware of the politics of race and colored identity, but they were the first signs of the possibilities of travel through music, and they were first heard in the kitchen, a place in which Sathima would spend much of her time when she settled in New York City to raise her children.

This body of vocal material was supplemented with the dance hall melodies originally played by several saxophones in Cape Town's dance bands; Sathima assumed the line of the saxophone in remaking the music, and then found the words in New York City's sheet music stores. Finally, she would add to her repertory the music she gleaned from recordings of Billie Holiday and Duke Ellington that traveled to South Africa in the postwar period. This music has been reconstituted in many moments of stillness through years of diaspora and after she settled in New York City, in which "an entire past sensory landscape was translated into a present act" of musical remembrance and celebration, a point I return to later on (Serematakis 1996, 16).

Phase Two: Falling in Love

British social psychologist Wendy Langford (1999) proposes two models for thinking about heterosexual women in love: the romantic and the democratic. In the romantic model Langford argues that falling in love produces

Figure 8.2. Sathima Bea Benjamin and Carol Muller meet at Penn Station in New York City, August 2010. Photo used with permission, taken by Dan Yon on Carol Muller's camera.

in women the feeling that they have the capacity for deep emotional connection, strong feelings of intimacy, attachment, and the freedom to be oneself. Falling in love means finding companionship; it fulfills a desire for a sense of security, and of course, enables women to move out of the controlled environment of being children in a patriarchal household into a space where the couple—the man and the woman in love—is autonomous and free to make decisions about their lives without interference from anyone else. In this model, nevertheless, there is also a moment of counterrevolution when disillusionment and disappointment in the male partner often sets in for a woman. At this point they fall back into the wife as mother figure in their relationship, rationalizing the incompleteness and weaknesses as would a mother her own child. The man in the relationship will then begin to view his spouse as either a good mummy—who is always forgiving and filled with unconditional love—or the bad mummy, one who tricks, teases, and makes demands he cannot hope to satisfy. In this model men ultimately begin to exert demoralizing control over their spouses, and women try to figure out what makes their partners tick.

The alternative model is the more democratic practice based on reason. In this model, individual women and men both know what they want, what is good for them, and how to negotiate an equitable place for themselves in the relationship. Despite the ideals of equality and freedom that a democratic model would appear to embody, Langford argues that this model produces similar outcomes to the romantic love process. She concludes her book suggesting that "love" remains a dubious ideal for most of heterosexual women in the contemporary world as it is elevated to the level of the spiritual and mysterious. Despite their best desires, love remains in Langford's model a form of dystopia.

The two models of romantic and democratic relationship, articulated as a kind of "revolution of the heart" are useful for framing the two moments in Sathima's early life of "falling in love." The first was when she chose to form a lasting relationship with Abdullah Ibrahim/Dollar Brand and not to pursue a marriage with then fiancé Sam Isaacs; and the second was her sense of "falling in love" with the music. There is no doubt that the two processes were intertwined, because as Sathima often recalls, it was the music of Duke Ellington and the song "I Got It Bad and That Ain't Good" that brought her and Abdullah together. These were two individuals who were truly in love with the music: it was through their passion for jazz that they formed a long-term relationship. Their romantic relationship was as much a rebellion as was their move into jazz. Love for the music, like love for each other, instilled feelings of freedom, intimacy, the capacity to be true to themselves, to take risks, and to move from one social status to another. Although theirs was a largely romantic revolution of the heart, much later in life, Sathima would begin to move toward the more democratic model particularly in her relationship to jazz performance. This is outlined in her discourse on jazz composition, performance, and recording later in this chapter.

Phase Three: Diasporic Reflection

Leaving home in 1962 and then living as a musical migrant was hard on Sathima—Europe offered occasional work but very little sense of home and familiarity. In this period she became far more introspective, reflecting on her heritage as a woman of mixed race and many origins. It was the memory of home and community that sustained Sathima in these years: she began to look inside herself for inner strength, to remember past repertories, and to read a wide range of subjects, all in search of a place in the world for a woman like herself. Personally and professionally these were challenging years.

Much of Sathima's time in Europe was spent taking care of the South African male musicians she traveled with. In the pain of exile there were severe bouts of substance abuse among these men. This was the period in which she was given the name "Sathima"—the one who listens (Xhosa) by South African bass player Johnny Dyani because she took care of him in his moments of deepest diasporic despair. She loved the idea of "Sathima" and so began to call herself Sathima Bea (short for Beatrice) Benjamin. She spent her time on the road wood-shedding and honing her vocal craft; her first compositions were "given" to her, and she began to formulate a set of ideas that would link her to the larger African diaspora and its community of jazz performers. Sathima recorded several times, but there is little commercially available beyond the *Morning in Paris* recording made with Duke Ellington in 1963 and released in 1996.[2]

Phase Four: Becoming a Woman in Jazz

Coming to New York City meant that Sathima had to begin to consolidate the range of musical, racial, political, and cultural experiences she had had and to make them work for her as a woman in jazz on her own terms. One of the key challenges was to make a way to do all the things she had to as wife, mother, and political activist while still finding time to make music, either alone in her kitchen, in the recording studio, or out in public. She couldn't be on the road very often; she wasn't able to perform live and thereby earn her keep or regularly rehearse with her trio. In other words, because she refused to give up on the music she had to devise alternative means for creating, performing, and distributing her music so she could remain at home; she also had to rely on Abdullah to fund her occasional projects in the recording studio. These were the compromises she made in order to fulfill her desire to be the best possible mother to her children.

In the domestic sphere, in the midst of the ebb and flow of everyday life, Sathima pulled out the old repertories she remembered from her childhood and then gave them to her musicians. Collectively they breathed new life into the old repertory in the language of jazz; or she composed new songs given as gifts to her "from God." She has created a distinctive Songbook by reintroducing songs from a past long forgotten by the trio but restored to their country of origin and newly made in performance as rare and beautiful things: beautiful in themselves, but equally poignant in the face of a history of injustice, oppression, gendered struggle, and forgetfulness.[3]

Imaginatively harnessing the principles of jazz performance Sathima has also constituted what Serematakis (1996) calls "moments of stillness" or what women often experience as "resting moments." "Stillness," writes Serematakis, "is the moment when the buried, the discarded, and the forgotten escape to the social surface of awareness like life-supporting oxygen."[4] Certain smells, practices, photographs, and reissues played on radio or digital television triggered the depths of childhood memory, bringing into being melodies or texts Sathima had sung or danced to in her Cape Town days. These tunes opened up the possibility of remembering—of an imaginative return to a particular place, event, or group of friends. Remembering in word and sound in a moment of stillness a very old body of songs was reconstituted as something new, even biographical, for the South African singer in New York City.

Phase Five: Going Home

This involves returning to South Africa, musically and personally. She has gone back for several performance events, though Sathima strongly desires to return home musically as well. Ideally this would mean being invited to teach young people about life and the world of jazz singing.

Sathima in Her Own Words

Music is the spirit within you, within you.
Deep within you, deep within you,
deep within you is music, music, music.
Find your sound then let it flow, free and easy and out.
    (Sathima Bea Benjamin, "Music" 1988)

In 1999, on a return trip to South Africa, Sathima expressed her beliefs about the early history of jazz in this way. "*Jazz*," she commented, "*is a cry. It is a survival skill for the spirit. I think it must have started with a woman who just let out a wail. Then came the accompaniment.*"[5] In other words, in Sathima's mind and imagination, the earliest sounds of what we now call jazz were the unaccompanied utterances of a woman crying out, a woman longing for healing and wholeness, a woman yearning to be free. When Sathima sings, her voice constitutes a momentary acoustical tie to, or echo of, those original moments. It is through song that she carves out a utopian place formed out of what she believes to be the ideal qualities of jazz music and its makers: spontaneity, love, respect, intuition, emotionality, subtlety, nuance, personal space, and human freedom. Music that reflects these qualities constitutes the poetic and emotional labor that Sathima produces in song performance.

Why jazz? For Sathima jazz is a personal music, a vehicle for you to express your very existence, to state what you feel about life. "*My message here is be true to yourself,*" she told students in a class I taught at Marymount College in Tarrytown New York in 1990; she continued:

Listen to my song, "Music" because the most important thing is to find your own sound. And when you do, everything gets easy. I wrote "Music" because we must all find our own individual sound. We all went through listening to other singers, you want to sound a little bit like them, or you just start in a vacuum.

Do you remember I told you we had the local bands, and this Cape Town sound of the saxophone stretching the lines? I sing those old songs from the 1920s. When I teach these songs to American musicians they say "Where did you find this, what is it?" They don't even know the music and it is actually from here. It went to Cape Town, and I am bringing it back to musicians in New York City. We give the song jazz changes, really hip changes underneath the melody, and I swing it. And then it sounds like I wrote it, but I didn't. It's just my memories of Cape Town that come back to me in New York City. Jazz is also a forward-looking, all encompassing music. It gives you freedom to do whatever you can imagine possible. All these musicians have this "fake" book. And they go through it and choose a song. I don't have a fake book. I don't even own one. Whatever I'm singing is in my repertory because I have heard it before and then it comes to mind again. There's a reason it comes to mind, and then you have to sing it.

On another occasion she explained:

The reason I am doing jazz is it affords you a certain amount of freedom of thought, freedom to be different and unique. And it dares you: it lets you pull out whatever courage you have. You have to take risks. That's the whole thing. I could have inherited this courage, I think even things like that come through in the genes. My mother had to take risks. Just growing up in South Africa not being White, you learnt how to survive and take risks. My grandmother taught me to be careful and stay out of trouble, but eventually I rebelled against that, that whole rebellion thing led me to jazz, I saw that as music of rebellion: maybe it wasn't but I think it really was. The music doesn't speak to my head, it speaks to my heart, and I listen only to that. I have never been able to listen to what my head tells me.

When I asked her how she sees herself in the American-centered jazz singer's lineage, she responded by saying that in addition to Billie Holiday, she sits between Betty Carter who inspired her to form her own record label, and Abbey Lincoln.[6] Why Abbey, I wondered? *"What I like about her is that she is just honest and forthright. But she has a very different approach from mine. When she sings she just goes on to the stage, and she's Abbey! It's like her audience is there, but you get the feeling, 'Listen, this is me here, I don't care if you don't like what I am singing because this is my show.' She takes total control."*[7]

It is curious, nevertheless, that while Sathima inserts a woman at the start of history—and it was Billie Holiday's voice that provided a feeling of place for the Cape Town girl—she never performs with other women because she sees her performance as a kind of musical unity formed between the heart of the female singer and her male trio, who in turn communicate to the hearts of their listeners. She explained:

What I know is that I love performing with men, combining the yin and the yang. You see I am an old-fashioned romantic. That is why I don't perform with other women—the struggles for women are too great—it is better to relax inside the music with male performers. I am always amazed at what happens when men blend their musicality with mine in performance. To do so they have to be spiritually inclined, have worked with themselves, and not allow their egos to get in the way of the music. My grandmother drummed into me that I had to be submissive to men: I had to fight hard to overcome that. I've changed but it took a very long time. I was raised to believe that men are the most important, and that I have to serve them. I love to serve all people—though a woman serving others is looked down upon in America. There is submission to each other in the music—we are a completely democratic unit.

While Sathima doesn't perform or interact much with other women in jazz, her approach to jazz is clearly as a woman. In this regard, she embraces the ideas traditionally associated with the Otherness of women—the spontaneous, intuitive, spiritual, and loving—and claims them as a core part of her personal strength, her voice in jazz, and her place in the world at large. It is a way of being that often brings her into conflict with those who seek out a more systematic and rational approach to life.

I am a complete romantic, jazz rules my life, and I live intuitively.

While living intuitively has cost her in personal ways, musically speaking, intuition and spontaneity have become the cornerstones of how she hears herself as a singer:

The older I get and the more I care about integrity, the more resonance I hear in my voice. I have turned into an artist. I am not just a singer. There are times when there is a lot of suffering going on in my soul, and I am not singing. I have to take care of the things with my family that you couldn't pay anyone for because no one would do it for money. It seems like such a life of self-sacrifice sometimes. I suppose every experience is thrown at you and you are supposed to run through that, and you get your heart squeezed. The next time I sing it will sound different. If I get squeezed too much, though, that will be the end of my art. But these are the times that I want to bring something musically new again. And it doesn't mean standing in front of an audience, it just means spending a couple of hours in a studio with me. That is the happiest. Those are the time[s] I don't feel like being visible as a physical person, because they are not going to see my soul. I am an unconditional lover.[8] The music has never let me down. What I get out of this is I get love back.

Remember, I am an interpretive singer. I love working with sound, its subtle-

ties and nuances. I have a natural gift much like Billie Holiday's approach. I urge musicians to feel free within a format. There is so much freedom and space within the music: you have to weave your voice in and out. Listen to what is happening and breathe your own thing into it. I heard Abdullah tell someone once that I am a renaissance woman. The jazz musicians will say, well you know, Sathima you have got to pay your dues. This jazz music that you do with your whole self, it is about total surrender to yourself. This is what its about: total surrender to the beauty inside so that you can bring it out. Ben Riley once said that you can't have too many people loving jazz because it's a very improvised way of looking at things: it makes you think for yourself, to be very free. If people aren't ready, you can have all the freedom in the world, but you have to be able to handle it. You have to listen with your heart. If your heart's open everything will tingle, that's why you hear the resonance in my voice. Some people will never hear it.

Sathima adds to her list of processes that define her musicianship: intuition, spontaneity, and inspiration (i.e., coming from the heart, in the moment, and without the mediation of music-writing).

I am just an inspirational composer, I don't sit down at a piano and say, I am going to write a piece. It just comes, and sometimes it doesn't come for a long time. I don't write down my own music. When I have a song, I have to ask somebody to write that down and you go through that whole process. But I think if I learnt to write, I would be interfering with my antennae and I don't want to do that. I gravitate to musicians like drummer Billy Higgins because he can hear subtleties and nuances, and he can help you punctuate them. It's wonderful to have someone like that in your orbit. And he's paid his dues.

How do I compose? I find that when I am walking through the streets and it's crowded, I get a lot of things because people impact on you. I don't have to walk down a lonely country road. It works for me to take long walks, even a subway ride. When I am standing on the platform waiting for a train, nobody can hear me singing. If I want to try something out, I try it out there and nobody hears it. Remember, Carol, when my children were young I used to take them to school—for almost ten years I did this every day during the school year. I had to go by subway or by bus, but always chose the subways to take them there, and then I would walk back at least a mile and a half each day, early in the morning. There were never many people about, so you are fresh, and then lots of things come to you.

My music is about essence and feeling. Betty Carter was very much like that too—I don't know about Abbey Lincoln. I can't write the feeling in the music down. The musicians, when they look at it, and they start dissecting it, and say "Oh my goodness!" Even my husband will say to me, "This is a really expensive song, Sathima." It's very difficult because I get impatient if I have to take someone on a gig when I can't get the real guys, and they can't play my music. And

I say, "But it's so simple" and my husband says, "It's not so simple. Besides the feeling, what is required technically is not that simple."

It's hard to explain how I write my music. The only way I can is to say that you have your antennae ready and they have to be clean. They have to be like laser beams so they attract—it's like what I call a lovelight. In the windsong, there's a lovelight. I don't have any control, I am just a channel of the music from the Creator. The antennae are actually inside. They have to be inside and then it comes. I think we are dealing with something that is very divine, that's not something that you can study. I don't know when a song will come. I just keep living my life until the Creator sends me something. So my heart must be clean.

People have ideas about singers, that they should be pretty and stand there looking great. That is an approach that people have come to expect, and I am not trying to be openly defiant, but I don't think it's necessary. I try to look less dramatic in the way I dress: I don't want people to come to see how I look. I really am very shy. Singing has helped me to overcome shyness.

People ask me about my sense of timing. The musicians ask about where in the measure they should come in. With me it is just between beat one and two, they count and so want to know exactly, but I can't tell them. Everything I do is completely intuitive. When I sing, I imagine myself dancing, and bass player Buster Williams, he knows just how to dance with me. The way you turn a corner in ballroom dancing—that is how his playing feels to me. I did a lot of ballroom dancing when I was young. I think that's got a lot to do with my sense of timing. Somewhere between one and two, before we get to that two I am going to be sliding in there.[9]

When I sing the words of a song, for me it's a story being told with the lyrics and the sound. It's a story you are telling. Everything has to make sense. I don't suddenly just sing a song. I will figure out what the story is here. That impacts on where I am going to put the accents and which word is more important in the line. Every song is a story. You might wonder, how on earth did you get this gift of storytelling in song? It comes to me when I am meditating in motion. I think about songs when I am walking in streets here amidst all kinds of people. I do not retire to some place and say, "OK, I am gonna write a song." It's not about that. It's very divine and inspirational.

Toward a Gendered Poetics of Self in Jazz

There can be no doubt that this is a woman's story: Sathima represents herself in traditional ways—as mother, wife, and singer—but she expands her world to become manager, political activist, composer, producer, record label owner, and organic intellectual. The home she has created in the music she makes is similarly formed from traditionally feminine attributes: spontaneity, intuition, caring, respect, love, and beauty, though she doesn't restrict these attributes to women. These are the qualities she looks for in the male musicians she invites to perform with her. She creates space in the musical fabric for each to express himself by performing feminine qualities; she urges them to embrace the freedom she offers to find the softer sides of their musical selves, and even to flirt a little in the moment of performance.

The depth of emotion Sathima feels toward the music parallels the passion evoked when a woman falls in love with a man. In her ensembles music-making is sensual in the moment of performance but never spills over into after-hours sexual pleasure. Of course, reaching the state of perfect union in the moment of performance is challenging: nothing comes easily; everything requires a level of struggle and the strength and courage to survive the difficulty. But once Sathima and her musicians have overcome the difficulties creating the charts for the sounds she hears; after she has convinced her musicians to listen closely to each other and to uncover the beauty inside themselves; and when they are in tune with each other musically and emotionally, they are able to make the most thrilling music together. At the end of an evening of live performance or a session in the studio, there is in Sathima's mind, a feeling of having reached a climactic moment of pure joy, akin to the momentary ecstasy that many experience when they have "fallen in love" or felt the pangs of romance.

Sathima's stress upon the feminine dimensions she expects her musicians to embody is juxtaposed with the more masculine elements of risk-taking that jazz improvisation and performance characteristically requires. In this sense, for Sathima jazz constitutes a place for exploring, even performing a mixed or yin and yang gendered self—its masculine and feminine dimensions. She would argue that her kind of music-making enables men to explore parts of themselves they would never dare to if they were in exclusively male ensembles. As such, Sathima's ensemble style provides a powerful counternarrative to the discourses of masculinity in jazz articulated in the autobiographies of some male musicians.

Hazel Carby, for example, characterizes Miles Davis's book *Miles: The Autobiography* (1990), in ways that overlap with, and diverge significantly from Sathima's story. At eighteen Davis travels to New York City from his home in Texas because, like Sathima, he believes New York City to be the center of jazz performance in the United States. He arrives there to explore the freedom that a major urban area like New York provides. Unlike Sathima, however, Carby argues that Davis's "concept of freedom remains limited to the misogynistic world of jazz, and it manifests itself principally in the musical relations among the male instrumentalists with whom he worked" (Carby 1998, 136). Davis's ideas of freedom include breaking loose from the confinement that women create for men, and he insists on the freedom to operate in a world defined by male creativity (ibid., 138). This is a world in which men and not mothers are his mentors and nurturers, and his lineage in jazz is a patrilineal one. Carby goes so far as to suggest that Davis thought of women, including his mother, as obstacles to his growth as a musician. His relationships with his first wife and child, and subsequent wives, are all tinged with a taste of disgust. For Davis, when his life with women thrives, the music goes badly. When the music is good, the way with women is rough (ibid., 141). Men are his resource for creativity, nurturance, and stimulation; women "exist to be exploited and to service his bodily needs" (ibid., 143).

Davis hears in one of his first experiences of live jazz performances in 1944, an intensity of emotion and passion that he likens to desire in a sexual relationship. While Sathima doesn't go quite this far in her description of the unity constituted in performance with her trio it is tempting to read that into her words. Nevertheless, Sathima's goals in performance are sensual more than sexual; possibly even maternal: she creates a musical space for her trio that she hopes will set them free, to find the vulnerable, feminine dimensions of their maleness. In return, she demands that they listen to her, enable her to perform her music by coming to understand her sense of timing, her intonation, and, indeed, to come to know something of her past from a place that is literally worlds away from theirs. This is not a position achieved without risk, pain, and struggle, but it is a place she hopes will ultimately produce real love, deep joy, and beautiful music.

In sum, Sathima is a woman in jazz who lives intuitively, with her heart, mind, and eyes open to new ways of doing old songs. She breathes life into songs from almost a century ago that intervene in the present as living witnesses to a past that cannot be simply forgotten. Each new rendition of a tune from turn-of-the-century British music hall, an early Hollywood musical, or a Strayhorn or Ellington composition, serves to remind its listeners of the fragments of a past many never knew. In return, it is Sathima's dream that one day jazz consumers in both of her home countries—the United States and South Africa—will finally find it in themselves to hear the emotive depth or beauty in her voice, to allow themselves to be decentered by the vocal presence nested inside the intricate lines of her trio, to come to know her story, and to relish the echoes of music in the voices of jazz men and women from the old and new African diasporas, echoes that crisscrossed the Atlantic Ocean many times in the twentieth century and continue to circulate back and forth in the twenty-first century.

Notes

1. See Muller and Benjamin (2011) for further discussion of issues of "mixed" racial heritage.

2. See Muller and Benjamin (2011) for a full discussion of the *Morning in Paris* recording, how it came to be made, its contents, and its outcomes.

3. The idea of beauty is not new to African diasporic or jazz thinking. Here I am reminded of the reflections on beauty by Ornette Coleman in his Atlantic Records collection, *Beauty Is a Rare Thing*; Frank Kofsky (1970) has a conversation with John Coltrane on beauty; see also Nutall (2007) and Nakedi (2006).

4. Serematakis 1996, 12–15.

5. Sathima Bea Benjamin as reported on by Jill de Villiers, *The Citizen*, June 24, 1999, p. 33.

6. Billie Holiday is thought to be the blues mother of jazz; Betty Carter and Abbey Lincoln, both of whom have died in the last decade, were pioneers as jazz singers. Carter established her own record label—as few other women have done. Lincoln, married to Max Roach for a period, was a singer who boldly sang political lyrics that inspired Sathima's own composition.

7. A similar release became necessary to Sathima's survival and capacity to thrive as a musician in the 1990s. She and Abdullah decided they needed to live separately, though he continues to support her financially.

8. Quote derived from Muller with Benjamin February 2000.

9. Derived from *All About Jazz* interview, April 2008, 6.

References

Carby, Hazel. 1998. *Race Men*. Boston: Harvard University Press.

Davis, Miles. 1990. *Miles: The Autobiography*, with Quincy Troupe. New York: Simon and Shuster.

Kofsky, Frank. 1970. *Black Nationalism and the Revolution in Music*. New York: Pathfinder.

Langford, Wendy. 1999. *Revolutions of the Heart: Gender, Power, and the Delusions of Love*. London: Routledge.

Muller, Carol, and Sathima Bea Benjamin. 2011. *Musical Echoes: South African Women Thinking in Jazz*, with compact disc. Durham: Duke University Press.

Nakedi, Ribane. 2006. *Beauty: A Black Perspective*. Pietermartzburg: UKZN Press.

Nuttall, Sarah, ed. 2007. *Beautiful/Ugly. African and Diaspora Aesthetics*. Durham: Duke University Press.

Serematakis, Nadia. 1996. "The Memory of the Senses, Parts I and II." In *The Senses Still: Perception and Memory as Material Culture in Modernity*. Chicago: University of Chicago Press, 1–44.

Wolf, Margery. 1992. *A Thrice-Told Tale: Feminism, Post-Modernism, and Ethnographic Responsibility*. Stanford: Stanford University Press.

Discography

Benjamin, Sathima Bea. 1997. *A Morning in Paris*. Munich: Enja Records, ENJ-9309 2.

———. 2006. *Musical Echoes*. New York: Ekapa (U.S.), Ekapa 004.

9. Sima's Choices

Negotiating Repertoires and Identities in Contemporary Iran

GAY BREYLEY

The earth is hot with thirst . . .
The stars have fever tonight . . .
I sing the *gharibi* [a song of separation and longing] because you
are far from me . . .
You sing *taleba* [a Mazanderani love narrative] and you leave your
lover alone
You are like the burnt heart of the *laleva* [a reed pipe played by
shepherds]
—"Thirsty," translated from the Tabari language, as sung by Sima[1]

In a village near the Caspian Sea coast in the northern Iranian province of Mazanderan, a group of old friends gathers in a private home. These friends are mostly middle-aged, with adolescent and adult children. They share news, reminisce, joke, and discuss current issues over kebabs grilled in the yard, with glasses that are constantly refilled. After eating, the host, Ahmad Mohsenpour, picks up his *kamanche* (a four-stringed spike fiddle), and one of the guests, Sima Shokrani, picks up her *tombak* (a goblet drum). The talk is soon hushed by the rich tones of Sima's singing voice. Her voice's low register, sustained notes, and improvised ornamentation shift between heartache and a graceful, knowing pleasure. Sima and Mohsenpour improvise on old Mazanderani songs that evoke longing, pleasure, and humor. The lyrics recount tales of love and separation, courage and hard work. These tales are set in the lush Mazanderani landscape and contain multiple layers of meaning, which address political, social, or spiritual matters, past and current, as well as other areas of local knowledge. As Sima sings into the night, her friends clap, click their fingers, occasionally sing along, and contribute calls of pleasure and encouragement between songs.[2]

Figure 9.1. Sima in
Mazanderani dress,
which she chooses
to wear at most
public performances.
Photographer
unknown.
© Sima Shokrani.

Performance Contexts

Sima's life and musical choices reflect her personal history and her roles and
positions in Iran's changing society. When she was twenty-one, in February 1979, Iran underwent its most significant modern turning point as its
monarchy was overthrown and the Islamic Republic was established. Before
and after the 1979 revolution, Sima continued singing through various constraints. These include a prerevolutionary prejudice against regional music
and a postrevolutionary law against solo female singing in the company of
unrelated men. Sima negotiates performance possibilities that both reflect
and shape intersecting aspects of her identity as an accomplished and creative
singer, a musical collaborator, a Mazanderani, an Iranian citizen, a woman,

and a senior educator in a country with a young population. Aspects of Sima's multiple identities are shaped and challenged by her roles in and relationships with her family and wider communities, as well as by her nation and its turbulent recent history.

I first met Sima at a private social gathering very much like the one outlined above. As a guest in Mr. Mohsenpour's home, I was looking forward to an evening of his music. However, it was Sima who stole the show with her singing. Since that initial meeting in 2006, I have spent time with Sima in Mazanderan, where she lives, and in Iran's capital city, Tehran, whenever we have both found ourselves in the same city. A private party, such as the one at which Sima and I met, is just one of the contexts in which she sings. Sima also performs at events organized by a women's nongovernment organization, at which she improvises vocally and accompanies herself on tombak. Other women musicians and singers sometimes join her, but she often performs solo. The organization is primarily concerned with improving opportunities in health and education for the local area's poorer families. Large groups of women and children attend these events, which involve discussions, speeches, eating, music, and dancing, a feature of most family and women's gatherings in Iran. In the absence of men, the women dance freely to Sima's improvisations. In Sima's words, these meetings are lively and the musical sessions are very joyous.

Sima also sings with the Shevash Ensemble at public, officially authorized concerts in Iran. These events, with mixed-gender audiences, are more formal and sedate. The ensemble includes Mohsenpour on kamanche; performers of other traditional instruments that are popular in Mazanderan, such as *laleva*, *dotar* (a two-stringed long-necked lute), and frame drum; two or three men vocalists; and at least one other woman singer. At these public concerts, Sima and the other woman vocalist must concentrate on singing in unison. In some pieces, the intensity of their combined voices builds up and dominates the ensemble's sound. To be officially authorized, these concerts' programs must be planned in detail and leave no space for improvisation. By contrast, at concerts in Germany, Sima responds to her audiences' requests and improvises in a manner similar to that used in her friends' homes in Mazanderan. Her audiences in Germany are largely made up of migrants from Iran but also include gradually increasing numbers of non-Iranian Germans who have come to know and appreciate Iran's traditional music. Sima's concerts in Germany are relatively lively, as audience members—especially those originally from Mazanderan—call out for the songs they wish to hear. Some sing along with Sima, while others become tearful.

Translating Voice: Sound and Call

In Persian, Iran's national language, voice is usually translated as *seda* and in some contexts as *neda*. One Persian-English dictionary defines *seda* as "1. sound, 2. voice" and *neda* as "call, summons" (Emami 2007, 574 and 910). These two definitions may be read as corresponding, respectively, with Steven Feld and Aaron Fox's notions of "embodied expression" and "social agency" (Feld and Fox, 2000, 161). *Seda* and *neda* are both relevant to the consideration of Sima's singing voice and the ways she uses it. The sound of her singing voice is her primary instrument. This is a deep, strong, flexible sound, arguably best suited to solo performance and improvisation, but also a sound that enriches and complements the sounds of other women's voices when they sing in unison. Sima developed her singing voice through a combination of informal listening to older women's voices and some formal training. The ways she has chosen to use the sound of her voice—and the lyrics she chooses to sing—relate to the definition of *neda*. Sima's singing practices have always played a primarily relational role in her life, representing an engagement with other people. This social engagement ranges from a vocal response to a beloved grandmother's voice, to a sung call or summons to fellow Iranians, inviting them to remember and respect the hard work of rural women. Since childhood, it has been important to Sima that she make her own choices about where, when, and how her singing voice is heard. She has chosen to use her voice to maintain and rearrange aspects of social relations in her local and national communities.

Martin Stokes suggests that performance "does not simply convey cultural messages already 'known' [rather, it] reorganises and manipulates everyday experiences of social reality, blurs, elides, ironises and sometimes subverts commonsense categories and markers" (2004, 101). Sima's performative choices reorganize various experiences of social reality and subvert some prescribed markers, such as those of gender, class, and ethnicity. For example, she performs songs of desire in the first person—in each of the contexts outlined earlier—which may have previously been ascribed to masculine narrators. At a time when popular songs praise or articulate the concerns of sophisticated urban young women, Sima sings in praise of, and empathy with, rural working girls, such as carpet weavers and goatherds. In a nation that has promoted the perceived cultural values of the dominant Persian ethnic group, Sima asserts the equality of her Mazanderani ethnicity by singing, reviving, and passing on the music of her childhood. In such choices, both the deployment of Sima's singing voice and the articulation of her sense of womanhood are crucial. The characteristics of Sima's sense of womanhood differ from those that have tended to dominate popular music industries in various world contexts. As well as love, desire, and poetic heartache, Sima's vocal articulation of womanhood encompasses the strength and beauty of women who work hard for their communities and the sense of fulfillment and agency of those who are deeply attached to their local environments. Her songs—mostly adaptations of traditional Mazanderani pieces—express complex women's emotions in ways that reflect Sima's negotiation of her identity as a woman who finds liberation in different places from those offered by some of her Western sisters. In her context, as a woman who grew up in Iran in the 1960s and 1970s, this is significant.

In the 1960s and 1970s, Iran underwent a process of rapid, if arguably superficial, cultural Westernization. Music was one of the industries most affected by this. Iran's all-time most popular singer, Googoosh, exemplified this period in Iran. Googoosh represented the sophisticated 1970s Iranian woman who articulated a complex range of emotions in a rapidly changing world. She did this with, among other things, a smooth, soulful voice and an ever-changing, trendsetting appearance that belonged to the new era of television. Sima is six years younger than Googoosh; like others of her generation, she grew up with the soundtrack of Googoosh's voice on radio and television. While she admires Googoosh, Sima's own singing practices are different in terms of her *seda*, or "embodied expression," and her *neda*, or "social agency." Sima's singing voice and the ways she chooses to use it serve to subvert 1970s (and, arguably, contemporary) notions that only Westernized women have agency and are in a position to articulate heartfelt emotions. Sima's voice and repertoire point to other possibilities than those of the urban superstar. Like Googoosh, Sima sings of women's strength and vulnerability. However, she does so with the locally grounded voice of her tradition and she sings of women who sweat over pots of rice or weaving looms as they wait for their lovers. Sima's heroines find forms of liberation in their relations with both social and natural environments, the fulfillment of their romantic desires, and the act of singing itself. These aspects of style and repertoire apply to all Sima's singing contexts—concerts in Iran and Germany, women's meetings, private gatherings and her recorded work.

Whereas women singers have played an extremely important role in Iran, especially in popular music, they have often been obliged to perform in conditions subject to the management and marketing structures of a masculinist industry. This is the case in popular music industries around the world. A range of studies of women and their musical possibilities has demonstrated the limitations that persist in diverse contexts (see O'Shea 2008; Magrini 2003; Koskoff 1989; Doubleday 1988). However, especially in the West, a presumption has persisted that the more traditional the context, the more extreme the restrictions. As Holly Randell-Moon suggests, "Because a moral and cultural superiority is ascribed to Western democracies on the basis of women's rights as fully realised, the negation of women's rights is presented as only occurring outside of Western democracies" (2007, 21). By contrast, Sima sees a range of restrictions on the musical choices of women in Westernized pop industries, especially singers. For her, even in Iran, with its unique limitations, the boundaries of traditional music are more easily and more interestingly pushed than those of Westernized pop singing. For example, the tradition of improvisation enables experimentation, and the traditional emphasis on vocal sound and feeling (rather than visual representations, catchy melodies, and regular or dance rhythms) allows the singer to focus on her voice and her emotions. Sima grew up in an Iran where popular notions of womanhood were shaped by the sounds and images of Googoosh, among others. These notions of womanhood intersected with ideas around emotion, beauty, vulnerability, and class. Sima's voice—her improvising *seda* and her *neda*, the call she puts out to other women wishing to push boundaries—responds to restrictive dominant notions by reorganizing perceptions of feminine emotion, beauty, and strength. The woman evoked both by Sima's singing voice and the repertoires she chooses is one who feels deeply and suffers, but also one who resists and overcomes her own suffering, along with that of others.

Childhood and Youth: Mazanderan

As Veronica Doubleday and John Baily point out, children "do not learn music in isolation; their development is very much a response to stimulation and encouragement—or censure and discouragement" (1995). Sima's personal relationships have always been central in her musical development and singing practices. From the age of four, she learned to sing traditional Mazanderani songs from her grandmother. As a child, she accompanied her grandmother as she worked in rice fields; many of the songs related directly to that work. Sima tells of her strong attachment to her grandmother and the crucial role this played in her love for her grandmother's songs. Throughout her life, Sima's first musical preference has remained for Mazanderani songs, especially those drawn from the realms of work and women's lives. This preference represents a counterpoint to dominant musical trends in Iran, which have tended to favor Persian art or popular music, urban settings (or romanticized, folkloristic views of the rural), and masculine perspectives.

Superficially, Sima's rural childhood with a loving extended family and close community might appear to have escaped the strictures of Iran's complex political pressures. However, even as a child, she was obliged to learn how to negotiate aspects of her identity. In the 1960s and 1970s, Iran's monarchic regime promoted a somewhat exclusive form of Persian nationalism, as well as the regime's notions of secularism and modernization.[3] Although the royal family itself originated from Mazanderan, the regime discouraged the use of Tabari, the Mazanderani language (which is closely related to Persian, but differs sufficiently to be classed as a language in its own right), and the singing of traditional Mazanderani songs. When Sima was a child in the 1960s, political and social pressure to Persianize, or to conceal differences, persisted. Sima enjoyed singing lessons at primary school but was obliged to submit to a strict rule against singing in her first language. She learned Persian pieces with pleasure, but recalls her strong feeling of indignation about the prejudice against her grandmother's songs. Still a child, Sima determined to defy the rules against the sounds that, for her, represented pleasure, as well as a sense of simultaneous freedom and security, of fresh air and communality. She continued to sing her beloved grandmother's songs outside school, in family and other community contexts, thus raising her Mazanderani voice—in both senses—and negotiating her primary identity as a member of a Mazanderani family.

When Sima was ten years old, the local radio station, which represented the music industry's primary means of dissemination in her community, invited her to sing on its musical programs. However, her father, whom Sima describes as conservative, refused to give his permission. While Sima's views differ from her father's in several areas, she later appreciated his reluctance to allow her to enter what he regarded as the music industry as a child. The question would arise again in her adolescence, when she had opportunities to enter the world of pop music. In Iran, it is common for children and teenagers, as well as talented adults, to perform at family and community events, especially the frequent private parties, to which large extended families are invited. Sima often sang on such occasions, and her voice and talent attracted the attention of people offering opportunities to perform in Tehran and to record. At the time, in the 1970s, Sima was interested in performing pop songs and taking up this opportunity. However, in retrospect, the adult Sima is glad her father obstructed that path too. She explains that, in her view, the prerevolutionary pop music industry sustained a culture in which men were free—or even expected—to develop unethical relations with young female singers. Sima feels that her father protected her from potential exploitation while also enabling her to maintain her taste for Mazanderani music. The latter remained difficult throughout her high school years. She enrolled at a private singing school in her home town of Sari but left after a few lessons, when her teacher demanded she give up her Mazanderani songs and sing only Persian pieces. In her adolescence, Sima's musical choices—to submit to her father's advice against singing pop songs in public and to defy the Sari singing teacher's advice against singing traditional Mazanderani pieces— consolidated the negotiation of her Mazanderani identity that had begun in childhood. They also initiated her life of negotiation as a woman singer. As a teenager, Sima determined to work only in equitable conditions, where collaboration was pleasurable for all concerned.

Early Adulthood: Revolution

One aspect of Sima's identity that she developed after she finished school was her political self, primarily her role as an Iranian citizen and activist. She moved from her family home in Sari to attend university in another Mazanderani town. Sima did not plan to become a professional singer at this time and, wishing to become financially independent, she studied accounting. It was the late 1970s and university students were not the only Iranians seeking political change, but they were at the forefront of a movement protesting the increasingly dictatorial regime of Iran's then Shah, Mohammad Reza Pahlavi. The Pahlavi regime had close ties to the United States and it imposed various programs of so-called modernization on Iran's population. These programs were welcomed by some, but they were resented by many Iranians. The regime had also banned political dissent and it sought to deter such dissent with, among other things, a pervasive intelligence agency and the execution of convicted dissidents. Sima's personal views soon appeared to find an ideological home among her leftist fellow students. These views included her support for freedom of expression, as reflected in her persistence with the Mazanderani songs that were not popular, either with the regime or with many members of her generation, and her opposition to the exploitation or suppression of the less powerful, as reflected in her allegiance to working girls and women (including her grandmother). As a student, Sima continued to sing—Mazanderani songs and revolutionary songs—for her own pleasure and when she was out with friends.

Sima was drawn to the ideals of the *Tudeh* (Workers) Party, Iran's most significant leftist movement in the twentieth century.[4] The ideals that were prominent in the 1970s, and shared by many in Iran who supported the coming revolution, included social justice, a return to so-called traditional values and a rejection of enforced Westernization, foreign control of oil revenue, state surveillance, and persecution of dissidents. In this context, leftist and revolutionary songs grew in popularity, although those who sang them risked prosecution. Sima enjoyed singing such songs with groups of young women as they climbed to the safety (from police) of the mountains. She also engaged with young men at university and in the movement. As she sought to buy cassettes of revolutionary songs, Sima met a fellow student who shared her passions and would soon become her husband. Today, Sima laughs as she remembers the revolutionary songs. She describes the genre as predominantly masculine, especially in its recorded form. The lyrics, melodies, and rhythms were rousing, in the Eastern Bloc tradition, and conducive to group singing. This intersection of ideology and music was especially appealing to students as they ended their teenage years. Where romance was also involved, as in Sima's case, the combination was intensified. Sima began to work actively toward the revolution, although its exact nature was not yet clear, and she sold cassettes of revolutionary songs herself to fellow students and other activists. She was not thinking of having her own singing recorded at this time. Most of the cassette recordings were hastily produced performances by groups of little known or amateur singers, with a preponderance of men. Although revolutionary songs dominated this period, Sima was pleased to discover that her husband also took great pleasure in her singing, among friends, of Mazanderani pieces.

As it became evident that it was possible for the revolution to move from the realms of fantasy into reality, an increasing optimism and sense of empowerment marked Sima's student years. In 1979, the Pahlavi regime was overthrown by what had come to be identified as the Islamic Revolution, and the Islamic Republic of Iran was established. It is useful to consider briefly the nature of Islamic practices in Iran. By the 1970s, after a century of rapid change, with diverse political, cultural, and spiritual movements, Iranian views of the world were as numerous as Iran's adult population. Notions of left and right, religious and secular, Eastern and Western do not adequately define the possibilities as individuals adopted various combinations of nationalism, anti-imperialism, Marxism, materialism, mysticism, modernism, liberal Islamism, and radical Islamism, among other isms. Sima's position in the spectrum of world views may be described as one that does not reject spiritual practices but sees issues of social justice as more significant. Her choices of dress reflect her views. For example, she does not wear the black chador favored by stricter Shi'a women and promoted by Iran's post-revolutionary government and she enjoys wearing the colorful traditional Mazanderani dress when she performs publicly (figure 9.1). The latter meets Islamic requirements, but it is beautiful, with intricate needlework, and each piece is individual, unlike the black chador. In casual contexts, Sima prefers the comfort of a Western-style T-shirt and trousers, while at the same time supporting the Revolution's rejection of more general cultural Westerniza-tion, especially in the area of music.

For Sima, the revolution and subsequent extreme political and sociocul-tural change brought both opportunities and restrictions. Finally, traditional and regional music had become more popularly acceptable than pop music as the country celebrated its new cultural independence from the United States and Europe. Initially, Sima also found a renewed respect for women and an end to the unethical gender relations that she believed had sustained the pop industry. She had observed that, before the revolution, many young women who recorded pop songs were pressured by their managers and producers to alter their personal appearance and/or to become involved in sexual re-lationships. Most pop music producers left Iran soon after the revolution. It was no longer possible for them to carry on their work in Iran because of the Islamic government's new laws against most forms of music. In 1980, Iran's postrevolutionary euphoria came to an abrupt end with the beginning of the Iran-Iraq War. Sima completed her university studies and she and her hus-band returned to Sari, where she gave birth to two daughters during the war. The war continued until 1988, with devastating effects for both Iran and Iraq. For Sima personally, these years were taken up with motherhood. Her prin-cipal singing activity during the 1980s was improvising on lullabies. Singing for pleasure or entertainment was considered unseemly by the government and many Iranians during the war. Casualties were very high, and the form of singing heard most frequently in public spaces was the melodic mourning performed by male cantors or Islamic reciters as they commemorated the lives of the hundreds of thousands of boys and men killed at war.

Adulthood: Creativity and Collaboration

In the 1990s, Sima's primary concern remained the care of her daughters, especially their education. However, Sima's daughters' educational success had an unintended consequence. Iran, like other countries, suffers from the emigration of many of its best-educated young people. The most difficult time in Sima's personal life was when her older daughter, Leila, migrated to Germany. Sima suffered depression and felt unable to sing—for herself or other people—for some time. However, it was a return to singing that later proved to be a crucial part of the solution to her depression. Ahmad Moh-senpour, the kamanche player mentioned at the beginning of this chapter, is also a prolific composer, arranger, and producer, as well as the head of

Mazanderan's House of Culture. He encouraged Sima to try singing again and taught her more about Mazanderani music. This renewed activity assisted her as she learned to live with the emigration of Leila and, later, her second daughter. Sima also began to take a new interest in her musical possibilities, especially improvisation. With deeper understanding of the structures of Mazanderani music and renewed confidence in her abilities, as well as the time and space—at home and in her friends' homes—to improvise freely, she developed her unique and sophisticated style.

"Intellectual" would not be the first word that Sima would choose to identify herself. However, it effectively describes her role in Mazanderan's musical life and her approach to the Mazanderani repertoire since the late 1990s. As well as the passion and talent that Sima has had for this music since childhood, she developed at this time a theoretical understanding that has enabled her to experiment musically, to analyze forms of experimentation, and to teach others. Sima joined a group of musicologists, composers, musicians, and educators who collaborate on various performances, recordings, and educational projects. Ethnomusicologist Sasan Fatemi notes that while the postrevolutionary government *imposed* seriousness on musical practice, demanding purposeful reflection rather than the frivolity or passion that was seen to characterize some Iranian music, a serious approach was also *proposed* by Mazanderan's intellectuals (arguably along with passion) (Fatemi 1997, 2002). However, these intellectuals' modes of seriousness differ significantly from those of the postrevolutionary authorities. Their desired effect is not a restriction, but rather an expansion of possibilities for pleasure and knowledge of selves and communities. Sima and her fellow Mazanderani intellectuals are not for forgetting the past but for remembering its overlooked aspects and its forgotten people. These people are not the revolutionary heroes and war martyrs who are commemorated elsewhere in Iran, but the workers, lovers, and poets who may continue to inspire. Workers and lovers are frequently the narrators and/or the addressees of traditional Mazanderani compositions, while the lyric writers, whose names have been lost in the case of many traditional pieces, are seen as poets, the professional category most revered by much of Iran's population. Sima and her colleagues seek to introduce the pleasures of all aspects of music-making, in all its Mazanderani contexts. She recounts a recent performance she gave for a group of young people in Sari, with a repertoire of work and love songs. Some of the youth in her audience expressed surprise that traditional songs could be so joyous. They explained that, previously, they had heard traditional singing only at funerals and had assumed that all such music was sad. Another aspect of Sima's work and repertoire is the decontextualization of the work songs she performs. Since her early childhood, Sima has not personally had to work in the fields or at a weaving loom, but she chooses to sing work songs in solidarity with those who are obliged to do such work. Of course, most songs performed at concerts or recorded and disseminated may be seen as decontextualized in some way.

While Sima's Mazanderani repertoire remains the most important in all her singing contexts, she has also begun to sing Persian art music since 2005. In 2009 she began to teach Mazanderani singing at Sari's House of Culture. Here, she takes great pleasure in the positive atmosphere, which contrasts starkly with her own childhood memories of singing lessons. She is pleased that girls and boys now work together in the classroom and learn to respect each other. Since childhood, Sima has been aware of the potential implications of musical encounter and difference, including the effects of notions of gender and ethnicity. Philip Bohlman provides a helpful analysis of these implications, suggesting that "even more than language, music is the key to understanding and to the power that will turn initial encounter into prolonged dominance" (2003, 46–47). The power of music, as outlined by Bohlman, played and plays significant roles in the varieties of "prolonged dominance" in Sima's world, including the dominance of notions of Persianness and that of restrictive notions of masculinity and femininity. Sima's consciousness of and resistance to such dominance has remained with her. This consciousness entails a knowledge that neither the Persian and the Mazanderani, nor the masculine and the feminine, represent binaries. For centuries, there has been interaction in musical and other areas, resulting in considerable overlap and constant change. When I ask Sima about the future for Mazanderani music, she sighs and says that, as in other countries, most young Iranians are more attracted to popular music than to traditional music. However, she remains hopeful, especially as Mazanderani music is very well established. Young and old continue to enjoy it, some young students are discovering it for the first time, and more accomplished musicians play it in innovative ways. Although Sima continues to perform, she sees her most significant future role as a facilitator of women's singing in Mazanderan. She does this especially through her teaching and also by organizing gatherings at which women are encouraged to sing.

The effects of postrevolutionary laws around music varied in different regions of Iran and in individual circumstances. In general, as outlined by Ameneh Youssefzadeh, restrictions immediately after the revolution and during the war were extreme, but they softened after the Revolution's leader Ayatollah Khomeini died in 1989 and "music slowly crept back into the broadcast programs and concert life of the Islamic Republic" (2005, 432[5]). In Sima's case, the main ongoing restriction is that when she performs in public in Iran, at officially authorized concerts in concert halls, theaters, and parks, with mixed-gender audiences, her singing voice must be accompanied by that of another woman. This expends her efforts and time that could otherwise be devoted to experimentation and improvement of her skills in vocal ornamentation and embellishment. Sima explains that men are able to develop their vocal styles freely, in every context, while women's development is slowed as they devote their public energies to adapting to their singing partners' styles. However, Sima makes up for this with intensified experimentation in private and women's contexts. She tells of the "very joyous gatherings" that ensue when she performs at women's events and invites others to collaborate. Sima also laughs as she explains that Iran has a history of dictatorships, and its people have always devised tricks to limit the restrictive effects of laws on life's pleasures, while also limiting their risk of punishment. For example, she and another woman singer were once denied permission to perform with their Mazanderani ensemble at a public concert that was being recorded. The two women negotiated with the recording crew that they would sing for their live audience, but with the volume turned down on the female voices' tracks, so that the recorded version sounds deceptively all male. Despite the restrictions, Sima says she is happy she can work in Iran and that difficulties are a necessary part of art.

Sima laughs again as she says how lucky she is with her marriage. According to her, men in Iran of her generation rarely encourage their wives to sing or play music, but her husband loves and promotes her singing. In 2005 he organized a concert tour of Germany for Sima and the Shevash Ensemble. They were invited back to Germany by a cultural association in 2008 and performed at the Iranian theater festival in Cologne. By then, both their daughters had moved to Germany and it had become very difficult for Sima and her husband to obtain visas to travel together. (If one partner remains in Iran, this is seen by the German government as a guarantee that the traveling partner will return.) Sima sighs as she reflects that international relations always affect performance possibilities for Iranian musicians, both outside and inside Iran. Like her music itself, Sima remains strongly attached to Mazanderan. Unlike many other Iranian women singers, she has no desire to emigrate, even in the face of her daughters' emigration.

Repertoire: Desire and Love

The intersection of politics, love, work, place, and spirituality features in the songs of Sima's Mazanderani repertoire. She explains that ostensibly simple narratives often carry several layers of meaning, which different listeners recognize or interpret in different ways. For example, the narrative of a wolf's attack on a shepherd's best sheep may simultaneously refer to a harsh regime's persecution of a community's most loved members and to the potentially harsh and dangerous life of a shepherd and the shepherd's attachment to his or her sheep. On another level, the same narrative might be understood in spiritual terms. Sima cites another example, this time representing the roles of women in political activity. Lyrics about a woman taking up her chador or another object may, in some contexts, refer to the role of women in secretly delivering messages to male fellow activists in difficult political times.

One song in Sima's repertoire is a love song in praise of a carpet weaver and her tireless work. Traditionally sung by carpet weavers themselves as they work, it includes these lines:

> Her face is red like fire
> Her eyes are like the sun . . .
> How I die for the light of her red eyes
> Which have not slept tonight . . .
> How I die for her tired body . . .
> How finely she has woven for her beloved.[6]

With its praise of a red face, red eyes, and a tired body, this song rearranges conventional notions of feminine desirability and beauty. While the imagery of Westernized popular music generally promotes the aesthetics of wide, clear eyes, and a pampered, fit body—especially for women—this song represents beauty as the effect of the working woman's devotion, strength, and love. It articulates an appreciation of those women whose bodies show the effects of a life fully lived, in all its beauty and brutality. As she sings this song, Sima's voice deepens and its volume and pace increase, reflecting the struggle of a working life. The song's melody and rhythms, especially toward the end, reflect the repetitive and tiring motions of weaving, provoking empathy with the working woman. Another piece in Sima's repertoire includes these lines:

> The dog is tied up - My love, come over tonight
> My grandmother is quiet - My love, come over tonight
> My little brother is asleep - My love, come over tonight
> My big brother is out with his friends - My love, come over tonight
> Our rice is cooking - My love, come over tonight . . .
> Your fiancé/e is the one reclining against the wall - My love, come over
>   tonight.[7]

This is one of the songs performed most passionately by Sima's ensemble in Iran, with Sima and another woman providing all the vocals. Some in Iran would find this a little subversive because the most common and "respectable" pieces with the theme of desire tend to have male narrators and singers. On hearing an officially approved recording of Sima and the ensemble performing this song, a colleague who researches music in another Iranian province suggested to me that such a performance would be unlikely to be granted permission there, mainly because the two women's individual voices are clearly audible. Thus, it seems that Sima and her colleagues in Sari have successfully negotiated a relatively open musical environment in Mazanderan.

In his discussion of music and identity, Simon Frith suggests that music "articulates in itself an understanding of both group relations and individuality" (1996, 111).[8] Sima's musical life and the voices she has adopted represent a rich example of such articulation. As with her singing, her life story is singular but carries collective significance at every turn. Sima's persistence with the hard work and the pleasure of singing, in the face of recurring obstacles, brings to mind novelist Shahrnush Parsipur's comment that "inevitably Iranian women have arisen" (2007). Singing has been crucial to Sima's capacity to "arise." As an Iranian woman, a Mazanderani granddaughter and mother, an artist, friend, and teacher, Sima negotiates her identities and repertoires with optimism, humor, generosity, and love. To reiterate Martin Stokes's notion, her singing voice "reorganises and manipulates everyday experiences of social reality, blurs, elides, ironises and sometimes subverts commonsense categories and markers" (2004, 101). Sima's particular modes of reorganization have adapted to exceptional historical circumstances and continue to inspire diverse musical communities.

Acknowledgments

Many thanks to the inspiring Sima and her husband Mr. Mazaheri for their generosity and warmth, and to the indefatigable Ahmad Mohsenpour and his family. Without the guidance, translation, and support of Sasan Fatemi, this research would not have been possible. I am grateful to Rezvan Khadjekan Ghalleh and the Mokhtabad family, who helped introduce me to Mazanderani music, and to Veronica Doubleday for putting us in touch and for her encouragement. Thanks also to Margaret Kartomi and the Monash University School of Music–Conservatorium for support.

Notes

1. Translated from the original Tabari, Sima's first language, by Sasan Fatemi and author.

2. Most of the information in this essay is based on my participation in such gatherings and on my interviews with Sima, conducted from 2006 to 2010. I am grateful to Sasan Fatemi for introducing me to Sima and assisting with all aspects of my fieldwork.

3. An analysis of this complex period is beyond the scope of this chapter, but useful analyses may be found in the work of historians such as Kashani-Sabet (2002), Abrahamian (2008), and Ansari (2007).

4. Again, detailed analysis is beyond the scope of this chapter. For further information about the movement, see Abrahamian 2008.

5. See also Youssefzadeh 2000.

6. Translated by Sasan Fatemi and author.

7. Translated by Sasan Fatemi and author.

8. I am grateful to Helen O'Shea for drawing my attention to this chapter.

References

Abrahamian, Ervand. 2008. *A History of Modern Iran*. Cambridge: Cambridge University Press.

Ansari, Ali M. 2007. *Modern Iran: The Pahlavis and After*, 2nd ed. Harlow, U.K.: Pearson.

Bohlman, Philip V. 2003. "Music and Culture: Historiographies of Disjuncture." In *The Cultural Study of Music: A Critical Introduction*, eds. Martin Clayton, Trevor Herbert, and Richard Middleton, 45–56. London: Routledge.

Doubleday, Veronica. 1988. *Three Women of Herat*. Austin: University of Texas Press.

Doubleday, Veronica, and John Baily. 1995. "Patterns of Musical Development among Children in Afghanistan." In *Children in the Muslim Middle East*, ed. Elizabeth Warnock Fernea, 431–44. Austin: University of Texas Press.

Emami, Karim. 2007. *Farhang Moaser Kimia Persian-English Dictionary*. Tehran: Farhang Moaser Publishers.

Fatemi, Sasan. 1997. *La Musique et la Vie du Mazandaran: Le Problème du Changement*, unpublished thesis, Mémoire de maîtrise en ethnologie, University of Paris X, Nanterre.

———. 2002. *Musiqi va Zendegi-ye Musiqâyi dar Mâzandarân: Mas'ale-ye Taqyirât*. Tehran: Mahoor.

Feld, Steven, and Aaron Fox. 2000. "Voice." *Journal of Linguistic Anthropology* 9(1–2):159–62.

Frith, Simon. 1996. "Music and Identity." In *Questions of Cultural Identity*, eds. Stuart Hall and Paul du Gay, 108–27. London: Sage.

Kashani-Sabet, Firoozeh. 2002. "Cultures of Iranianness: The Evolving Polemic of Iranian Nationalism." In *Iran and the Surrounding World: Interactions in Culture and Cultural Politics*, eds. Nikki R. Keddie and Rudi Matthee, 162–81. Seattle: University of Washington Press.

Koskoff, Ellen. 1989. "The Sound of a Woman's Voice: Gender and Music in a New York Hasidic Community." In *Women and Music in Cross-Cultural Perspective*, ed. Ellen Koskoff, 213–23. Urbana: University of Illinois Press.

Magrini, Tullia, ed. 2003. *Music and Gender: Perspectives from the Mediterranean*. Chicago: University of Chicago Press.

O'Shea, Helen. 2008. "'Good Man, Mary!' Women Musicians and the Fraternity of Irish Traditional Music." *Journal of Gender Studies* 17(1):55–70.

Parsipur, Shahrnush, interviewed by Mohammed Al-Urdun. June 19, 2007. "Iran's literary giantess is defiant in exile . . . but missing home." *Camden New Journal—Middle East Eye*. http://www.shahrnushparsipur.com (accessed March 2012).

Randell-Moon, Holly. 2007. "Secularism, Feminism and Race in Representations of Australianness." *Transforming Cultures eJournal* 2(1). http://epress.lib.uts.edu.au/journals/TfC.

Stokes, Martin. 2004. "Place, Exchange and Meaning: Black Sea Musicians in the West of Ireland." In *Popular Music: Critical Concepts in Media and Cultural Studies, Volume IV: Music and Identity*, ed. Simon Frith, 101–16. London: Routledge.

Youssefzadeh, Ameneh. 2000. "The Situation of Music in Iran since the Revolution: The Role of Official Organizations." *British Journal of Ethnomusicology* 9(2):44–48.

———. 2005. "Iran's Regional Musical Traditions in the Twentieth Century: A Historical Overview." *Iranian Studies* 38(3):417–39.

10. Zainab Herawi

Finding Acclaim in the Conservative
Islamic Culture of Afghanistan

VERONICA DOUBLEDAY

In 1968, accompanied by her husband and children, twenty-seven-year-old Afghan singer Zainab Herawi[1] traveled to Kabul to make recordings at Radio Afghanistan. The long journey—seven hundred miles from her home city of Herat—was her first trip to the capital and a turning point in her singing career. No other woman singer in her musician clan had been accorded this honor, and the invitation gave her preeminence. Ever afterward Zainab liked to boast to her clients and rivals that she and her family had been guests of Radio Afghanistan for two weeks.

Zainab's host, the head of music at Radio Afghanistan, was Abdul Wahab Madadi, a native Herati and a distinguished singer in his own right. An excellent judge of talent, he was on the lookout for new singers to broadcast at a time when Radio Afghanistan was busy popularizing regional music. While visiting Herat he had recently invited Zainab and other prominent musicians to a recording session in their local theater, and these broadcast recordings received such a good nationwide public response that he invited the best singers to make new recordings with the Radio Afghanistan orchestra in Kabul. From each singer's repertoire he personally selected appropriate items on the basis of their originality and the quality of the melodies and poetry (Madadi, pers. comm. 2008).

For Zainab it was an exciting but daunting prospect. She was an unsophisticated provincial entertainer and wedding ritualist and had never experienced the demanding standards of a national recording studio—especially working with the Radio Afghanistan Orchestra. Her normal musical milieux were noisy, long-drawn-out female festive gatherings, crowded with women and children. She was used to gender-segregated social situations and singing in the company of women. In Kabul she would meet members of a predominantly male musical community focused around two locations: Kucheh Kharabat, the hereditary musician quarter in the old city, with its esteemed *ustad*s (master musicians), and Radio Afghanistan, with its hub of men and women singers and male instrumentalists, composers, and arrangers (many from the Kharabat) all working to create a new popular radio style.[2] But it seems that she was most in awe of her female counterparts, the radio stars whose songs and names she already knew. Her nephew Amir accompanied her to the radio station, reporting that she asked, "With Rokhshana and Parwana and Jila and Mahwash there, how can I sing?" Very likely she felt her abilities and performance would be measured against them.

The recordings went well, and the *ustad*s and singers were impressed by her, praising her as a true artist and singer.[3] Madadi remembers the occasion too, saying she was "very quick and good" and "so in tune."[4] She recorded five songs,[5] among them her famous *chaharbeiti* lament, "Shirin Dokhtar-e Maldar" ("Sweet nomad girl"). *Chaharbeiti* is a plaintive and ancient style of sung folk poetry, performed in a free rhythm,[6] and this piece received particular praise, being commended as totally authentic and original. Madadi subsequently took it into his own vocal repertoire, and in the light of its reception in Kabul this became Zainab's most prized song.[7]

Madadi offered contracts for work at Radio Afghanistan to Zainab and a few other selected singers. She was honored but did not accept. Her husband opposed the move, and she told me that in any case she was not fond of Kabul—it was "dirty and crowded." Besides, she felt she had too many children to take on such a formal commitment. Not long afterward another professional opportunity came: a German radio team offered her a generous fee to go to Kabul and make further recordings. But Zainab was in the late stages of a pregnancy and felt unable to travel. In 1973, when I arrived for my first year's residence in Herat, Zainab was generally hailed as "the best woman singer of Herat," but she had not managed to capitalize on several career opportunities.

Several obstacles thwarted and impeded her progress. In general terms these related to gender, religion, and family. Another important disadvantage was her birth in a geographical location far from the capital city. Working at Radio Afghanistan would have greatly extended her musical development, but Madadi told me she made a sound decision because the Radio Afghanistan salary was small, and she was making a good income at Herati weddings. In reality Zainab did not have the resources to stay in Kabul—and she had no family or connections there. Also, had she stayed, stardom was by no means assured. As Madadi pointed out to me, a female singer's fame depended on other aesthetic criteria beyond vocal ability. "Zainab was not too beautiful," he said, noting that "unfortunately, the Afghan public like to hear singers who are beautiful." Even for radio singers, this aesthetic discrimination applied.[8] Besides this, other aspects of her social background served to undermine her prospects for national fame.

Prejudice against Musical Performers

From around the age of eight or nine, when she became an apprentice musician, Zainab had a strong experience of social disapproval. She was classed as a *sazandeh*, a term for musicians (literally, "instrumentalist") that carries negative connotations (see Baily 1988, 149–52). A disreputable image clung to the Herati women's *sazandeh* bands, who were popularly known as "the Golpasand bands" after the professional musician and patriarch Golpasand.[9] Despite the fact that they were in great demand at thoroughly respectable lavish all-women festivities, their work was considered to be morally questionable. In Afghanistan prejudice against professional musicianship has its roots in a complex history of theological debate on the status of music in Islamic culture,[10] essentially linking music with pleasure and seeing it as a distraction from work and prayer.

There were other reasons for Zainab to grow up with a sense of being an outsider. She came from a low-status barber-musician background associated with male performance on the *sorna* and *dohol*, the celebratory and ritually auspicious shawm and drum pair found right across the Muslim world, and beyond (see Poché 1984). Barbers also performed male circumcision, and the profession was seen as unclean. People from this background were set apart in terms of marriages, seating and eating arrangements, and places of burial. In Herat members of these communities were derogatorily known as "Jats," and they lived in particular areas of the city or in specific villages.[11] Among themselves they used a kind of secret language, which was especially useful in their work. They could say to each other things such as "This is a bad person," "Let's get out of here," or "They won't give any more money."

A notable Jat artistic tradition—obsolescent in the preconflict period of the 1970s and perhaps now defunct—was the outdoor performance of bawdy satirical theatrical sketches.[12] For this the actors daubed themselves with flour makeup, cracked lewd jokes, and dressed up as women or animals—clownlike behavior that was considered highly unrespectable. Zainab's mother came from Deh Tappeh, a Jat village with its own theatrical troupe (Baghban 1977, 65–66), and in her social comportment Zainab embodied some aspects of Jat behavior. She could be loud, argumentative, and rudely assertive—or, when well treated, effusively polite.[13] She also had a talent for comic mimicry.

Zainab grew up inured to the prejudices surrounding music and performance, but she was at pains to hide her outsider identity, fearing it would damage her professional image. Mixing with her clients and their guests, she was evasive when questioned about kinship relationships. Also, when interviewed in 1972 by Lorraine Sakata, she untruthfully said she was a "Burakzai Pashtun," and the "daughter of Golpasand" (2002 [1983], 88 and 207).[14] Zainab was not the only member of her family to hide details of her identity: her eldest son told me none of his classmates had any idea his mother was a *sazandeh*. He kept it secret, because it was shameful. All in all, Zainab's marginalized social upbringing was a disadvantage.

Education and Musical Training

Zainab did not attend school, nor did she send her own daughters to school, because she wanted them available for work in her band.[15] Like the other women in her community, she was illiterate. In Kabul most of the women radio singers were reasonably well educated, and literacy was convenient for learning songs and collecting song texts in notebooks. This situation surely undermined Zainab's confidence at the prospect of radio work. But she did have an advantage in her long experience as a singer. She had been performing at women's festivities from around the age of ten: first in the band of Sabo, Golpasand's youngest wife, and then later leading her own band. Zainab spoke very fondly of Sabo, who became her mentor and later her mother-in-law.[16] Sabo was a small, beautiful woman, whom older Herati women still remember warmly. She recognized Zainab's potential as a singer and said she was her "nightingale" (*bolbol*), a considerable compliment in a culture that reveres this songbird as a poetic symbol for intense mystical love and emotional expressivity (see Schimmel 1975, Chapter 7).[17] In Zainab's early years, out at weddings, Sabo was sometimes harsh when Zainab made mistakes, clearly wanting to avoid repetition of errors. However, Sabo was good to Zainab at home. Professionally and domestically, they were close. Zainab lived in Sabo's home, doing her housework, cooking meals, and helping to mind her children. Together they ate food from the same hearth. Sadly for Zainab, Sabo died before reaching the age of forty, so she lost an ally in her.

Like her peers, Zainab learned to sing and play instrumental music through a process of observation and imitation, watching and following skilled band members at weddings. Having observed the next generation of learners, I was able to analyze their patterns of musical enculturation and concluded that in this community there was little musical tuition apart from the correction of faults. Senior musicians such as Sabo encouraged and praised learners, but ultimately motivation was left to the individual, learning by imitation (see

Doubleday and Baily 1995, 440). Baghban's assessment of the related tradition of Jat buffoonery broadly supports my conclusions, stressing two main ideas: learning from a young age and learning from a skilled elder (1977, 59).[18]

Singers like Zainab grew into confident performers, but they had no theoretical understanding of their craft. In terms of musical apprenticeship and training, there are interesting parallels with *sazandeh* traditions in neighboring Bukhara, in Uzbekistan. Theodore Levin notes that the musical culture of Herat "shares many features with that of Bukhara" (1996, 300 n.31), and he quotes a venerable Bukharan musician Tohfaxan (born around 1928) describing her apprenticeship: "Older *sâzanda*s took me on as a pupil. They'd be going to a wedding and they'd say, 'Come with us.' And I went. They didn't teach me. I just watched them dance and absorbed what they did" (ibid., 119). Across a broad cultural area extending well beyond Afghanistan's borders, entertainment singers and performers learned in this way, inheriting professional expertise through long hours of musical exposure. The apparent emphasis on apprentices learning to dance is interesting and similar to the situation in Herat, where young band members developed a song-and-dance act as their first performance piece.

As a young apprentice, initially Zainab simply watched and listened, running errands and minding the older band members' children as necessary, but before long she was allowed to sing. Fledgling band members were encouraged to display their talent as early as possible, and Zainab was naturally extrovert. Speaking of those early days, she described herself as uninhibited, comic, cheeky, and outward-going. She was a natural entertainer and good at making the guests dance. She used to do comic naughty dances herself, thrusting her bottom from one side to the other, and she also amused her audience with vocal imitations of instruments.[19] Sometimes the women laughed so much they told her to stop.

Usually held in the lavishly decorated courtyard of a large house, the women's parties lasted almost twenty-four hours and required considerable vocal and physical stamina. Musically, the women's bands imitated the sound of male urban Afghan music in their use of the hand-pumped portable Indian harmonium and *tabla* (North Indian drum pair), to which they added one or two frame drums (*daireh*) as the rhythmic backbone of Afghan women's music. All the band members sang, providing a varied repertoire of popular and ritual songs (figure 10.1).

The atmosphere was crowded and chaotic, with children running around and a lot of noise. Musical precision was not emphasized. Hosting a family event, Zainab's female employers required a vibrant atmosphere and plenty of dance music. The numerous guests wanted to chat, admire one another's

Figure 10.1. Zainab Herawi (on the right, in a white headscarf) with her band, taking a break at a wedding party, Herat city, April 1977. Photograph by Veronica Doubleday.

colorful new dresses, listen to a bit of singing, watch some lively dancing, and make detailed mental notes about the relative expense and grandeur of the occasion. In such settings they were easily distracted and not particularly discriminating listeners. As city dwellers they were alert to new fashions, and they might request the latest radio songs, so new musical material was always coming into the repertoire. Zainab developed an excellent ear. As a mature musician she was able to learn new songs very quickly by listening to the radio, to recordings, or to other performers she might hear. These skills would have served her well in radio work.

Zainab had no interest in musical terminology, abstraction, or theory, and no command of the standard terms for rhythms or modes employed by male professional musicians. Her male professional counterparts did not share their specialist knowledge with their female *sazandeh* relatives: in an intensely competitive male musical hierarchy, they were presumably keen to retain a position of authority and superiority over them.[20] When I asked Zainab about technical terms, she dismissed such talk as "a matter for the *ustads*." She did not want to play the men's game of intellectual one-upmanship and apparently had no use for their jargon. This closed intellectual mindset left her ill-prepared for potential activities at Radio Afghanistan. Recording her own songs was one matter; following the demands of music directors might be quite another.

Modesty and the Evil Eye

In a city where women were largely veiled and secluded, Islamic female modesty was a crucial issue for women performers. This applied to actresses and dancers in the local theater, and privately hired musicians like Zainab. Zainab wore the *burqa* veil in public space, but she and her peers were notorious for flouting the rules of purdah (the practice of preventing women from being seen by men). They had to negotiate fees and conditions face-to-face with male clients (the men of the families giving the wedding). At weddings the women musicians appeared gaudily dressed in full view of unrelated men— the bridegroom and bridegroom's father at least, and usually others. Often they had to travel to the venue in a car with their male hosts. These aspects of their work aroused strong social disapproval. Zainab and her peers developed strategies for coping with this. Coming from the lower echelons of society, they readily brushed off insults, but they also recognized the value of forging supportive links with patrons. Zainab's boisterous and outgoing humorous personality was an asset in performance, but she was also concerned—as far as possible—to project a public image of personal respectability. She especially wanted to distance herself from the "disreputable girls" who worked on stage singing and dancing for sexually avid audiences of men at the Herat theater.

The Herat theater had originally used all-male casts (with female roles taken by young men and boys). At some point, perhaps in the 1960s, as part of a government policy aimed at improving the position of women in the arts, women were introduced onto the stage as actresses, singers, and dancers. Paradoxically, this resulted in a lowered status for the theater because "the only women who could be recruited to perform before audiences of men were courtesans, who used the theatre to advertise themselves, as well as earning surprisingly large salaries" (Baily 1988, 134). The theater women were not sophisticated or highly trained like the courtly entertainers of North India (e.g., see Qureshi 2006), so the term "courtesan" may be misleading: Baily intended to indicate a more refined form of sexual availability than common prostitution.[21] Furthermore, they were not talented singers, and audiences were mostly interested in the thrill of seeing glamorous women, especially when they danced.[22] "Their work is bad," Zainab told me. "They stand up for men to see them and get excited. We play sitting down, just for women, which is quite different." I suspect that these concerns made her wary of the unfamiliar free-living mixed-gender environment of Kabul.

Sex and overt sexuality were delicate issues. Afghanistan and its surrounding areas (Central Asia, Iran, India) have a long history of links between female professional singing, dancing, and prostitution (e.g., see Floor 2008;

218–22, Doubleday 2000, 815). Many Herati men held a general conception that Zainab's female musician milieu was implicated in sex work. This was certainly not true of Zainab and her family, but she was vulnerable to spiteful or misinformed rumors and accusations. In general, the image of women performers in Islamic cultures has long been problematic, especially for dancers, because dance places its central focus on the body and Zainab's disapproval of the theatrical women relates to this.[23]

But in Afghanistan and other Islamic societies women singers are strongly implicated in issues relating to personal allure. Codes about female veiling and seclusion heighten public interest in a woman's face and body and in the erotic power of the voice. Added to this is the dominance of romantic themes in song lyrics.[24] To achieve success, a woman Afghan singer needs to harness more or less all these alluring qualities, but in so doing she attracts disapproval and censure. Strictly speaking, it is not necessary to have a really beautiful face: a singer may create this allure through the sensuous qualities of her voice and her ability to infuse the lyrics with heartfelt meaning. In Zainab's case, her wedding audiences were female—or primarily female—and the few men that attended were normally respectful, keeping their eyes fairly downcast. Accordingly, the erotic content of the vocal repertoire was not a cause for shame or embarrassment: it was not as though Zainab was singing about love while maintaining eye contact with a male patron, thereby arousing sexual desire, as in the courtesan traditions of North India.

According to Afghan aesthetics, a woman singer needs to dress glamorously, with glittering clothes and fashionable makeup and jewelry (even if the clothing is modestly long and loose). For their audiocassette covers, Kabuli women radio stars tended to cultivate elaborate hairstyles and exaggerated makeup, influenced by the image of Hindi film stars. Artificial coiffures and heavy makeup are also standard features of an Afghan bride's appearance on her wedding day.[25] But Zainab was rather diffident about self-adornment. By the time I knew her she was already a mother of eight, and she normally dressed for weddings in a relatively quiet style, although the other band members compensated with boldly colored eyelids and shining lip gloss. Zainab's perceived unpolished appearance detracted from her commercial success in Herat. Wealthy female clients wanted glamour, and some were more concerned about visual impressions than musical standards. Young elegant dancers were a great attraction, and the most successful musicians invested in flashy gold jewelry and rich dresses. The need for good looks—a pretty face and lithe, sexually appealing body—in a singer is hardly confined to Afghanistan and has frequently been discussed and documented in other cultural contexts (e.g., see Koskoff 1989; Kimberlin 1990).

In Islamic societies, physical self-presentation has been a perennial problem for women singers. Given their visual prominence and romantic songs, they attract sexual interest, and it seems hard to find a middle way between brazen beauty and respectable downplayed modesty. As Racy notes, in traditional Arab societies female singing is recognized as "an effective conveyor of musical ecstasy" (2003, 17), but, along with this, he points out the general belief that "for women, pursuing the music profession is incompatible with private family life and with the established norms of social decorum" (ibid., 16). To varying degrees this compromised image pervades the Islamic world. Even in the relatively secularized context of Azerbaijan, Inna Naroditskaya notes that "although the question of female morality did not arise, since the female performer [/singer] worked in women's company, the image of a woman entertainer was morally ambiguous" (2000, 240 and 243–44).

In Afghanistan the role of the professional woman singer has never been comfortable. One of the first women to sing on Radio Afghanistan, in 1951, was Parwin. She came from a noble family in Badakhshan, in the traditionalist and remote mountainous northeast, and had the support and encouragement of powerful men, including the well-known painter Abdul Ghafur Breshna, then director of the newly inaugurated radio station (Rahimi 1986 [1977], 89). However, in 1972, in an encounter in Badakhshan, Lorraine Sakata, then a young researcher, recounted that her jeep driver refused to stop and give Parwin a ride: he did not approve of women like her "and didn't want to have anything to do with her" (2002 [1983], 98). Sakata points out that by this time women singers were no longer a rarity, and many of them, like Parwin, had been awarded the King's Gold Medal in recognition of their talents, but "the majority of the population who knew of her [Parwin's] presence felt the same way [as the jeep driver]" (ibid.). Similar negative attitudes could be found in Herat, among the more conservative city dwellers and certainly in the countryside.[26]

Zainab and her peers flouted the rules of purdah by making their voices heard in the company of men from outside their own family circles. As well as singing to entertain, they called out and sang ritual blessings. At certain points in the ceremonies, Zainab and her girls would get up to lead the bride and groom, singing bridal songs as they slowly processed to their special "throne." It was also the musician's job to display bridal gifts—loudly advertising the items one by one, like an auctioneer. Apart from singing, Zainab was a storyteller, and she might entertain women with anecdotes based on her own experiences.[27] Furthermore, she sometimes indulged in a bit of theater. On leaving a wedding she was prone to demand further payment or gifts in an embarrassing shouting match that was a typical Jat strategy for getting extra rewards or money. Overall, her voice commanded attention, and was assertive rather than modest.

However, for all her brazenness at weddings, Zainab was wary of gaining too much public exposure. In 1977 a Herati music shopkeeper invited her to make some commercial recordings, but she refused. Probably the financial offer was not particularly enticing, but other factors came into play. "What do I want with a cassette with my photo on it?" she asked me. The photo seemed to be a real issue. Herati veiling involves the action of covering the face with the *burqa*—it is called "*ru gereftan*" (to "take" or cover the face)—and the act of publicly revealing her face apparently concerned her. One wonders how might she have projected herself? She had no truck with eye makeup and contrived hairstyles, and in company always wore a loose head covering over her hair. Perhaps she thought: why should I reveal my face anyway?

Belief in the evil eye is widespread in Afghanistan: it is thought that an admiring gaze may inadvertently damage or destroy the object of admiration, and I think in this instance Zainab was wary about attracting the destructive impact of an evil eye. Added to this, she felt beleaguered by the presence of so many rival women musicians around her, all vying for work. "They're all jealous of my success, and they want to steal my patrons," she told me. She was comfortable in all-women or family contexts, but her sense of Islamic modesty made her nervous about launching herself into the world. It is not surprising that the prospect of living and working in the unfamiliar liberal atmosphere of Kabul did not appeal.

Family Constraints

Many factors deterred Zainab from accepting the Radio Afghanistan offer: concerns about Islamic modesty and public exposure as a woman; distrust of the libertarian values of Kabul, and perhaps fear of prejudice against Jats in an unfamiliar environment. But financial concerns were probably paramount. Zainab was the main breadwinner of the family. Her barber husband earned rather small daily sums of money—just enough to pay for some groceries—but he insisted on relative comfort and luxury. Over the years, he was a serious drain on her financial resources. In particular he entangled her in a hard legal battle, by tricking her into accepting a co-wife in a deal involving the marriage of their eldest daughter. The arrangement misfired and the daughter was whisked away to a remote village, barred from contact and unavailable for work. Zainab spent large sums of money on legal fees before finally managing to regain her much-loved and much-needed band member.[28] Hard-won earnings were wasted and Zainab was forced to sell all her gold jewelry. Among Afghan women gold is a great indicator of prestige, and the loss of this diminished her public image. Not only was Zainab short on gold and glamorous clothes, she could not even afford good instruments. Her *tabla* drums were often in poor repair, and for a time her harmonium had several notes that stuck. By contrast, one of her rivals had a loudspeaker system for the band—a great attraction for clients.

Physical constraints also loomed large with regard to Zainab's career prospects. She was a fertile woman unable to control the size of her young family. "I'm unlucky," she told me. "I conceive even when I'm still breastfeeding. I get pregnant every two years." Many Afghan women breast-feed their babies for a good two years: breast-feeding often delays the return of menstruation, thereby offering a natural form of contraception. This was not the case for Zainab, who quickly became pregnant again. When I met her, one of the first things she asked me was whether I could give her contraceptive pills. Motherhood was sapping her energy and financial resources. Her breasts sagged and her abdomen was distended by many pregnancies, causing her to lose interest in self-adornment and glamour.

Another family constraint hampered Zainab's career. Band membership was based on family connections, and Zainab's kinship network was limited.

Figure 10.2. Zainab Herawi with her daughter Anar Gol and one of her sons, relaxing at a social gathering with music, Herat city, May 1977. Photograph by Veronica Doubleday.

"It would have been good if I'd had lots of daughters!" she said to me. By the mid-1970s she had two daughters working, but the younger one was still only a promising apprentice. Her other two band members lacked vocal talent, but she had no other relatives to recruit. In 1972, when she recorded some pieces for Lorraine Sakata, she used male accompanists: her nephew on goblet drum (*zirbaghali*), and Sakata's teacher, Ghulam Haidar, on *dutar* (Sakata 2002 [1983], 129–32 and 144–45). Zainab obviously appreciated the precision of polished male accompanists, but the all-women context of her normal work precluded such collaborations.

By this point, the one person who inspired Zainab had died—Sabo, her mother-in-law. She had no one to help her develop her career. If you look at any successful Afghan woman star, you'll find a male sponsor has worked to support her. This is true of Afghanistan's most famous woman singer, Us-tad Mahwash, who now lives in exile in California and enjoys international fame. Her husband is a music-lover and a good businessman who strongly promoted her career.[29]

Dreams of Fame

Despite her apparent diffidence, Zainab still entertained faint dreams of greater fame. One day, when I was visiting, she fantasized that when I went back to England maybe (through me) someone would invite her to come and make some recordings. She would take her husband and elder daughter with her, she said. Then, in the next breath, she said she did not know when she would go to Kabul to record more songs on the radio. She planned to sing more of the traditional folk material that people like Madadi had appreciated so much.

But she had lost her opportunity, and events took over. With the Marxist coup d'etat of 1978, the onset of civil unrest in Herat affected all musicians, making working conditions dangerous. Women musicians were especially vulnerable to criticism and harassment from Islamist factions. At the same time, under communist rule, music flourished in Kabul, and another Herati girl did go there and became a national star. Setara (meaning "star") was an actress, singer, and dancer from the local theater. Her singing was not es-pecially distinguished: it was her pretty face, tender smiles, slim figure, and delicate, precise, and understated dancing that made her famous. Around 1980, when television transmissions began, this sweet-faced girl made her name with a signature song: "Man dokhtar-e Heratam" ("I'm a Herati girl"). Footage exists of her performing this song on Afghan television. She stands demurely dressed with a cap and filmy veil, sequins pasted on her brow, in front of a semicircle of seated musicians who are the cream of Kabul's male performers. Her enduring fame is fueled by a persistent but incorrect rumor that she was murdered for her dancing by the *mujaheddin*. Symbolically it is almost true: she fled from Afghanistan in the 1980s and has shunned public life. Today she lives in privacy with a Canadian husband near Toronto, but she is fondly remembered, and her televised performances are available on YouTube. Zainab was a more talented singer, but she never even achieved national fame. Although audio recordings of her songs exist, including those in the Radio Afghanistan archive, very little has remained to keep her memory alive.

In the 1980s, as violence and political instability spread across the country, the role of music was a hotly contested issue. All women professional singers were in a perilous position. Well before the advent of the Taliban, women radio and television stars were in real danger of assassination, so they escaped to other countries, preferably ending up in Europe or North America (see Baily 2001, Doubleday 2007). Zainab stayed in Afghanistan, but her luck turned. One of her children was killed, caught in cross fire and shot in the head. Her husband became ill and died. Patrons were leaving to take shelter in Iran. She herself became ill, suffering from a neurological disease that paralyzed and eventually killed her in 1985. Her singing career was cut short.

Only members of an older generation of Herati women now remember Zainab, and sometimes they get confused between her, her sister, and other entertainers from her Golpasand community. For Herati women, weddings were important social gatherings: they gave only partial attention to singers and their music. It was male connoisseurs and musicians such as Madadi or Ali Ahmad, Sabo's son (who loved Zainab's singing), who appreciated Zainab as "Herat's best female singer" of the time. Her female patrons were barely aware that she had the distinction of making the recordings in Kabul.[30]

Interlaced Stories:
No Fame but a Lasting Legacy

Around a month before my departure from Herat in 1977, Zainab took me to visit a young woman relative who had recently returned from living in Russia. She had married a Kandahari man who was studying in Moscow, and they were making a return visit home. Strongly influenced by Soviet values, he deplored the bad position of music in Afghanistan. He said in any other country his wife would have been a singing star—with her stunning good looks and voice. Zainab agreed, but said Afghan people varied in their treatment of musicians: some were respectful, whereas others were rude. She said she had some good Herati patrons who helped her, lent her money, and listened properly to her singing, but plenty of her employers were ignorant about music and not too respectful. However, she went on to say that none of the women in their Golpasand alley who went out as musicians were happy to do so, but they "do it because they're forced to by economic circumstances." Any Afghan woman singer would most likely agree that the music profession is psychologically stressful. One is open to denigration, as Sakata's story about Parwin illustrates.

Although Zainab loved performing, and wanted greater recognition, vocal talent and performance ability are not sufficient attributes in themselves for an Afghan woman singer to achieve success and acclaim. Zainab was held back by many other factors: her uneducated and marginalized upbringing, her poverty and lack of social connections, her heavy family obligations, and a fear of exposure beyond certain familiar bounds. This fear was a complex mix of provincial Islamic female modesty, an awareness of malicious rivals, and a sense of potential supernatural destructive forces liable to attack people in the limelight. Also, crucially, Zainab lacked the active protection and support of a male promoter. Such a person—typically a father or husband—can make a world of difference in the life of an aspiring female singer.[31] This is especially true in Islamic societies, where public performance may bring women into disrepute. The career of the famed Egyptian singer Umm Kulthum illustrates this point: her father was totally committed to promoting and supporting her, and later in life many influential and important mentors and backers followed (Danielson 1997). Also, to achieve national fame one must be in the capital city, and Umm Kulthum's story also demonstrates this. As Umm Kulthum's singing career in the Nile Delta region flowered, "numerous people encouraged her father to move to Cairo in order to advance her career. He was reluctant to do this for he did not know the city and had no close relatives or any assurance of work there. The subject of Cairo remained under discussion for several years" (Danielson 1997, 33). Zainab was at a similar disadvantage. Without moving to Kabul she had no hope of expanding her fame on a national level.

As Zainab's student, performer, and biographer, I am also part of her story. I continue to acknowledge Zainab as my teacher, and some of the songs she taught me are quite special and original, powerfully evoking a former period of Afghan life.[32] In this way my singing perpetuates Zainab's name. If you do an internet search for Zainab Herawi, you find her name linked with mine. For those Afghans who have read my book, I have perhaps also transformed their perception of her and other musical entertainers in Afghanistan.[33] Zainab's limitations and achievements serve to illustrate the contradictory forces surrounding any aspiring Afghan woman singer. Intractable customary prohibitions against female public performance stand pitted against a deep cultural appreciation of music and sung poetry. This is, after all, a country where the female voice is seen as controversially seductive and where censorship of women singers still applies. A woman's voice is eroticized, and its allure is linked with the need for attractive physical self-presentation in a performer, and Zainab was unable to enter that domain of sophistication and glamour.[34]

Notes

1. This was her approximate age. I have written extensively elsewhere about Zainab under the pseudonym of Shirin in my narrative ethnography, *Three Women of Herat* (2006a [1988]). In that work I used pseudonyms (and modified certain details of the action) in order to mask people's identity and protect their privacy (see author note, Doubleday 2006a,xi).

2. For further information on the activities of Radio Afghanistan, see Baily 1981, 1994, and 2001. There is also much relevant information in Sarmast 2004.

3. Amir, taped interview with John Baily, 1985. Their terms *honarmand* (artist) and *khanandeh* (singer) are polite and appreciative, as opposed to another rather derogatory term *sazandeh* (musician/instrumentalist), discussed later.

4. Madadi, pers. comm. 2008.

5. The songs were "Shirin dokhtar-e maldar/Sarhadi," "Ze hejranat aziz-e man hamishe cheshm-e taram," "Ahesteh buro," "Olang olang," and "Yar yar yar."

6. One track on the companion website contains two examples of Zainab singing in this form (sung consecutively). Also see Doubleday 2011 for detailed information about the performance of *chaharbeiti* in Afghanistan.

7. For a recording (as a duo with myself), see Track 10 in Madadi et al. 2005. In 1972 she recorded it for Lorraine Sakata, with the alternative title *Sarhadi*. The two titles relate to two different systems of categorization: *Shirin dokhtar-e maldar* is the chorus line, the normal mode of identifying Herati folk songs, and *Sarhadi* is its melodic designation, as identified by local instrumentalists. Sakata provides an analysis of this song (2002, 129–32 [1983]), and her recording is Example 8 on her accompanying CD. When I first met Zainab in 1976, she also sang this song for me.

8. Madadi, pers. comm. 2008.

9. For a factual account of the Golpasand musician community, with actual names, see Baily 1988. The data on the women's bands was imparted by Zainab to me.

10. See, for example, Nasr 1997; Neubauer and Doubleday 2001. Neubauer is the author of the section on the theological debate. My role was to expand and update other parts of the article.

11. In other parts of Afghanistan Jats are linked with other professions, including music and prostitution (see Rao 1982). Another more polite term, *gharibzadeh*, translates roughly as "stranger."

12. See Baghban 1977.

13. In villages Jats had a customary right to collect a portion of the harvest, but they often had to behave assertively (and insultingly) in order to receive this payment for their services.

14. Zainab had no blood relationship with Golpasand. Her father was an artisan and instrument maker from Kandahar, and it is most unlikely that he belonged to the Burakzai tribal group. Tribal Pashtuns do not enter the musician profession; they employ people from outside their tribal system, and such people are identified as *Dom* (see Mills 2003, and Schmid on low-status Dom musicians in northern areas of Pakistan, 2000, 794–95).

15. This did not apply to all the Golpasand *sazandeh*; a few younger women had received several years of school education.

16. Sabo arranged Zainab's marriage to her orphaned nephew in order to keep her in her band because the bands were organized on the basis of kinship.

17. Sabo died around the early 1970s, before I met Zainab. My information is based on what Zainab told me and also on discussions with various Herati women in Canada and Australia.

18. As Baghban explains, in the traditional Herati system of education "enculturation takes place through apprenticeship which utilizes informal instruction, observation, and participation," a pattern of learning applied "virtually across the board" (1977, 221).

19. Amateur girls sometimes imitated instrumental music when playing dance rhythms on the *daireh*, e.g., Track 3 ("O bacheh aughan") in my CD of field recordings (Doubleday 2002). This vocal imitation of instrumental sounds would seem to underline Afghan female performers' lack of access to melodic instruments (as discussed in Doubleday 2006b [1999]).

20. See Baily 1988. For a classic account of male musicians' power play in North Indian classical music circles, see Neuman 1980.

21. I repeatedly heard that these women were sexually available for a negotiated fee.

22. The professional male musicians who accompanied them thought little of their talent, complaining that they often sang out of tune and took a long time to rehearse new songs (Baily 1988, 135).

23. See, for example, Karin van Nieuwkerk's 1995 work on Egyptian dancers *"A Trade Like Any Other": Female Singers and Dancers in Egypt* (Austin: Texas University Press).

24. See Racy's excellent analysis of *tarab* lyrical conventions in the Arab world (2003, Chapter 6).

25. See Rodriguez 2008, 56.

26. Zainab's husband's provincial relatives strongly disapproved of Zainab's profession, and they refused to attend their wedding.

27. Zainab openly confided details about her life in the company of sympathetic clients, as described in Doubleday 2006a [1988]: Chapter 24. Nasruddin Seljuqi told me when he was a child Zainab's sister Gol Dasteh had regaled the women of his family with a long story about her involvement in a car accident, moving many of them to tears (pers. comm. 2008).

28. See Doubleday 2006a [1988]: Chapter 24.

29. Born in Kabul in 1947, Ferida Mahwash made her name as a singer through broadcasting on Radio Afghanistan. In 1977, in a bid to improve the status of women, the government

publicly awarded her the title "Ustad" ("master musician"). This was an unprecedented distinction, and she is still frequently described as "the first woman *ustad*."

30. A Herati woman now living in Copenhagen confirmed this point in a telephone conversation in 2009. She asserted that no one much remembers Zainab nowadays. She had no idea that Zainab had made recordings at Radio Afghanistan.

31. Among various possible examples, Naroditskaya's work in Azerbaijan provides an interesting parallel in Sakina Ismailova. Her husband was initially unhappy with her singing vocation, but her father-in-law approved of her talent and took an active role in supporting her (Naroditskaya 2000, 247–48).

32. In 2007, after a concert in Hamburg, an Afghan woman insisted on meeting the next day. She was so grateful for my songs that she wanted to give me a beautiful dress of great sentimental value to her. Later in an email, she said "To meet you and your music from Herat has reawakened my afghan-music-spirit. Since I know you and your music the melodies are flowing under my skin, I'm singing them when I'm awake and I'm singing them when I'm asleep. I thank you for this precious gift that you have made us" (April 2007).

33. Recent research among Herati women in Germany and Canada revealed quite positive memories of the Golpasand female musicians as good, respectful, and honest women. Attitudes may have sweetened with temporal and geographical distance.

34. Published recordings of Zainab's singing are to be found in Doubleday (2002) (Tracks 1, 4, 16, 17, 20, and 22); in the CD accompanying Sakata 2002 (Tracks 8 and 18); and Track 11 of Baily and Doubleday (2002) *Afghanistan: The Traditional Music of Herat.* Unesco/Audivis CD.

References

Baghban, Hafizullah. 1977. *The Context and Concept of Humor in Magadi Theater*. Doctoral Thesis, Indiana University. Ann Arbor: University Microfilms.

Baily, John. 1981. "Cross-Cultural Perspectives in Popular Music: The Case of Afghanistan." *Popular Music* 1:105–22.

———. 1988. *Music of Afghanistan: Professional Musicians in the City of Herat*. Cambridge: Cambridge University Press.

———. 1994. "The Role of Music in the Creation of an Afghan National Identity, 1923–73." In *Ethnicity, Identity and Music: The Musical Construction of Place*, ed. Martin Stokes, 45–60. Oxford: Berg Publishers.

———. 2001. *"Can You Stop the Birds Singing?" The Censorship of Music in Afghanistan*. Copenhagen: Freemuse.

Danielson, Virginia. 1997. *The Voice of Egypt: Umm Kulthūm, Arabic Song, and Egyptian Society in the Twentieth Century*. Chicago: The University of Chicago Press.

Doubleday, Veronica. 2000. "Afghanistan: Music and Gender." In *The Garland Encyclopedia of World Music, South Asia: The Indian Subcontinent*, volume 5, ed. A. Arnold, 812–16. New York: Garland Publishing.

———. 2006a [1988]. *Three Women of Herat*. London: I. B. Tauris.

———. 2006b [revised] [1999]. "The Frame Drum in the Middle East: Women, Musical

Instruments and Power." In *Ethnomusicology: A Contemporary Reader*, ed. J. C. Post, 109–33. New York and London: Routledge.

———. 2007. "9/11 and the Politics of Music-Making in Afghanistan." In *Music in the Post-9/11 World*, eds. Jonathan Ritter and J. Martin Daughtry, 277–314. New York and London: Routledge.

———. 2011. "Gendered Voices and Creative Expression in the Singing of *Chaharbeiti* Poetry in Afghanistan." *Ethnomusicology Forum* 20(1): 3–31.

Doubleday, Veronica, and John Baily. 1995. "Patterns of Musical Development among Children in Afghanistan." In *Children in the Muslim Middle East*, ed. Elizabeth Warnock Fernea, 431–44. Austin: University of Texas Press.

Floor, Willem. 2008. *A Social History of Sexual Relations in Iran.* Washington D.C.: Mage Publishers.

Kimberlin, Cynthia Tse. 1990. "'And Are You Pretty?': Choice, Perception and Reality in Pursuit of Happiness." In *Music, Gender, and Culture*, eds. M. Herndon and S. Ziegler, 221–39. Wilhelmshaven: Florian Noetzel Verlag.

Koskoff, Ellen. 1989. "An Introduction to Women, Music, and Culture." In *Women and Music in Cross-Cultural Perspective*, ed. Ellen Koskoff, 1–23. Urbana: University of Illinois Press.

Levin, Theodore. 1996. *The Hundred Thousand Fools of God: Musical Travels in Central Asia (and Queens, New York).* Bloomington: Indiana University Press.

Mills, Margaret A. 2003. "Dom." In *South Asian Folklore: An Encyclopedia*, eds. Margaret A. Mills, Peter J. Claus, and Sarah Diamond, 164. New York and London: Routledge.

Naroditskaya, Inna. 2000. "Azerbaijanian Female Musicians: Women's Voices Defying and Defining the Culture." *Ethnomusicology* 44(2): 234–56.

Nasr, Seyyed Hossein. 1997. "Islam and Music: The Legal and Spiritual Dimensions." In *Enchanting Powers: Music in the World's Religions*, ed. Lawrence E. Sullivan, 219–35. Cambridge MA: Harvard University Press.

Neubauer, Eckhard, and Veronica Doubleday. 2001. "Islamic Religious Music." In *The New Grove Dictionary of Music and Musicians*, volume 12, 2nd ed., ed. Stanley Sadie, 599–610. London: Macmillan Press.

Neuman, Daniel. 1980. *The Life of Music in North India: The Organization of an Artistic Tradition.* Detroit: Wayne State University Press.

Poché, Christian. 1984. "Zurna." In *The New Grove Dictionary of Musical Instruments*, volume 3, ed. Stanley Sadie, 905–8. London: Macmillan Press.

Qureshi, Regula Burckhardt. 2006. "Female Agency and Patrilineal Constraints: Situating Courtesans in Twentieth-Century India." In *The Courtesan's Arts: Cross-Cultural Perspectives*, eds. Martha Feldman and Bonnie Gordon, 312–31. Oxford: Oxford University Press.

Racy, Ali Jihad. 2003. *Making Music in the Arab World.* Cambridge: Cambridge University Press.

Rahimi, Fahima. 1986 [1977]. *Women in Afghanistan.* Liestal: Stiftung Bibliotheca Afghanica.

Rao, Apurna. 1982. *Les Gorbat d'Afghanistan: Aspects économiques d'un groupe itinerant "Jat."* Paris: Institut français d'Iranologie de Teheran.

Rodriguez, Deborah. 2008. *The Kabul Beauty School: The Art of Friendship and Freedom.* London: Hodder and Stoughton.

Sakata, Hiromi Lorraine. 2002 [1983]. *Music in the Mind: The Concepts of Music and Musician in Afghanistan.* Washington and London: Smithsonian Institution Press.

Sarmast, Ahmad. 2004. *A Survey of the History of Music in Afghanistan, from Ancient Times to 2000 AD, with Special Reference to Art Music from c. 1000 AD.* PhD thesis. Melbourne: Monash University.

Schimmel, Annemarie. 1975. *Mystical Dimensions of Islam.* Chapel Hill: The University of North Carolina Press.

Schmid, Anna. 2000. "Northern Areas of Pakistan." In *The Garland Encyclopedia of World Music, South Asia: The Indian Subcontinent,* volume 5, ed. Alison Arnold, 792–801. New York and London: Garland Publishing.

Discography

Baily, John, with Veronica Doubleday. 2002 [1996]. *Afghanistan: The Traditional Music of Herat.* Unesco/Audivis CD.

Doubleday, Veronica. 2002. *Afghanistan: Female Musicians of Herat.* Unesco/Audivis. CD.

Madadi, Abdul Wahab, Veronica Doubleday, and John Baily. 2005. *Sweet Nomad Girl: Folk Music from Afghanistan.* Metier Sound and Vision. CD.

Afterword

ELLEN KOSKOFF

Upon first reading the essays in this extraordinary collection, I was struck by two contradictory ideas: on the one hand, the articles seemed to lack any overarching, connecting themes, save the one mentioned in the Introduction, written by editor, Ruth Hellier; on the other hand, this very resistance to thematic construction seemed to give a vibrancy, a realness to the individual voices and to the multiplicity of voices (even within one individual) that sing in each of the chapters. I was so engaged with these individual women (not to mention the individual authors) that connecting them to each other began to seem something of a violation. This is not your usual collection of articles on women and music—this is both an illuminating set of biographical case studies—and, more importantly, a tour de force, illustrating the engaging use of creatively experimental writing that, like the music it discusses, flows gracefully through these pages.

The one thread linking all of the essays together, according to editor Hellier, is a concentration on individual women living in a variety of musical cultures, who use their voices, both literal and metaphoric, to create, negotiate, and perform various, sometimes changing and conflicting, identities. The interplay between the literal voice—its timbre, its range, even its use as a sonic tool for gender confusion—and the metaphoric voice—seen here as a means of creatively expressing agency, activism, sexuality, and of creating often multiple strategies to ensure that one is heard and taken seriously— resonates deeply throughout this work.

Hellier also outlines in her Introduction various other threads, partial themes, or, as she says, "clusters" that link some of the essays together, such as the importance of families and supporters, risks and opportunities, the role of new technologies, and various legacies left by these extraordinary sing-ers, so I will not dwell on those here. Rather, I ask, as she does, that readers be interactive with this text, doing their own work in seeking meaningful connections. I concentrate here on two issues that, for me, seemed to hold these essays together with a kind of liquid and gently flowing glue: feminist activism as everyday practice and creativity in self-identity construction.

Hellier clearly states that this collection is not feminist in its orientation, and, to the degree that it is not theoretically situated in feminist theory, or explicitly relating to it, I would agree. However, each of the articles illustrates an individual woman doing the work of feminism—that is, creating strate-gies that enable her to perform various identities, often in conjunction with so-called traditional ones, that resist and critique issues of gender within her specific context. This is what feminism looks like when it is individually performed on a daily, often mundane, basis. Stripped of its theory, feminism is simply living a life guided by resistance (small or large) to inherited or imposed gender norms, as found in specific cultural and historical moments. Creative writers are often cautioned to "show not tell"; each of the stories contained here shows a life of integrity, purpose, and commitment to music but does not tell us that these are feminist lives.

Feminist acts become Political, in the sense of conscious activism, when they are explicit and public, voiced with the goal of social change. But, as feminists (and others) often remind us, every social act is political in some sense; how conscious the actor is of performing a political act, however, can vary consider-ably. Some examples from this collection: when Akiko Fujii makes the decision to continue performing *jiuta*, or when Zainab Herawi decides not to continue performing on Kabul Radio, it is doubtful if either of them saw their decisions as feminist Political acts (they may have done so, but we cannot tell from the stories presented here). However, readers of these accounts, on the outside looking in, may interpret these acts as feminist, as the women are performing counter-narratives to their specific gender norms. Such readers may even go on to use these data to construct their own feminist theories, although Akiko and Zainab might be uncomfortable with this use of their musical lives.

On the other hand, when Amelia Pedroso opens a gay-friendly house for female Santería drummers, or when Lexine Solomon, feeling the triple-in-visibility of being a woman, a Torres Strait Islander, and simply an "islander" living in Australia, composes songs that reclaim and document the lives of women in her community, they clearly must have been conscious of these as Political acts, ones that would, no doubt, cause a lot of attention and criticism but might possibly also promote social and cultural change, especially for marginalized women. They might be proud to be called feminists, but as the

Iranian singer, Sima Shokrani reminds us, what, exactly is a feminist outside of the western academy? Thus, each of the women presented here is doing the on-the-ground political work of feminism within her own specific context, but feminist Political action might or might not have been the conscious goal.

As we read on through the collection, we can see that the individual women here not only had different goals from each other but also different and sometimes changing goals for themselves as they progressed through life. Achieving a goal usually requires a strategy, that is, a workable plan that can be adapted at a moment's notice to fit some unforeseen circumstance. And, in order to work, a plan must be situated within a specific environment. Here, I discuss some of the wonderfully creative and flexible strategies, some of which evolved consciously, others not, that grew throughout these women's musical lives to enable them to achieve (at least some of) their goals, however P/political.

At the heart of all of these essays lies the issue of agency, the ability to act based on one's position within a changing matrix of self/other identities and contexts: "agency is concerned with the social conditions for, and requirements of, action, as well as with the internal and external barriers to action" (Deveaux 2000, 15). Each of the women here is an agent in her own social and musical actions. To achieve their goals, the women often had to construct and reconstruct appropriate identities contingent upon changing social, political, and familial conditions. What is unusual here is that we rarely see the details of this kind of agency in a standard ethnography, so this comes as a wonderful surprise and contributes much to the book's overall vividness. Here are four examples illustrating different forms of agency:

Shokrani, the Iranian activist and singer, despite religious and political restrictions, consciously chooses to privately sing songs that celebrate women's agency within the family. She also currently participates publicly in Iran's classical music tradition, while at the same time passionately adhering to her traditional role as mother. One of her goals, as we learn, is to caution western feminists to become more sensitive to cultural differences. What happens in the United States cannot happen in Iran, she states—but *something* can happen in Iran. During her young life to midlife, Shokrani took out time from her musical activism to care for her growing children, but she continued not only to perform in her birthplace, Mazandaran, but also to resist the growing Persianization of this local repertoire. As she grew older, Shokrani began to perform and teach Persian art music, a practice that has certainly contributed to her stature as a mature musician, despite her gender. Respected as a performer, supported by her husband and community, yet tempered somewhat by her role as mother, Shokrani has successfully balanced multiple identities and political realities to achieve her goals.

Kyriakou Pelagia, the singer from rural Cyprus, devoted much of her younger life to caring for her family and working with them in their fields while also singing locally within her community. Public, professional singing for women in Cyprus in the mid–twentieth century, although not prohibited, did carry some social stigma. However, in the 1990s, somewhat serendipitously, when Pelagia was already an older woman, new music call-in shows on the radio provided her with a unique opportunity: to record the traditional folksongs she had learned as a child. Protesting loudly and often that this whole venture was "ridiculous," Pelagia somehow managed to parlay this moment into national fame and a successful career. How was this possible, given her original dismissal of this as ridiculous? It was possible because Pelagia (consciously/unconsciously?) understood both the silliness of this situation and its political potential. Her loud protests proclaiming her empowering status as a housewife, as well as her "nasal" voice quality that led her audiences to associate her with traditional village life, allowed her to carve out a space to construct another, less conventional, identity—Star of Cyprus.

Determined to rap at a young age, Ayben Özçalkan, the "Girl's Voice in Turkish Rap," was enabled by her brother (already a known rapper) to perform on his new CD recording, effectively launching her career. Taking a break to care for her dying mother, Özçalkan returned more determined than ever to infiltrate the male-dominated world of rapping. She gradually became famous and, risking censure, chose consciously to perform and compose rap songs that addressed women's issues in Turkey, hoping to speak to them and to the wider society through a "woman's" voice. The author of this essay, Thomas Solomon, comments more than once upon Özçalkan's unusual attention to clear articulation and vocal quality—attributes that have certainly contributed to her success in Turkey by helping to distance her from the often highly sexualized, violent, and casual performance styles of some of her U.S. contemporaries. Located in Istanbul, she has had easy access to recording studios and concert venues, thus continuing to sustain a successful career. In public performances, costumed in the baggy pants and tank tops of the American rappers she idolized as a youth, Özçalkan walks the line between possibly bringing disapproval onto her family and international stardom.

And, finally, Amelia Pedroso, the openly gay Cuban ritual singer and drummer, despite all odds, provides a possibility for women to perform ritual drums, considered a strictly heterosexual male activity in Cuba. To do so, Pedroso successfully used the growing interest in the Santería tradition outside Cuba to promote her feminist Political agenda. Forming an all-woman drumming ensemble, she toured the United States and Europe—contexts that were more accepting than those in Cuba. And, although she did not marry or have children, she nurtured and cared for scores of women who came to study and be inspired by her. Perhaps of all of the women presented here, Pedroso was positioned (or situated herself) as the "most outside" her own cultural norms, protesting and defying the expected through her performances.

What these four examples, and, indeed all of the articles in this collection also share, in addition to agency is the ability to creatively play with self and other constructive strategies that carve out musical spaces to perform any number of sometimes conflicting identities—some that could be described as "fully natural," others as "completely constructed." Although this has been commented upon by many others (see Butler 1990, for example), what is so interesting here is that we can closely watch and hear how these women walk/sing such fine lines between their accepted (some said, "empowering") roles as mothers and caretakers and their rebellious (perhaps personal) roles as resisters and fighters against their own culturally specific gender norms. This attention to detail is perhaps the most positive feature of biographical writing like that presented in this collection.

The sonic space of musical performance seems to create for these women a sort of safe space or zone that takes both performer and audience into another reality. Here, I call that safe space "enchantment." Enchantment, in its earliest usage in the thirteenth century, meant to cast a magic spell, bewitch, or charm through singing. Ixya Herrera, the Mexican American singer presented in Hellier's chapter, explicitly mentions this term, associating it with a specific performing directive—grace. Thus, for Herrera, to enchant means to perform with the grace of flying birds, and all that she does on stage—costuming, movement, vocal quality—works toward that end. That is how she sees herself and how she wants to be seen by others. If she can create a space of safe enchantment, then her messages of resistance and advocacy can be heard more easily.

Enchantment is a safe place, out of time and space, that is open for both performers and audiences to play, experiment, remember, fanaticize, mourn, connect with others, experience pure joy, or discover parts of themselves they never knew existed—whatever they wish. Performers, though, generally control, often in tandem with their audiences, the flow and pacing of enchantment—the real-time events that structure this space. That is their job—to take themselves and their listeners to that place and to bring them safely back. To do this, performers must walk a fine line: they must captivate, charm, and bewitch, but not go so far as to encourage aggression or violence in their audiences or censure for themselves.

So, when Pelagia states that she is a "housewife, not a singer," despite her national fame as a publicly performing woman, or when Özçalkan asserts that she is "still the girl next door," despite her overtly political lyrics, these women are balancing objectified essentialist social norms against their own subjective, and perhaps risky or threatening, resistance to those norms. Often, as we see in these pages, they use the devices of poetry, such as metaphor, irony, or playfulness in their lyrics. These are ways of deflecting direct, and potentially dangerous, statements while at the same time making P/political ones. As any good comic knows, these devices serve to both enable social realities to be contested—and to defuse the fear and anger that inevitably arise in these circumstances.

One of the most poignant essays in this collection beautifully illustrates the potential for self-construction through musical performance. Here, it works, not to promote an overtly Political act but, rather, to provide a space for one person to work out painful family relations—a localized and personal political act. Akiko Fujii, the singer of Japanese jiuta, uses her musical performances to bring her audiences back to the older performance style and context previously associated with this all-male tradition. In order to do this Fujii had to first face and deal with considerable anger and resentment toward her own mother and teacher, as well as her brother, who inherited the position of head of the school associated with their lineage. Her brother, having had no intention of becoming a musician, changed his mind and entered Tokyo University of Fine Arts and Music, thus pushing Fujii into second place for succession. Fujii recounts that her brother only wanted to be a "superior teacher," whereas she wanted to "save jiuta."

To do so, Fujii broke with her family and began performing jiuta alone, outside the context of her school. She distanced herself from the tradition she had been given by her mother by returning to more intimate performance spaces and renewed her commitment to performing jiuta in the strong, gritty voice of her grandmother, acknowledging that she had crossed a gender line. In short, Fujii used her anger productively, creating a safe performance space for herself—an enchantment—that enabled her to achieve many goals: to become a successful performer who could enchant her audiences by taking them back to an older time, to fulfill her dream of saving jiuta (perhaps from her brother?), and to become more emotionally healthy and independent. Thus, the two themes discussed in this section, those of feminist everyday P/political activism and of creative identity construction, seem to link all of the essays in this collection together into a meaningful and satisfying whole.

• • •

My "theme-seeking self," who wrote the text above and who needs to link people together in some meaningful way to help her build a convincing theory, will now step aside and be replaced by my "theme-resisting self," a more playful identity, who advocates for different, individual voices (who cares if they connect?) and for creative experimental writing (who cares if it works?). I am not suggesting that one of these identities is better than the other—simply different, and difference itself, as this identity believes, is good.

One of the best features of this collection is its resistance to linking the details of these women's lives together for the explicit purpose of theory building. So, in this section, I concentrate on the other half of the conundrum mentioned in the first paragraph of this Afterword: the delight I felt, not only in getting to know the individual women in this volume, but also reading about them in prose that, in some cases, comes closer to poetry or music. In doing so, I hope also to show how this book contributes to the current ethnomusicological/anthropological literature as well as to contemporary feminist values.

I begin with a response from Nicoletta Demetriou (2010) to a personal communication from Hellier, asking her to be more theoretical in her article:

> When I tried to incorporate more theory into my chapter, I got the sense that Pelagia was turning into a caricature of herself, that I was moving from the living, breathing individual that I know Pelagia to be towards an abstract theoretical entity.

Theoretical writing forces the researcher/subject to objectify the researched/object; biographical writing, on the other hand, is more intersubjective; here, it is based on fieldwork, on face-to-face discussions and actions between living people who are (hopefully) equally invested in the work. Fieldwork lends itself to intersubjectivity: it allows subject and object positions to be shared, passed back and forth, collapsing boundaries between these binaries. It is difficult to truly objectify a person with whom you have shared a part of your life, with whom you have performed music, or to whom you have told secrets.

What is truly powerful in these articles is that one can feel the interconnectedness between the partners presented in each of the individual chapters. Many of the authors have known their partners for years and have, in essence, become a part of their families. Others were raised in the same geographic and cultural milieu as their partners, thus coming to this work with a store of shared knowledge. Still others, not personally knowing their partners well, have followed their lives and careers for years. There is true investment here on both sides to present the lives of these singing women as "accurately" as is possible, given the constraints of writing. I am not so naive, however, as to believe that the intersubjectivity of fieldwork alone can erase the power differential in the subject/object binary, even here; after all, each of the authors "presents" her/his partner to us through this collection (somewhat like a reified object), so, try as they might to mitigate this, the author/subject binary still controls and mediates these interactions to some degree.

This attempt to collapse the subject/object binary through fieldwork and its inherent intersubjectivity, although laudatory, has been a pesky problem within feminist anthropology and ethnomusicology for a while now. In the decades following the so-called Second Wave of feminism,[1] feminist anthropologists began to isolate two problems they were experiencing—one outside their field and one within. First, I will address the outside issue (see more on the inside problem later).

One of the hallmarks of feminism's Second Wave was the passing of a great deal of legislation that prohibited sex discrimination of any kind, domestic abuse, and many other consequences of unequal gender relations, as well as providing many positive opportunities for women and girls, such as the right to an abortion, or to play on a school sport's team. In short, the decades between 1960 and 1980 were amazingly productive in legally addressing many social ills that were regarded as being rooted in centuries-old attitudes and laws that normalized gender inequality. In order to accomplish this, Second-Wavers (both men and women) had to conceptualize women as a single, monolithic group, all of whom faced similar issues: second-class status, nonaccess to education or work opportunities, and so on. These sweeping generalizations enabled them to make a powerful and effective case for change.

Soon, however, some, like writer and activist bell hooks, and many other people of color, began to point out that these changes were being driven largely by white, middle-class perspectives and interests and cautioned their white sisters to also consider class and race as separate, yet intertwined, issues within feminism. This challenge came about within the context of 1960–70s race relations in the United States, and resonated generally with the anger and frustration of radical African American thinkers: "Even before race became a talked about issue in feminist circles, it was clear to black women (and to their revolutionary allies in struggle) that they were never going to have equality within the existing white supremacist capitalist patriarchy" (hooks 2000, 4).

Feminist anthropologists and ethnomusicologists were initially delighted that there was now an opportunity to put women into the picture, and many articles and books appeared at that time positioning women at the center, not at the margins, of culture. (See Tick, Ericson, and Koskoff [2001] or my forthcoming book, *A Feminist Ethnomusicology*, for a fuller discussion of this history.) However, some, like those feminists of color mentioned above, began to see mainstream feminists as both too limited and monolithic in their idea of what a "woman" (or "man") was, and were also hampered by their general lack of knowledge and seeming disinterest in non-Western cultures. After all, the anthropologists said, we conduct fieldwork all over the world, where white/black racial tensions, like those found in the United States, are largely irrelevant. Much more relevant, they said, are the effects of colonialism and European (albeit white) hegemonies. Thus, in addition to the problem of the monolithic and essentialist "woman," they saw Second Wave feminism as not especially sensitive to cultural and historical differences. This very valorization of individual differences by feminist anthropologists, however, made categorizing, or linking many different women together, far more difficult and cross-cultural comparison all but impossible.

Then, along came postmodernism, saving us by revolutionizing how we see (or rather, construct) "reality." Postmodernism and its twin, poststructuralism, suggested that we abandon binaries altogether because they were the result of crude and rigid power relations that were no longer relevant. Instead, we should play with language and other human creations to expose the preposterousness of power, of Truth claims that positioned some people in and others out. No one voice or position was any more True than any other, they said; everything could be interpreted through the flow of constantly moving social interactions, perspectives, and constructions. (In the spirit of transparency, I acknowledge that I'm playing with, and glossing over, many different strands of postmodern thought here, but this is my lighthearted identity speaking.)

During the 1980s and 1990s, mainstream feminism and feminist anthropology also began to change as more and more of these ideas trickled into their discourses. Younger women in the United States (who mainly saw feminism as the "new f-word") were also beginning to deconstruct essentialist notions of woman, concentrating their efforts on destabilizing controlling binaries and celebrating individually different voices. Rebecca Walker, who coined the term, "Third Wave" in response to the complacency she saw in the 1980s and 1990s that proclaimed feminism's goals had been accomplished, writes in the Introduction to her call-to-arms, *To Be Real* (1995, xxxiv):

> As they [the authors in her collection] formulate a feminism they can call their own, they debunk the stereotype that there is one lifestyle or manifestation of feminist empowerment, and instead offer self-possession, self-determination, and an endless array of non-dichotomous positions.

This statement effectively flips the subject/object positions seen in the rhetoric of Second Wave feminism from a top-down, subject-imposed label

(You are a feminist if you believe and do X) to a bottom-up, self-selected label as a source of empowerment (I can be a feminist and do anything I want). Walker continues:

> These voices are important because if feminism is to continue to be radical and alive, it must avoid re-ordering the world in terms of any polarity, be it female/male, good/evil. . . . It must continue to be responsive to new situations, needs, and especially desires, ever expanding to incorporate and entertain all those who wrestle with and swear by it, including those who may not explicitly call its name (xxxv–xxxvi).

This shift in thinking from the other-to-self and from the monolithic to the multiple, allowed more space in anthropology and ethnomusicology to address not only gender differences, but also other relevant cultural differences researchers saw outside of the United States that were intertwined with gender in the specific cultural contexts they documented. Many monographs, such as those of Veronica Doubleday (1990), Jane Sugarman (1997), and Virginia Danielson (1997) as well as collections, such as Diamond and Moisala (2000), Magrini (2003), and Bernstein (2004), and others too numerous to mention here, began to appear in the ethnomusicological literature. Alongside this blossoming of literature, however, another trend was taking hold in anthropology: the "New Ethnography"—the second (inside) issue to which I referred earlier.

The New Ethnography was one outcome of anthropology's powerfully self-reflexive moment in the 1980s, sometimes referred to as the "crisis of representation." Briefly, this moment dealt with the power structures within anthropology itself: its method (fieldwork), its representation of others (interpretation), and its presentation of data (ethnography). Ushered in by James Clifford and George Marcus (1986), and later Clifford Geertz (1988), among others, the new ethnographers suggested that fieldwork was a form of academic colonialism, where the (usually western) ethnographer used the work of the (usually non-western) other for his/her own benefit. Further, the end result of fieldwork (ethnography), in order to be written so that academics and others (but not necessarily the people studied) would understand and be moved by its rhetoric, was certainly partially fiction, constructed by the author and bearing a closer resemblance to the novel than to a full and accurate documentation of living cultural informants. Since there was no longer a Truth to be had, older ethnographic writing soon went out of style and newer experimental writing was adopted, where the authors began to position themselves in their work, and where different styles of writing were used to present a multiplicity of voices and perspectives.

The collection of essays here beautifully captures the spirit of this creative, experimental writing and of the multiple voices that lie at the heart of the new ethnography. Like the interactive and personalized collection of Diamond and Moisala mentioned earlier, this collection plays with reflexivity and intersubjectivity in ways that could not have been possible twenty years ago. Three articles here stand out as models for new ways of writing that come closer to the internal flows of conversation. Carol Muller's essay on South African singer Sathima Bea Benjamin, for example, uses the device of different voices to tell and retell her story. Inspired by Marjory Wolf's *A Thrice-Told Tale: Feminism, Post-Modernism, and Ethnographic Responsibility* (1992), Muller clearly presents the device of using three different narrative forms in her essay: biography, where Muller outlines the basics of Benjamin's life; autobiography, where Benjamin tells her own story; and finally conversation, where the two previous voices interact and blend to provide a convincing analysis. This works because all of the subject/object positions are visible and positioned adequately to help make this a wonderfully convincing story.

Hellier's article on the Mexican singer Ixya Herrera takes another tack: assigning creative headings to different sections (e.g., Seven, Twelve, Father, Future Unknown). This serves not only to position Ixya in her own life, but also to further personalize it for us. Hellier also seems to flit back and forth between her own voice, often captured in its embodied presence—how she felt emotionally and physically while speaking—as well as its informational presence—the literal meaning of what she was saying—and Ixya's voice captured in lengthy field notes. In this way, Hellier plays with intersubjectivity, sometimes leaving open for a time the answer to the question of whose voice is speaking. This is nice because, in contrast to a constant authorial/narrator voice, this kind of dual-voice writing gets us closer to the process and feeling of a real exchange between two situated people.

Finally, Katelyn Barney's article on Torres Strait Islander, Lexine Solomon, incorporates a form of dramatic writing, especially in the heading of the first "scene," where she introduces her partner: "A singing workshop in the classroom: Introducing Lexine." Here, she writes the scene using her own voice, that of Lexine, and the voices of her students, using both a narrative and dialogic writing style. One would think that this moving from one style to another would hamper the feel of this scene, but, in fact it seems to enhance the realness of this experience, to engage us in its "you are there" feeling, much as the feeling of living inside a novel while reading it. This form of dialoguing and describing, without the usual authorial interpretation and analysis, gently diffuses not only Lexine's Political messages so that they can be heard more easily, but also diffuses the power dynamic between author and subject. Thus, like the ironic or comic devices discussed earlier, Barney, as well as Hellier and others within this collection, couch the utter seriousness of their work in creative and entertaining forms—enchantments of a different kind.

This kind of playing with narrative or poetic forms may not be everyone's cup of tea, but these authors should be congratulated for their courage to try something different; and, to the degree that these essays go beyond the written words of academic discourse to expose and blur boundaries between self and other, individuality and generalization, and speech and song, they make an important and valuable contribution to a new kind of feminist ethnomusicology.

Postmodern critical theory tells us that our identities are multiple, fragmented, contingent, and situated, always changing in relation to social interactions and environments. If we accept this notion, then we must always ask the question, as Louise Wrazen does in her article on the Polish Górale singer, Marysia Mąka: If identities are multiple, then who is the who in "Who is singing?" If we answer that question through carefully detailed and nuanced portraits like those presented here, the Who will not only become clear, but also the Why and the What of musical and P/political performances.

Notes

1. The designation of First, Second, and Third Wave is a contentious topic that is discussed elsewhere. I am using it here, however, because it is familiar to most readers interested in this topic.

References

Bernstein, Jane A., ed. 2004. *Women's Voices across Musical Worlds*. Boston: Northeastern University Press.

Butler, Judith. 1990. *Gender Trouble: Feminism and the Subversion of Identity*. New York: Routledge.

Clifford, James, and George E. Marcus, eds. 1986. *Writing Culture: the Poetics and Politics of Ethnography*. Berkeley: University of California Press.

Danielson, Virginia. 1997. *The Voice of Egypt: Umm Kulthum, Arabic Song, and Egyptian Society in the Twentieth Century*. Chicago Studies in Ethnomusicology. Chicago, Illinois: University of Chicago Press.

Deveaux, Monique. 2000. "Agency." *Encyclopedia of Feminist Theories*, ed. Lorraine Code. New York: Routledge.

Diamond, Beverley, and Pirkko Moisala, eds. 2000. *Music and Gender*. Urbana: University of Illinois Press.

Doubleday, Veronica. 1990. *Three Women of Herat*. Austin: University of Texas Press.

Geertz, Clifford. 1988. *Works and Lives: The Anthropologist as Author.* Stanford: Stanford University Press.

hooks, bell. 2000. *Feminism Is for Everybody: Passionate Politics.* Brooklyn: South End Press.

Koskoff, Ellen. (forthcoming). *A Feminist Ethnomusicology.* Urbana: University of Illinois Press.

Magrini, Tullia, ed. 2003. *Music and Gender: Perspectives from the Mediterranean.* Chicago: University of Chicago Press.

Sugarman, Jane. 1997. *Engendering Song: Singing and Subjectivity at Prespa Albanian Weddings.* Chicago: University of Chicago Press.

Tick, Judith, Margaret Ericson, and Ellen Koskoff. 2001. "Women in Music." In *The New Grove Dictionary of Music and Musicians,* 2nd ed., ed. Stanley Sadie. London: MacMillan.

Walker, Rebecca, ed. 1995. *To Be Real: Telling the Truth and Changing the Face of Feminism.* New York: Anchor Books.

Wolf, Margery. 1992. *A Thrice-Told Tale: Feminism, Post-Modernism, and Ethnographic Responsibility.* Stanford: Stanford University Press.

Threads, Themes, Connections, and Clusters

Outlines for Each Singer

In Part Two of the introductory chapter we provided a medley of threads, themes, connections, and clusters, giving an overview of each attribute and idea, mostly without reference to specific singers. Here we develop that section of the introduction, presenting a summary as related to each singer, which enables readers, who so desire, to have the extrapolated themes set out for them.

As noted in the Introduction, with such rich, multifarious, and diverse material, creating order is problematic because issues are shared, overlapping, and interfacing. A diagrammatic and schematic expression would capture some of the intricacies; however, a linear format is rather limiting. One issue could be mentioned under one subheading, but could equally fit with another. The inclusion of repetitions in the summaries emphasizes the interconnectedness of issues. Within each topic the explanatory summaries are mostly given in chapter order, using the singer's name to guide readers to each specific chapter. As in the Introduction, the eight topics are

> Repertoire and Function: "Sing what?" and "Why sing?"
> Vocal Aesthetics and Self-Crafting: "Sing how?"
> Bodies and Clothes: "What to wear?" and "How to move?"
> Childhood, Families, and "Home"
> Journeys and Migration
> Risk, Tensions, Opportunities, and Activism
> Recording and Broadcast Technologies
> Legacies

Repertoire and Function:
"Sing what?" and "Why sing?"

Akiko in Japan engages the tradition of *jiuta* song, following in the path of two women—her grandmother and mother—who had innovated a long-held men's tradition. Akiko made a career choice, thereby aiming to provide herself with an income, endeavoring to perpetuate the tradition, even while transforming certain elements. She connects with her local, intimate audience in Tokyo.

Amelia in Cuba was immersed in spiritual practices and popular music, studying Santería and also performing as part of a rumba group. Through her role in Santería she appropriated men's musical prerogatives. She sang to lead her religious devotees in Cuba and internationally.

Ayben in Turkey took on the male-dominated genre of rap and challenged the notion of the impropriety of women's vocality. Her career choice is driven by creativity and empowerment. Ayben creates rap that connects with Turkish women to empower them and with Turkish men to cause reflection on women's issues.

Ixya in the United States of America sings a selection of old Mexican songs, nurturing an often unfamiliar repertoire and dealing with cultural heritage. In contrast to Ayben, Ixya chose to go back to older songs, resisting overt genre-breaking activism. Ixya chose a career as a singer, compelled by a passion for singing, aiming to enchant and thrill her audiences, connecting with her Mexican heritage, and subtly engaging with Mexican American or Chicana politics.

Kyriakou in Cyprus "does" tradition, engaging the art of making improvised couplets, known as *tsiattista*, and challenging the notion of the immorality of women's vocality by appropriating a man's privilege. She sings her local repertoire, has also learned new selections of Cypriot music, and sang with a young hip-hop singer. Kyriakou is an incredulous and reluctant star who became famous in her fifties simply through her desire to participate, vocalizing in public a lifelong skill that she had practiced mostly in private. She connects with all Cypriots, but especially with the youth, and also sings to connect with her village roots.

Lexine in Australia creates her own repertoire, drawing on Torres Strait Island music and church music, and composing lyrics to express her family history as Torres Strait Islanders. Her transformation to professional singer was an almost imperceptible shift as she discovered her own capacity in adulthood. Through her career in singing she enables marginalized women to reflect on their lives, believing song and singing to be a "stronger way of expressing identity." Lexine sings to connect with Torres Strait Islanders, especially women; to celebrate women; for her siblings and family; and for future generations. For herself she sings to connect with her family and her Torres Strait Islander identity.

Marysia in Canada is rooted in traditional Górale music from the Podhale region in southern Poland, having been immersed in this as the daughter of a well-known fiddler. After migrating to Canada she continues the same repertoire, adapting the lyrics to her new circumstances. By singing in her local community, she creates connections between her Górale roots in Poland and the current context in Canada, enabling her children to recognize who they are. In Poland she sang to connect with the landscape and mountains; in Canada singing helps her to define a home for herself and her family, assuring her of a much broader personal identity.

Sathima in the United States of America is wrapped up in a world of jazz, with all the associations of the genre, and aware of the jazz lineage, drawing on the jazz "greats," especially Billy Holliday. As a child in South Africa she listened to British music hall and Hollywood musical classics, and as an adult she breathes life into these songs from almost a century ago. As a professional jazz singer she has accomplished a long career. When she sings, Sathima connects with South Africa and with a larger African diaspora, and also with a broad jazz-loving audience. For herself, singing helped Sathima overcome her shyness. She sings to connect with South Africa and the Cape Town days of her childhood; with New York; and with "original moments," fulfilling a yearning to be free.

Sima in Iran sings the music of her childhood, which is rooted in the local Mazanderani ethnicity. Her repertoire includes songs of women and women's lives, including those in praise of rural working girls, and songs of desire in first person. Following university study, she turned to singing as a career. Wishing to push boundaries, and to resist and overcome suffering, Sima sings as form of social agency, putting a call out to other women and singing in solidarity with those who have to work. In Germany she connects with Iranian migrants, especially from the Mazanderani province. For Sima, singing expresses her localized identity, giving her personal pleasure, endurance, and sustenance. She has been unable to sing when depressed and then has also used singing to draw her out of this state.

Zainab in Afghanistan performed local traditional music for wedding celebrations, having to deal with the prohibitions of female singing. Apprenticed as a child, she became a professional singer and principal breadwinner for the family. Zainab loved performing, and sang to connect with, and entertain, the women guests at weddings.

Vocal Aesthetics and Self-Crafting: "Sing how?"

Akiko received lessons from her grandmother and mother. She follows both of these women, who developed a very different aesthetic from the gendered vocality of the inherited men's tradition, but she draws on the stark contrasts between their voices, describing her mother as logical and her grandmother as passionate and robust. Her grandmother found strength in her voice through the use of her entire body. Akiko aspires to achieve an intimate, gentle, and robust vocality.

Amelia was taught by her uncle and grandmother. She developed a very direct sound, with no vibrato, and used a lower register and chest voice, which was often perceived as androgynous.

Ayben taught herself at home by listening, rapping along, and recording herself on her computer in order to develop her style, which she transformed from simple to sophisticated. She played with the pitch, register, and volume of her speaking voice as she experimented with her rap.

Ixya began by listening to recordings and attempting to emulate what she heard. From the age of twelve onward she took formal singing lessons, engaging in a daily practice. Ixya aims for power, versatility, range, clarity, and purity, controlling her vibrato to sing different genres. She engages a falsetto technique to demonstrate enchantment and control, and plays with the register of her speaking and singing voice.

Kyriakou received no formal training, learning aurally in her village. She deploys a nasal timbre with no vibrato, creating reception that invokes notions of homemaker with village authenticity.

Lexine learned to sing in church and developed her vocality to display power and strength.

Marysia began singing in her village community in Poland, resonating with the vastness of the mountains and landscape. She encompasses a hearty and resonant chest timbre, emphasizing the physicality of her voice.

Sathima grew up listening to the radio as a child, copying the singing voices, and developing her rhythm through ballroom dancing.

Sima learned songs from her grandmother when she was a very young child. She also developed her vocality through informal listening to older women and through formal training. She uses a low register, with an emphasis on sustained notes, creating a deep, strong, flexible sound.

Zainab became skilled as a child, learning by listening to her elders and to the radio and recordings.

Bodies and Clothes: "What to wear?" and "How to move?"

Ayben dresses in tank top and baggy low-slung pants of hip-hop fashion. Movementwise, Ayben jabs at the air with her hands, using staccato and chopping actions.

Ixya engages an aesthetic of grace and enchantment, wearing a long evening gown and *rebozo* (shawl). She regards this as sensual but not sexual, saying that "no one wants to see the girl next door." Ixya practices corporeal gracefulness and legato movements, enabling her to move smoothly across the stage.

Kyriakou wears the "normal clothes" of an older village woman and "housewife." When she shares the stage with a woman pop star, who displays an overt sexiness with her scantily clad body, she sets up an interesting contrast.

Sathima aims to focus on the sonic element, saying, "I don't want people to come to see how I look," believing that it is not necessary for a singer to stand there looking great.

Sima prefers to focus on her voice and emotions, engaging the traditional emphasis on vocal sound and feeling, rather than visual representations.

Zainab was subject to prohibitions and a strict dress code in Afghanistan, which regulated her clothes. In a complex and rather dichotomous situation she was required to cover her body and face, but also to dress "glamorously." Paradoxically, covering women's bodies and faces created an "erotic voice," through a profound sense of suggestions and restriction. Issues of "gaze" were also related to the notion of the evil eye and connected with theater women and glamorous dancing women. For Zainab a corporeal distinction was crucial, stating: "We play sitting down, just for women."

Childhood, Families, and "Home"

Akiko was born into a prestigious musical family in Tokyo, with a famous grandmother and mother, both of who were jiuta singers. As a young child she was apprenticed to her mother, blurring the lines between home and profession as she experienced the roles of daughter and apprentice-musician, thus creating a problematical childhood environment. Home was a site of intense music-making and difficult family relations. She expected to inherit the position of head of school from her mother, but without warning her mother gave it to her brother. Choosing to marry, partially as a form of escape, she found herself with the same pressures that her mother had experienced with an unsupportive husband. She made the decision to divorce and to carve out a career as a single woman. Her choice also enabled her to become the caregiver for her mother until her mother's death. Her grandmother was highly influential with regard to the vocal aesthetic of passion. In Akiko's family three generations of women singers encapsulate some of the predominant tensions of being a professional musician, raising a family, and living without full cooperation within marriage. Akiko's grandmother broke with a traditional men's practice as musician, and her mother made the decision to combine the position of career-woman (as a musician and head of school) and the traditional role as housewife to a businessman, the consequences of which were then experienced by Akiko in her own life as a singer.

Amelia studied Santería song repertoire as a young child with her uncle, and song liturgy with her grandmother, within the context of a musical family in Havana. As an adult she adopted a daughter and maintained a lesbian relationship, although many in her blood family did not accept her sexuality. Through her religious and musical contexts she developed a god family, which included a network of lesbian drummers. For Amelia her ritual home was predominant, central to religious practices as a place for singing and music-making.

Ayben was inspired as a child in Istanbul by the New York–based rapper RZA from the group Wu-Tang Clan. Within her bedroom she listened to her idol and had posters of him on her wall (at age twenty-two she briefly shared the stage with him). Her older brother, likewise a rap star, also acted as musical role model for her, both validating and encouraging her. As part of a traditional familial and neighborhood environment Ayben was well supported. She maintained her conventional role in the family and became the caregiver for her mother until her mother's death. Ayben's family home, and in particular her bedroom, were spaces where she practiced rapping and undertook home-recording, specifically developing her skills while nursing her sick mother.

Ixya, immersed from birth in a musical family home in Oxnard, California, experienced an epiphany at the age of seven when listening to a recording of the renowned singer Linda Ronstadt, and by chance had the opportunity to sing with her on stage when just twelve years old, marking the start of her career. As a teenager she began to take lessons, performed many concerts, and recorded her first CD. Through childhood and into adulthood she has had the practical and emotional support and guidance of parents, brothers, and sisters. Her father and brothers provide the musical accompaniment for her concerts, and she has a special relationship with her father, who acts as agent and producer. The living room in Ixya's home is a special place of musical resonance: as a young child it was the place for live music-making with family and visitors, additionally becoming the rehearsal space as she moved into the professional world.

Kyriakou was precluded from singing publicly as a child because she was a girl in a traditional Cypriot context where festivals and fairs were events at which only men were allowed to sing. However, as her father was a poet-singer who desired to interact musically with his children, she recited with him within the confines of family life. For Kyriakou home life, family, children, grandchildren, and village are fundamental for her. She has a deep concern for her husband, making him her priority and arranging her career around him. As her role as housewife and grandmother are intrinsic to her fame, elements of respectability, modesty, piety, and her private domain are strategically part of her career. Kyriakou's narrative is rooted in her kitchen within her village home, both of which are central to her life even as a national star.

Lexine sang in church and often made up songs as a child growing up in Australia. As a teenager she sang at a wedding, an experience that led to her making a career from singing and composing. As part of a large family with roots in the Torres Strait Islands, yet raised by her father on mainland Australia, Lexine experiences a sense of disconnection and a profound desire to sing to create belonging and connection. She sings of her family (grandmother, mother, aunties, sisters, girlfriends) and for her family (particularly her siblings), even producing a CD for them. Within her home in Queensland she has a home studio where she records her own productions for international distribution. In this special space her ephemeral singing voice and songs are transformed into tangible documents that will reach many others in their lives and homes.

Marysia grew up with live music around her in her village in the Tatra Mountains of southern Poland. Her father was a well-known fiddler, and she learned the local Górale repertoire and sang for special occasions at church. As a young adult she and her husband ran a song-and-dance troupe from their home, sharing and collaborating within their marriage in their musical endeavors. At the center of Marysia's life is a happy marriage and active motherhood. With twelve children, her life is for them, and she sings for them to shape their lives. Within her kitchen in her home in the village in southern Poland she taught local girls the Górale traditional songs. In her home in Toronto she replicates the context and perpetuates the tradition.

Sathima heard popular songs on her grandmother's radio while doing chores in the kitchen as a child. She remembers being deeply moved and wanting to sing them. As a black child in apartheid South Africa she secretly created a repertory and from the age of eleven, sang in competitions during the intermission at the movies. During her childhood her grandmother taught her to be submissive to men, a position that she had to overcome in her musical endeavors. As an adult, romance and marriage have been crucial to her life. Her husband is a musician, but not part of the same jazz group, because Sathima has her own. Sathima raised two children, and with the decision to bear children came the tensions of caring for them and enabling her husband to maintain his musical career, therefore squeezing her own musical practices into the routine demands of everyday life. For Sathima home in New York was a space for caring for her growing children and developing her jazz.

Sima experienced a rural childhood within a loving extended family in Iran. At age four she learned traditional songs from her grandmother in the rice fields, and at age ten her local radio station invited her to sing, although her father refused her permission. She attended a private singing school where she was pressurized to Persianize; however, she defied the rules and continued to sing Mazanderani songs. While studying at the university she fell in love with, and married, a man who has been intrinsic to her career as a singer, both promoting her and delighting in her singing. As the mother of two children, Sima's singing shifted temporarily to a private domain when her daughters were young. As young women both daughters migrated to Germany, which, despite the distress, has provoked Sima to travel and arrange concerts there. Sima's home has been a place for improvising her traditional Mazanderani songs and for singing lullabies to her children.

Zainab began singing as an apprentice musician at age eight or nine, and at the age of ten she commenced public performances. Her childhood was therefore one of musical training. As a young married woman, already with children, she was invited to sing for Radio Afghanistan in Kabul. However, her husband both opposed her singing and also made the familial decisions, resulting in Zainab turning down further recording work. Zainab expressed unhappiness in her marriage and also with her ability to have children, stating she was unlucky because she became pregnant too easily, but also paradoxically she needed daughters who would sing with her in the all-women musical contexts. Significantly, she lived with her mother-in-law, who also became her singing mentor; therefore the everyday tasks of homemaking were enmeshed with her life as a singer.

Journeys and Migration

Amelia's experience as a singer in Cuba encompassed the facility to travel beyond her national border when others were denied such a possibility. Her journeys involved visits to the United States of America, Canada, and Europe—travel that was recip- rocated by her students and devotees who traveled to Cuba, generating a network of non-Cuban women, and numerous European and North American godchildren. As embodied in her religious beliefs, her own journey continued after death, forming links between this world and the "other world."

Ixya's identity in the United States of America is rooted in her Mexican heritage and culture, expressed in her self-identification as Mexican (and also Chicana, a Mexican woman living in the United States of America). Although she has lived in the United States of America since birth her sense of profound Mexicanness and Mexico as "homeland" blurs territorial borders and engages the notion of Mexico as people, rather than place. Through her singing Ixya lives a notion of "home" as

Mexico, engaging a diverse repertoire of Mexican genres and performing concerts in Mexico and the United States of America, touching not only people with Mexican connections, but also all audiences for whom she sings.

Kyriakou's life is rooted in her village in Cyprus. Until recently she refused any invitations to sing anywhere in Cyprus that was too far from home (Cyprus is 150 miles long and 62 miles wide), preferring to remain close to her husband and village life.

Lexine's experience is as a dislocated Torres Strait Islander living on mainland Australia. Encompassing the idea of diasporic imagination, she sings to connect with her home islands, and also makes literal journeys to the islands to sing. As part of her goal to enable connection and belonging she also undertakes world tours, giving concerts, teaching, and facilitating workshops.

Marysia spent her childhood and early adulthood in the Tatra mountains of southern Poland, where singing centered on village life and her Górale ethnicity. After her parents migrated to Toronto, Canada, for work purposes, she decided to make the same journey with her husband and children. In Canada Marysia sings the Górale repertoire, fulfilling an inner need and compulsion and enabling her children to connect to their homeland.

Sathima's life takes in three continents: she lived her childhood years in Cape Town, South Africa, which was followed by incessant travel in Europe in search of work as a jazz singer, finally settling in the Americas, in New York, where she developed her career with her jazz ensemble. Her sense of dislocation and diasporic imagination has compelled her to return to Cape Town to record an album.

Sima's singing career is rooted in the Mazanderani region of Iran. Unlike other singers, she chose not to migrate during the times of great political change. Her daughters, however, both decided to migrate to Germany, and Sima therefore travels to Germany to visit them. Taking the opportunity to connect with the diasporic community from Iran, she also gives concerts in Germany.

Zainab grew up in the Herat region of Afghanistan, traveling locally to sing at weddings. Her one long journey was as a young woman and entailed traveling seven hundred miles to the capital Kabul, where she had been invited to record for Radio Afghanistan. She did not, however, stay in Kabul but returned to Herat, a decision that had a lasting impact upon her career.

Risk, Tensions, Opportunities, and Activism

Akiko suffered from a complex home-professional life through childhood and into adulthood, losing the opportunity to follow in her mother's footsteps and then deciding to create her own career as a single woman, after divorcing her husband. She risked social disapproval and financial difficulty, particularly because of the declining popularity of the musical form of *jiuta*. However, acting as innovator, entrepreneur, and agent, she created an intimate performance setting in a small venue, transforming elements of the genre by incorporating speech about her family and creating a close relationship with her audiences, and in doing so she risked disapproval by her mother and her audiences.

Amelia demonstrated explicit, radical resistance to gender boundaries in the music of Santería, ascending to the top of a mainstay of male power. Using her status as priestess and ritual singer she was an innovator who crossed a traditional gender line, challenging a men-only prerogative. She formed her own mostly female ensemble, took on a man's musical role, and contested the discrepancy of divisions between Cuban and non-Cuban women. As a lesbian in a homophobic environment she became a role model for many.

Ayben enacts an overt relationship between the metaphorical and literal voice, shifting barriers and removing obstacles through her vocality in the triple affiliations of gender (woman), religion (Islam), and genre (rap). Within the context of a religiously conservative Muslim population and neighborhood, specific values of her local community and her family placed expectations on her as a young woman to be a homemaker. By performing in public and in the specifically male-dominated genre of rap she risked bringing disapproval on herself and her family. When she was seventeen, her older brother encouraged her to rap on his album. She took the risk and experienced self-assurance and a supportive family, acknowledging her brother's patronage, while simultaneously asserting her unique voice. The tension of career and family role was played out through taking on the task of caregiver for her mother until her death, while still working on rapping skills at home. Through her personal rapping style and self-penned song texts, dealing specifically with the treatment of women, she proclaims her agency of womanhood in her rap, transforming the gendered genre and giving voice to other women.

Ixya chose to "be" a singer at seven years old, displaying a bold sense of self-definition. At twelve years old she was invited to sing on stage with her idol, Linda Ronstadt, marking the start of her career. As a Chicana or Mexican American in the United States of America her choice of repertoire and language are a form of activism. Although not highly commercial and marketable, she sings songs "of the past" in Spanish, and engages an aesthetic of graceful enchantment, risking disapproval from peers who might prefer a different model of femininity. Elements of her vocality, particularly falsetto, high, and long notes, create a context of risk of failure.

Kyriakou grasped the opportunity, as a woman in her fifties, to phone in to a radio show in order to recite and sing on air, using the musical form of tsiattista that was reserved for men. She challenged the restrictions on the public expression of art, which regarded such behavior as improper and disrespectful for women, claiming the airwaves and then the stage for women and showing that being a woman singer can be respectable. She risked disrupting her family life and producing village gossip with her fame through public exposure. Her role as a housewife and senior woman in control of her house and family is an empowering one, and by engaging this as her public persona she creates a context of respectability, enabling her to sing with and share the stage with a young woman pop singer.

Lexine has contested power through her vocality, displaying an overt connection between the metaphorical and literal voice. As a Torres Strait Islander woman in Australia who is disenfranchised and marginalized through gender and indigeneity, she specifically sings about her life experiences. As a singer, composer, producer, teacher, and workshop leader she enables her own family and women in many international contexts to create a sense of connection. As a self-directed entrepreneur she manages her own career and chooses to record and release albums independently to retain artistic control over her sound. By choosing to record songs about home-truths, she risked disapproval by her close family.

Marysia has devoted much of her life to the music of her home region—that of the marginalized ethnic identity of the Górale people of southern Poland. As a young woman in her village in Poland she actively led a music and dance ensemble, with her husband, teaching many girls to sing and developing her own vocal style. After migrating to Canada she became an activist and innovator who chooses to teach music exclusively from the Podhale region, rather than a medley from a variety of regions, and who composes new texts to known tunes, reorienting the poetics and images as relevant to Canada, risking disapproval from her fellow community members because of new ideas.

Sathima is an innovator and entrepreneur who has shaped the discourse of jazz to her own purpose. Experiencing "mixed race" segregation in South Africa, the transition to apartheid and its demise, as a child she took risks by singing songs considered to be inappropriate for her racial context. As a young adult pursuing a vocation in jazz she was required to leave South Africa, experiencing the tensions of sustaining her husband's musical career, caring for her family, and undertaking the mundane tasks of everyday life. By pursuing a career as a jazz singer she risked losing her marriage because few jazz musicians survive as couples. As a songwriter, producer, manager, and record-label owner she has seized upon the freedom to be unique and different, regarding jazz as the music of rebellion and crafting her contrasting, woman-centered vocality and narrative to the masculinity in jazz.

Sima has challenged and overcome many restrictions and prohibitions with her voice, not least the constraints of the postrevolutionary law against solo female singing in the company of unrelated men. Even as a child she defied her teacher's advice, choosing to sing the traditional music of her Mazanderani ethnicity, which was marginalized in centralist terms. As an adult she has devised tricks to limit the restrictive laws, saying that "boundaries of traditional music are more easily and more interestingly pushed than those of Westernized pop," aware as she is of the masculinist nature of the pop industry. She asserts her regional Mazanderani ethnicity, and as a form of activism sings a repertoire that encompasses women's lives, particularly songs in praise of rural working girls and songs of desire sung in the first person. Her roles as a senior woman and facilitator of women's singing are significant.

Zainab sang within a contradictory conservative Muslim context, with prohibitions against female performance and associations with immorality, set against a deep cultural appreciation of music and sung poetry. Although aware of regulations of gender segregation in social situations, requiring women to sing in the company of women, she flouted the rules of purdah by singing in the company of men outside the family. Such actions proved to be psychologically stressful in the period when radio and TV stars were in danger of assassination. Her low-status barber-musician background; the male musical hierarchy, which compelled a successful woman star to need a male sponsor; her bodily image (she was not considered to be beautiful); and her fear of rivalry from other women, the evil eye, and supernatural forces—all created insurmountable problems for Zainab. Yet she was a professional career singer and the principal earner for the family (because her husband earned only small sums of money), demonstrating Zainab's steadfastness and capability in managing her own career and vocality.

Recording and Broadcast Technologies

Akiko's career and vocal style were shaped through recordings made by both her mother and grandmother. When Akiko was a child, her mother performed as a *jiuta* singer on both TV and radio. As an adult Akiko listened to tape recordings of her grandmother's voice, hearing subtle aesthetic facets that she had not heard when being taught live by her grandmother, and she implemented these facets in developing her own vocality.

Amelia made audio recordings, therefore enabling her voice to be heard even after her death and giving her religious devotees access to her powerful vocal aesthetics.

Ayben was heavily influenced by recordings of other rappers, including her own brother, who bolstered her self-confidence by encouraging her to rap on his album. In the privacy of her home she developed her unique rapping style by recording herself on her computer and then listening back. In her public career, recordings have been crucial, along with TV appearances and an internet presence through websites and YouTube.

Ixya's decision to become a singer occurred when listening to cassettes at home as a child of seven. She then went on to record her first CD when just sixteen and has followed this with other recordings and an internet presence.

Kyriakou's career was set in motion through the medium of radio, when she phoned in to participatory shows that gave her the opportunity to express herself vocally in a way that was previously almost impossible. Her voice was broadcast to thousands of listeners and led to the offer of making a recording, an idea that at first she refused, thinking it "ridiculous," but then later agreed to. With the ensuing national celebrity status, she makes radio and TV appearances.

Lexine records albums in her home studio, preferring to be the executive producer of her own recordings, even though she has been offered a contract with a production company. Her recordings are available to an international market.

Sathima heard songs on her grandmother's radio as a child that inspired and stirred her to sing. In developing her own style she has listened to many recordings of jazz greats, contributing to the same trajectory by making her own recordings. She has her own record label and produces her own work.

Sima was invited to sing and record for a radio station locally and in Tehran but did not accept the invitations. As a university student, cassettes of revolutionary music inspired her to political action. In adulthood she devised the means to circumvent the strict laws on live and recorded women's voices.

Zainab recorded for Radio Afghanistan in her local region of Herat. Her voice was broadcast nationally and she was invited to record in Kabul, by the same radio station, and by a German recording company; however, she declined both.

Legacies

As Zainab and Amelia are no longer living, we cherish and acknowledge the lives of these two women.

Zainab touched many listeners as a singer for wedding celebrations, yet following her death she was repositioned in a realm of obscurity. However, her traditional legacy exists through the singing and narratives of Veronica Doubleday, who performs the songs she learned from Zainab and continues to disseminate her life through published narratives.

Amelia shaped issues of gender in the music-making of Santería, creating a lasting impact upon her followers, in Cuba and internationally, and upon the accepted norms of sexuality. Posthumously she continues to guide and inspire through her recordings, through the perpetuation of her practices, and through the belief of Egun and the spirit world.

Akiko propagates the lineage of jiuta, as developed by her grandmother and mother, even as she creates a new path in her own manner, inspiring other women to challenge traditional cultural patterns.

Ayben is only twenty-eight, yet through her career since the age of seventeen she has carved out a high-profile role for women rappers in Turkey and created lyrics that challenge men's actions toward women.

Ixya has given voice to a young and graceful Chicana presence and has brought into circulation older and less well-known Mexican songs.

Kyriakou has afforded senior and older women a public place as singers.

Lexine empowers Torres Strait Islanders and Aboriginal women to reflect on their lives and become activists.

Marysia enables Górale migrants and their offspring who have not lived in Poland to connect with their homeland and repertoire.

Sathima reinforces the lineage of jazz women, creating a place for South African women through her recordings and live performances.

Sima has solidly established the importance of Mazanderani songs in national and international contexts.

Contributors

SHINO ARISAWA is a Lecturer in Japanese Studies at the Tokyo Gakugei University. She received her doctoral degree in Ethnomusicology from the School of Oriental and African Studies (SOAS), University of London with the thesis "Changes in the Transmission of 'Traditional' Music: The Case of Japanese *Jiuta-Sōkyoku.*" Prior to her current position, Arisawa was a Post-Doctoral Research Associate at SOAS, where she also taught Japanese music courses in the Department of Music.

KATELYN BARNEY is a Project Manager and Researcher in the Aboriginal and Torres Strait Islander Studies Unit at the University of Queensland, Australia. Her main research interests include collaborative research with Indigenous Australian women performers, teaching and learning approaches in Indigenous Australian studies, and facilitating support for Indigenous Australian postgraduate students. She has published across these areas and also teaches piano privately. Her recent publications include articles in *Perfect Beat: The Pacific Journal of Research into Contemporary Music and Popular Culture, Teaching in Higher Education*, and *Music and Politics* and she co-edited the volume *Musical Islands: Exploring Connections Between Music, Place and Research* (2009).

GAY BREYLEY is an adjunct research associate in the School of Music–Conservatorium at Monash University in Australia. In 2010, she was an Endeavour research fellow (Austraining International) in the Department of Music at the University of Tehran, Iran. With Sasan Fatemi she is coauthor of *Iranian Music and Popular Entertainment: From Motrebi to Losanjelesi and Beyond* (Routledge, 2011). Her other publications include articles in *Musicology Australia, New*

Formations, Antipodes, Life Writing, Ethnomusicology Forum, Prose Studies, Journal of Australian Studies, and *Borderlands.*

NICOLETTA DEMETRIOU is currently the Alistair Horne Visiting Fellow at St. Antony's College, Oxford University, where she is working on a book of creative nonfiction. She holds an MA in Life Writing from the University of East Anglia and a PhD in Ethnomusicology from the School of Oriental and African Studies (SOAS), University of London. A trained classical singer, she has also been a performer of Cypriot folksong since childhood.

VERONICA DOUBLEDAY is a visiting lecturer in the School of Historical and Critical Studies at the University of Brighton, United Kingdom. Her numerous publications on Afghanistan include a narrative ethnography, *Three Women of Herat* (1988), and *I Cried on the Mountain Top* (2010), a volume of archive photographs accompanied by traditional Persian-language lyrics with her own English translations. Other research revolves around women's music, gender issues, and musical instruments, and she guest-edited a themed issue of *Ethnomusicology Forum* on musical instruments and gender (2008). As a vocalist and drummer Doubleday is an acclaimed performer of Afghan traditional music, and over the years she has given concerts all over the world.

RUTH HELLIER [HELLIER-TINOCO] is a professor in the Departments of Music, Theater and Dance at the University of California, Santa Barbara, where she engages areas of performance studies, ethnomusicology, theater and dance studies, applied arts, and Mexican and Latin American performance. After childhood training at the Guildhall School of Music in London (piano and violin), she gained a degree in Music, Drama and Dance (Birmingham 1983), which included opera training at Birmingham Conservatoire. She undertook a successful career as an actress, singer, and community arts facilitator, followed by positions as Head of Music at two large high schools. With a fascination for Mexican cultural history, she undertook a PhD in Mexican performance and politics, leading to an academic position at the University of Winchester, United Kingdom. She has published widely, including *Embodying Mexico: Tourism, Nationalism and Performance* (OUP 2011), chapters and articles on power relations, ethics, and cultural memory, and *Performing Memory and History: Contemporary Theatre and Performance in Mexico* (forthcoming).

ELLEN KOSKOFF is Professor of Ethnomusicology at the University of Rochester's Eastman School of Music and is the director of ethnomusicology programs. She also directs and performs with the School's Balinese Gong Kebyar and Angklung gamelans. She has published widely on Jewish music, on gender and music, and is the editor of *Women and Music in Cross-Cultural Perspective* (1987). Her book, *Music in Lubavitcher Life* (2000) was the winner of the 2002 ASCAP Deems-Taylor award. Koskoff is a contributor to the *New Grove Dictionary of Music and Musicians*, is the general editor of the *Garland Encyclopedia of World Music*, vol. 3, "The United States and Canada," and the series editor of the University of Rochester Press's, Eastman/Rochester Studies in Ethnomusicology. She has just completed a collection of essays on music and gender to be published by the University of Illinois Press entitled, *A Feminist Ethnomusicology: The Ellen Koskoff Reader*. She is a former President of the Society for Ethnomusicology.

CAROL MULLER is a Professor of Music (ethnomusicology) at the University of Pennsylvania, Philadelphia, who has published widely on South African music, both at home and in exile. Her intellectual interests include the relationship between music, gender and religious studies, migration and diaspora studies, and critical ethnography. Muller has published on South African jazz, religious performance, traditional and popular musics including: *Shembe Hymns* (Univ. of KwaZulu Natal 2010); *Focus: South African Music* (Routledge 2008); *Rituals of Fertility and the Sacrifice of Desire: Nazarite Women's Performance in South Africa* (Chicago 1999). In 2011 Muller led a combined online and live summer abroad program in South Africa at one of the world's largest arts festivals. Muller is also a seasoned gumboot dancer.

THOMAS SOLOMON is Professor in the Grieg Academy–Department of Music at the University of Bergen, Norway. He has previously taught at New York University, University of Minnesota, and Istanbul Technical University. He has done field research in Bolivia on musical imaginations of ecology, place, and identity; and in Istanbul on place and identity in Turkish hip-hop. His publications include articles in the journals *Ethnomusicology*, *Popular Music*, *European Journal of Cultural Studies*, and *Yearbook for Traditional Music*, as well numerous papers in edited volumes. He is also editor of *Music and Identity in Norway and Beyond: Essays Commemorating Edvard Grieg the Humanist* (Fagbokforlaget 2011).

AMANDA VILLEPASTOUR is an ethnomusicologist with a focused research interest in Yorùbá music and religion in Africa and the African diaspora. Villepastour completed her MMus (1998) and PhD (2006) at the School of African and Oriental Studies in London and has since published her first monograph, *Ancient Text Messages of the Yorùbá Bàtá Drum: Cracking the Code* (Ashgate 2010). Her past research and teaching positions include Goldsmiths College, University of London, The Smithsonian Institution, Bowling

Green State University (Ohio), and The Musical Instrument Museum (MIM) (Arizona). Villepastour is currently an ethnomusicology lecturer at Cardiff University in the United Kingdom.

LOUISE WRAZEN is Chair and Associate Professor in the Department of Music at York University, Toronto. Her research on the music and dance of the Górale of southern Poland has focused on transnationalism, transmission, and gender and has been published in various journals, including *Yearbook for Traditional Music, Ethnomusicology, Intersections,* and *The Anthropology of East Europe Review.* She is currently coediting a volume on performing gender, place, and emotion.

Index

gracefulness: as aesthetic, 20, 28, 213, 217,
230, 235, 238; embodied, 28, 99, 104, 130;
vocal, 28, 48, 92-111
"Grain, of the Voice." *See* Barthes, Roland
grandfather. *See* family
grandmother. *See* family
graphing. *See* author; ethnography; narrative; writing
Greece, 20, 119, 126
Greer, Germaine, 11

Havana, 54-72
Hayes, Eileen, 5
hegemony, 59, 63, 68, 102; vocal, 4
Hellier, Ruth [Hellier-Tinoco], 1-37, 92-111,
227-38
Herat, 194-212
Herawi, Zainab, 1, 9, 11, 15, 24-31, 30, 194-
212, 227-38
heritage, 26, 27, 43, 51, 92, 94, 101, 103,
109n18, 137, 139, 167, 175n1, 228, 233
Herrera, family, 94, 108n4
Herrera, Ixya, 1, 9, 11, 15, 19, 24-31, 92-111,
217, 223, 227-38
herstories, 1-37, 110n24. *See also* biography;
ethnography; narrative; story; writing
heterosexuality, 18, 59, 66, 68, 102, 106, 165,
167, 216. *See also* sexuality
Heyes, Cressida, 14
hip-hop, 19, 26, 73-91, 103, 119, 120, 124. *See
also* rap
Holiday, Billie, 33, 165, 170, 171, 176n6
home, 22, 24, 26, 27, 28-29, 30, 42, 74, 80-81,
93-94, 113, 134, 146, 147-48, 150, 152, 158,
161, 162, 169, 177, 187, 227-38. *See also* bedroom; kitchen; living room; recording,
home studio
homemaker, 7, 20, 23, 25, 141, 235. *See also*
housewife; housework
homophobic, 67, 71n7, 235
homosexuality, 54-72. *See also* bisexual;
lesbian; sexuality
hooks, bell, 220
housewife, 20, 28, 42, 51, 112-30, 216, 218,
230-32, 235. *See also* homemaker; wife
housework, 40-41, 77, 118, 150, 197. *See also*
cooking; homemaker
husband, 19, 20, 22, 23, 24, 28-29, 41-42, 51, 82,
112, 118-19, 147, 148, 150, 152-53, 157, 163, 172,
185, 186, 189, 181, 194, 195, 203, 205, 206, 207,
215, 227-38. *See also* family; marriage; wife

hyperfemininity, 26, 106
hypermasculinity, 73

"I," as pronoun for narrative, 8, 16, 17-24.
See also authors; biography; ethnography;
ethnomusicology, and the individual;
methodology; narrative; subjectivity
"I Belong," 137, 139
Ibrahim, Abdullah (Dollar Brand), 23, 163,
167
iconic status, 18, 55, 56, 65, 69, 105
identity: class, 194-212; construction, 2, 9,
11, 12, 14, 17-24, 217, 224; multiple, 1, 14,
23, 215; traditional, 118, 124, 164; woman/
man, 6, 12. *See also* age; ethnicity; gender;
Indigenous; language; nationality; race;
religion; sexuality
ideology, 1, 4, 10, 11, 23, 30, 55, 102, 184, 185;
and gender, 6
illness, 17, 43, 50, 80. *See also* cancer; caregiver; death
improvisation, and singing, 107, 113, 122,
126n4, 172, 177, 179-80, 182, 186, 187, 228,
233
Indigenous, 15, 21, 131-45, 238, 239. *See also*
identity
individuality, 2, 39, 81, 146, 169, 191, 221, 224.
See also difference; individuals; self
individuals, 1-37, 158, 213, 215, 219; and ethnography, 7-16, 147-48, 219 (*see also* "I");
and voice prohibition, 191. *See also* ethnography; ethnomusicology; self; selves;
subjectivity
"in-ness," 100
interconnectedness, 219, 227
internet, 5, 8, 32n3, 78, 82, 83, 88n2, 107, 134,
206, 207, 237. *See also* Facebook
intersubjectivity, 219, 220, 223. *See also* subjectivity
interviews: as method, 2, 6, 8, 16, 17-24,
33n13, 39, 63, 66, 75-76, 78, 80, 83, 85,
87-88, 112, 118, 132, 142, 168n3, 191n2; and
conversations, 8, 16, 18, 22, 33n13, 39, 132,
148, 159n2, 223. *See also* ethnography;
fieldwork; methodology; power; recording
Iran, 2, 9, 15, 23, 24, 26, 29, 177-93, 200, 206,
215, 229, 233, 234
Islam, 9, 26, 29, 33n9, 76, 77, 178, 185-86, 188,
194-212, 235
Istanbul, 18, 19, 73-91, 216, 231

The University of Illinois Press
is a founding member of the
Association of American University Presses.

Composed in 10.5/13 Minion Pro Regular
by Celia Shapland
at the University of Illinois Press
Manufactured by Thomson-Shore, Inc.

University of Illinois Press
1325 South Oak Street
Champaign, IL 61820-6903
www.press.uillinois.edu